Unity Shaders and Effects Cookbook

Discover how to make your Unity projects look stunning with Shaders and screen effects

Kenny Lammers

BIRMINGHAM - MUMBAI

Unity Shaders and Effects Cookbook

First published: June 2013

Production Reference: 1110613

Published by Packt Publishing Ltd.
Livery Place
35 Livery Street
Birmingham B3 2PB, UK.

ISBN 978-1-84969-508-4

www.packtpub.com

Cover Image by Erol Staveley (erols@packtpub.com)

Credits

Author
Kenny Lammers

Reviewers
Vincent Lim
Christian 'XeviaN' Meneghini

Acquisition Editor
Edward Gordon

Lead Technical Editors
Joel Noronha
Chalini Snega Victor

Technical Editors
Jalasha D'costa
Amit Ramadas

Project Coordinator
Leena Purkait

Proofreaders
Dirk Manuel
Aaron Nash

Indexer
Tejal Soni

Graphics
Ronak Dhruv

Production Coordinator
Aparna Bhagat

Cover Work
Aparna Bhagat

About the Author

Kenny Lammers has been working in the games industry for 13 years now. He has worked for companies such as Microsoft, Activision, and the late Surreal Software. He currently runs two companies; the first is Creative TD, where he does Unity3D consulting / asset creation for companies such as IGT, Microsoft, Janus Research, and Allegorithmic, and the second company he owns and operates, with his business partner Noah Kaarbo, is Ozone Interactive. Ozone specializes in creating interactive applications and high-quality design with a focus on Untiy3D, for companies such as Amazon, E-line Media, Microsoft, and Sucker Punch games. His games industry experience has given him the opportunity to create characters using Zbrush and Maya, to write real-time Shaders and post effects, and to program full games in Unity3D using C#. He is currently working on a few games and developing toolsets within Unity to expedite the game creation process.

There are so many people I would like to thank, that it would take up a whole chapter by itself. First and foremost I would definitely like to thank my mom, for always telling me to keep working toward my dreams and always being there for me! I would like to thank my business partner Noah Kaarbo, for supporting me throughout the writing of this book and being my friend. I want to thank all the people I have worked with in the past, but most importantly I want to thank the few individuals who always urged me to push my skill sets even further and opened new worlds of the industry to me. These people are Ben Cammerano (MGS), Paul Amer (MGS), Fillipo Costanzo (5D Institute), Alessandro Tento (Lakshya), James Rogers (MGS), and Tony Garcia (Unity Technologies). I wouldn't be where I am today without any of these people, and they have my utmost respect!

About the Reviewers

Vincent Lim is a graduate from The One Academy with a Diploma in Digital Animation and Game Development. He joined Big Ant Studio immediately after graduation, where he was sculpted into a game developer. Spending a couple of years with them, Vincent has learned much, from low poly modeling to tiling textures to terrain sculpting, a little bit of programming and MEL scripting. With the variety of tasks he encountered during his active employment with Big Ant Studio, Vincent has equipped himself with knowledge about the game engine, how certain Shaders work, and the workflow pipeline. He was given several opportunities to construct or restructure certain pipelines for better efficiency. His MEL scripting skills were fostered through practical implementations within the pipeline. This enabled him to create the tools artist could use to speed up the process and shorten the gap to get a 3D model from a base mesh to in-game. With these experiences from Big Ant Studios, Vincent has been broadening his knowledge by learning new software and reading up about game mechanics and game engines. This has allowed him to discover Unity, and he has been experimenting with it as he strives to make his learning curves sky rocket.

Christian 'XeviaN' Meneghini is the young owner and enthusiast of Sinclair ZX Spectrum. He started to snoop the game development world with hardcoded sprites in basic and assembly languages. Years passed by and he worked with great technologies such as C64, the glorious Amiga, and all the PC's family processors, using all the video cards from Hercules and CGA from the first 3D accelerators to the actual ones. He felt an addiction to real-time rendering and demo scene, while specializing in graphics programing and performance optimization. Christian also composes music in his spare time.

After years of night-hour works with friends and colleagues, studying tech books, writing engines, and working for third-party companies, Christian founded a small studio in 2011, along with his friends Marco Di Timoteo and Luca Marchetti, and called it STUDIO EVIL. The first product of STUDIO EVIL was Syder Arcade, an old-style retro Shoot 'em up with actual 3D graphics for PC and Mac platforms, subsequently ported to iOS, Android, and OUYA platforms.

I'd like to thank all of my Italian game-developer friends for their commitment in growing the game development industry in our country.

www.PacktPub.com

Support files, eBooks, discount offers and more

You might want to visit www.PacktPub.com for support files and downloads related to your book.

Did you know that Packt offers eBook versions of every book published, with PDF and ePub files available? You can upgrade to the eBook version at www.PacktPub.com and as a print book customer, you are entitled to a discount on the eBook copy. Get in touch with us at service@packtpub.com for more details.

At www.PacktPub.com, you can also read a collection of free technical articles, sign up for a range of free newsletters and receive exclusive discounts and offers on Packt books and eBooks.

http://PacktLib.PacktPub.com

Do you need instant solutions to your IT questions? PacktLib is Packt's online digital book library. Here, you can access, read and search across Packt's entire library of books.

Why Subscribe?

- Fully searchable across every book published by Packt
- Copy and paste, print and bookmark content
- On demand and accessible via web browser

Free Access for Packt account holders

If you have an account with Packt at www.PacktPub.com, you can use this to access PacktLib today and view nine entirely free books. Simply use your login credentials for immediate access.

Table of Contents

Preface

Welcome to *Unity Shaders and Effects Cookbook*! This book is your guide to becoming familiar with the creation of Shaders and post effects in Unity3D. You will start your journey at the beginning, creating the most basic Shaders and learning how the Shader code is structured. This foundational knowledge will arm you with the means to progress further into each chapter and produce Shaders that simulate human skin, Shaders that handle dynamic reflections, and will also develop post effects such as night vision.

By the end of each chapter you will have gained new skill sets that will increase the quality of your Shaders, and even make your Shader-writing process more efficient. These chapters have been tailored so that you can jump into each section and learn a specific skill, from beginner to expert. Or, for those new to Shader writing in Unity, you can progress through each chapter, one at a time, to build on your knowledge. Either way, you will learn the techniques that make modern games look the way they do.

Once you have completed this book, you will have a set of Shaders that you can use in your Unity3D games, as well as the understanding to add to them, to accomplish new effects and address performance needs. So let's get started!

What this book covers

Chapter 1, Diffuse Shading, teaches the foundations of Shader writing by explaining how to structure a Shader in Unity3D. It then applies that knowledge to creating default diffuse lighting, and provides tips and tricks from the industry for creating custom diffuse lighting.

Chapter 2, Using Textures for Effects, describes how to utilize textures to create different effects. You will learn how to animate textures on a sprite sheet through a Shader, as well as how to utilize the different channels of a texture to make your Shaders more efficient. By the end of this chapter you will have the power to use textures to create your own custom effects.

Chapter 3, Making Your Game Shine with Specular, teaches you everything you need to know about creating the most widely used Specular type, Blinn and Phong. You will learn how to apply these Shader effects to create masked specular, metallic specular, and will even learn a technique to create anisotropic specular. By the end of the chapter, you will feel confident enough to create your own custom specular effects for your own custom Shaders.

Chapter 4, Reflecting Your World, gives you a peek into one of the more popular effects for modern games and that is to incorporate reflection techniques into Shaders. This chapter will teach you everything from the basics of reflections in Unity3D Shaders to setting up your own simple dynamic reflection system using C#.

Chapter 5, Lighting Models, begins the process of creating more complex Shaders. You will learn how to create your own lighting models to achieve your own types of surfaces. Each recipe demonstrates different techniques to accomplish different tasks, all meant to enhance your Shader-writing skill set. By the end of the chapter you will have created your own skin shader, your own Lit Sphere shader, and your own car paint shader.

Chapter 6, Transparency, shows you that, at some point in a games production, transparency becomes a necessary technique. Just about every game employs transparency to some extent, for things such as GUI, foliage, decals, and so on. In this chapter you will learn how to use transparency in Unity3D and how to deal with issues that might arise when incorporating transparency.

Chapter 7, Vertex Magic, covers how to access the information that is stored in each vertex of our 3D mesh. You will learn how to take this information and utilize it in a Shader to produce effects such as texture blending and animation.

Chapter 8, Mobile Shader Adjustment, is all about looking at ways in which you can utilize Unity3D's built-in flags and values to reduce the overhead of your Shaders. This becomes especially important when dealing with Shaders on a mobile platform.

Chapter 9, Making Your Shader World Modular with CgIncludes, shows you that it is necessary to learn how to re-use code that you have written, over and over again, in order to make your Shader-writing more efficient. This chapter shows you how to create your own CgInclude files to store all the repetitious code for re-use.

Chapter 10, Screen Effects with Unity Render Textures, starts off with a look at how any modern game utilizes screen effects, sometimes called post effects, to alter the look of the final rendered image of a game. You will learn how to create your own screen effects, and learn the secrets behind how to add color adjustments and texture overlays to produce different visual looks in your game.

Chapter 11, Gameplay and Screen Effects, takes the knowledge you have learned about screen effects a step further, and shows you how you can create screen effects that heighten a moment in a game. You will learn how to create an old movie screen effect as well as a night vision screen effect.

What you need for this book

The following is a list of required and optional software for completing the recipes in this book:

- Unity3D (Unity3D Pro is required for Chapters 10 and 11)
- A 3D application such as Maya, Max, or Blender (optional)
- A 2D image editing application such as Photoshop or Gimp (optional)

Who this book is for

This book is meant for all Unity3D developers, beginner- to advanced-level. It is best if you have experience with C# or JavaScript, and feel comfortable enough creating simple assets inside of the Unity3D editor. It is recommended that you take a look at Packt Publishing's *Unity 3.x Game Development by Example Beginner's Guide* (`http://www.packtpub.com/unity-3-x-game-development-by-example-beginners-guide/book`), to get a solid grounding on the use of Unity3D basics.

Conventions

In this book, you will find a number of styles of text that distinguish between different kinds of information. Here are some examples of these styles, and an explanation of their meaning.

Code words in text are shown as follows: "Enter the following code into the `Properties` block of your Shader."

A block of code is set as follows:

```
void surf (Input IN, inout SurfaceOutput o)
{
  float4 c;
  c =  pow((_EmissiveColor + _AmbientColor),  _MySliderValue);

  o.Albedo = c.rgb;
  o.Alpha = c.a;
}
```

New terms and **important words** are shown in bold. Words that you see on the screen, in menus or dialog boxes for example, appear in the text like this: "This creates a Cubemap swatch in the **Inspector** tab and allows a user to drag-and-drop a Cubemap into the Shader."

Reader feedback

Feedback from our readers is always welcome. Let us know what you think about this book—what you liked or may have disliked. Reader feedback is important for us to develop titles that you really get the most out of.

To send us general feedback, simply send an e-mail to `feedback@packtpub.com`, and mention the book title via the subject of your message.

If there is a topic that you have expertise in and you are interested in either writing or contributing to a book, see our author guide on `www.packtpub.com/authors`.

Customer support

Now that you are the proud owner of a Packt book, we have a number of things to help you to get the most from your purchase.

Downloading the example code

You can download the example code files for all Packt books you have purchased from your account at `http://www.packtpub.com`. If you purchased this book elsewhere, you can visit `http://www.packtpub.com/support` and register to have the files e-mailed directly to you.

Downloading the color images of this book

We also provide you a PDF file that has color images of the screenshots/diagrams used in this book. The color images will help you better understand the content of the chapter. You can download this file from `http://www.packtpub.com/sites/default/files/downloads/5084OT_Images.pdf`.

Errata

Although we have taken every care to ensure the accuracy of our content, mistakes do happen. If you find a mistake in one of our books—maybe a mistake in the text or the code—we would be grateful if you would report this to us. By doing so, you can save other readers from frustration and help us improve subsequent versions of this book. If you find any errata, please report them by visiting `http://www.packtpub.com/submit-errata`, selecting your book, clicking on the **errata submission form** link, and entering the details of your errata. Once your errata are verified, the errata will be uploaded on our website, or added to any list of existing errata, under the Errata section of that title. Any existing errata can be viewed by selecting your title from `http://www.packtpub.com/support`.

Piracy

Piracy of copyright material on the Internet is an ongoing problem across all media. At Packt, we take the protection of our copyright and licenses very seriously. If you come across any illegal copies of our works, in any form, on the Internet, please provide us with the location address or website name immediately so that we can pursue a remedy.

Please contact us at `copyright@packtpub.com` with a link to the suspected pirated material.

We appreciate your help in protecting our authors, and our ability to bring you valuable content.

Questions

You can contact us at `questions@packtpub.com` if you are having a problem with any aspect of the book, and we will do our best to address it.

1
Diffuse Shading

This chapter will cover some of the more common diffuse techniques found in today's Game Development Shading Pipelines. You will learn about:

- Creating a basic Surface Shader
- Adding properties to a Surface Shader
- Using properties in a Surface Shader
- Creating a custom diffuse lighting model
- Creating a Half Lambert lighting model
- Creating a ramp texture to control diffuse shading
- Creating a faked BRDF using a 2D ramp texture

Introduction

The beginning of any good Shader always relies on having a foundational diffuse component or lighting model. So it always makes sense to start the Shader writing process with the diffuse component of the Shader.

Previously in computer graphics, diffuse shading was done with what was called the **fixed function lighting model**. It gave graphics programmers just a single lighting model that they could tweak, using a set of parameters and textures. In our current industry, we have access to much more control and flexibility with Cg, and especially in Unity with its Surface Shaders.

The diffuse component of a Shader basically describes the way light reflects off a surface in all directions. That might sound very similar to the description of how a reflective mirror works, but it is actually different. A reflective surface actually reflects the image of the surrounding environment, while diffuse lighting takes all the light from light sources, such as the sun, and reflects its light back to the viewer's eye. We will be covering reflections in a later chapter, but for our purposes right now, this will help us differentiate between the two.

To achieve a basic diffuse lighting model, we will have to create a Shader that will include an emissive color, an ambient color, and the total light accumulated from all light sources. The following recipes show you how to build up a complete diffuse lighting model, and also show some various industry tricks that come in handy for creating more complicated diffuse models using only textures.

By the end of this chapter you will have learned how to build basic Shaders that perform basic operations. Armed with this knowledge, you will be able to create just about any Surface Shader.

Creating a basic Surface Shader

As we progress further into the recipes in this book, it is important that you know how to set up your workspace in Unity, so that you can work efficiently, and without any pain. If you are already quite familiar with creating Shaders and setting up Materials in Unity 4, you may skip this recipe. It is here to ensure that newcomers to surface shading in Unity 4 can work with the rest of the recipes.

Getting ready

To get started with this recipe, you will need to have Unity 4 running, and must have created a new project. There will also be a Unity project included with this cookbook, so you can use that one as well and simply add your own custom Shaders to it, as you step through each recipe. With that completed, you are now ready to step into the wonderful world of real-time shading!

How to do it...

Before getting into our first Shader, let's create a small scene for us to work with. This can be done by going to **GameObject** | **Create Other** in the Unity editor. From there you can create a plane, to act as a ground, a couple of spheres, to which we will apply our Shader, and a directional light to give the scene some light. With our scene generated, we can move onto the Shader writing steps:

1. In the **Project** tab in your Unity editor, right-click on the **Assets** folder and select **Create** | **Folder**.

> If you are using the Unity project that came with the cookbook, you can skip to step 4.

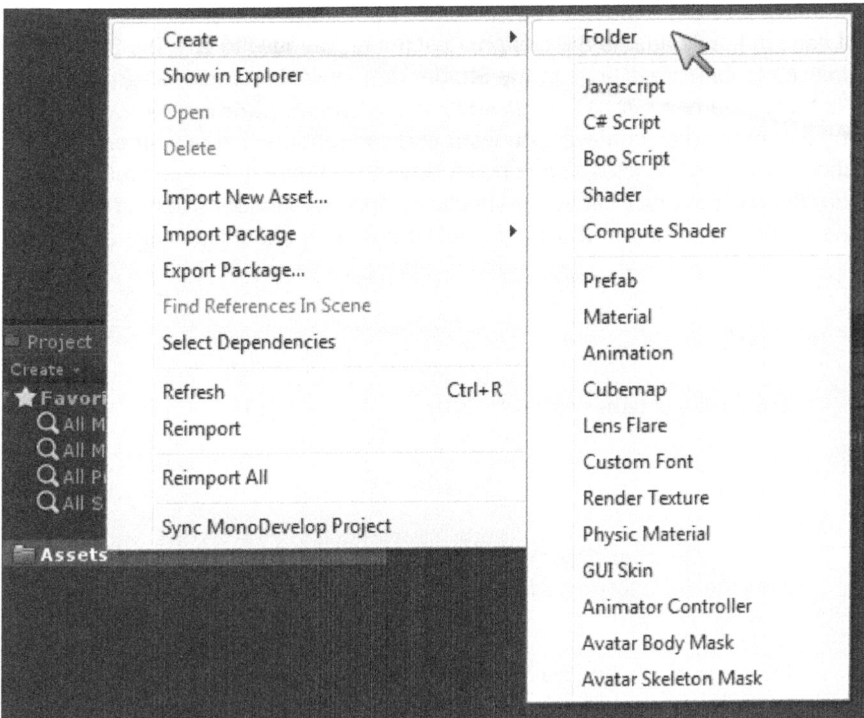

2. Rename the folder that you created to `Shaders` by right-clicking on it and selecting **Rename** from the drop-down list, or by selecting the folder and hitting *F2* on the keyboard.
3. Create another folder and rename it to `Materials`.
4. Right-click on the `Shaders` folder and select **Create** | **Shader**. Then right-click on the `Materials` folder and select **Create** | **Material**.
5. Rename both the Shader and the Material to **BasicDiffuse**.
6. Launch the **BasicDiffuse** Shader into **MonoDevelop** (the default script editor for Unity) by double-clicking on it. This will automatically launch the editor for you and display the Shader code.

You will see that Unity has already populated our Shader with some basic code. This, by default, will get you a basic diffuse Shader that accepts one texture. We will be modifying this base code so that we can learn how to quickly start developing our own custom Shaders.

7. Now let's give our Shader a custom folder from which it's selected. The very first line of code in the Shader is the custom description we have to give the Shader so that Unity can make it available in the Shader drop-down list when assigning to Materials. We have renamed our path to `Shader "CookbookShaders/BasicDiffuse"`, but you can name it to whatever you want and can rename it at any time. So don't worry about any dependencies at this point. Save the shader in MonoDevelop and return to the Unity editor. Unity will automatically compile the Shader when it recognizes that the file has been updated. This is what your Shader should look like at this point:

```
Shader "CookbookShaders/BasicDiffuse"
{
  Properties
  {
    _MainTex ("Base (RGB)", 2D) = "white" {}
  }

  SubShader
  {
    Tags { "RenderType"="Opaque" }
    LOD 200

    CGPROGRAM
    #pragma surface surf Lambert

    sampler2D _MainTex;

    struct Input
    {
      float2 uv_MainTex;
    };

    void surf (Input IN, inout SurfaceOutput o)
    {
      half4 c = tex2D (_MainTex, IN.uv_MainTex);
      o.Albedo = c.rgb;
      o.Alpha = c.a;
    }
    ENDCG
  }
  FallBack "Diffuse"
}
```

8. Select the Material called **BasicDiffuse** that we created in step 4 and look at the **Inspector** tab. From the **Shader** drop-down list, select **CookbookShaders | BasicDiffuse** (your Shader path might be different if you chose to use a different path name). This will assign your Shader to your material and now make it ready for you to assign to an object.

To assign a material to an object, you can simply click-and-drag your Material from the **Project** tab to the object in your scene. You can also drag a Material onto the **Inspector** tab of an object, within the Unity editor, to assign a Material.

Not much to look at, at this point, but our Shader development environment is set up and we can now start to modify the Shader to suit our needs.

How it works...

Unity has made the task of getting your Shader environment up and running, very easy for you. It is simply a matter of a few clicks and you are good to go. There are a lot of elements working in the background, with regard to the Surface Shader itself. Unity has taken the Cg Shader language and made it more efficient to write, by doing a lot of the heavy Cg code lifting for you. The Surface Shader language is a more component-based way of writing Shaders. Tasks such as processing your own texture coordinates and transformation matrices have already been done for you, so you don't have to start from scratch any more. In the past, we would have to start a new Shader and rewrite a lot of code over and over again. As you gain more experience with Surface Shaders, you will naturally want to explore more of the underlying functions of the Cg language and how Unity is processing all of the low-level **graphics processing unit** (**GPU**) tasks for you.

So, by simply changing the Shader's path name to a name of our choice, we have got our basic diffuse Shader working in the Unity environment, working with lights and shadows and all that, by just changing one line of code!

See also

For more information on where to find a large portion of the built-in Cg functions for Unity, go to your Unity install directory and navigate to `Unity4\Editor\Data\CGIncludes`. Within that folder there are three files that are of note at this point, the `UnityCG.cginc`, `Lighting.cginc`, and `UnityShaderVariables.cginc`. Our current Shader is making use of all these files at the moment.

We will go more in-depth with CgInclude files in *Chapter 9, Making Your Shader World Modular with CgIncludes*.

Adding properties to a Surface Shader

Properties of a Shader are very important to the Shader pipeline, as they are the method you use to let the artist or user of the Shader assign textures, and tweak your Shader values. Properties allow you to expose GUI elements in a Material's **Inspector** tab without you having to use a separate editor, which provides visual ways to tweak a Shader.

With your Shader opened in MonoDevelop, look at the block of lines 3 through 6. This is called the **Properties block**. Currently, it will have one property in it called **_MainTex**. If you look at your Material that has this Shader applied to it, you will notice that there is one **texture** GUI element in the **Inspector** tab. These lines of code, in our Shader, is creating this GUI element for us.

Again, Unity has made this process very efficient in terms of coding and the amount of time it takes to iterate through changing your properties.

How to do it...

Let's see how this works in our current Shader called **BasicDiffuse**, by creating our own properties and learning more about the syntax involved:

1. In our `Properties` block of our Shader, remove the current property by deleting the following code from our current Shader.

```
_MainTex ("Base (RGB)", 2D) = "white" {}
```

2. Now enter the following code, save the Shader, and re-enter the Unity editor.

```
_EmissiveColor ("Emissive Color", Color) = (1,1,1,1)
```

3. When you return to Unity, the Shader will compile and you will see that our Material's **Inspector** tab now has a **color** swatch, named **Emissive Color**, instead of a **texture** swatch. Let's add one more and see what happens. Enter the following code:

```
_AmbientColor ("Ambient Color", Range(0,10)) = 2
```

4. We have added another Color Swatch to the Material's **Inspector** tab. Now let's add one more to get a feel for other kinds of properties that we can create. Add the following code to the properties block:

```
_MySliderValue ("This is a Slider", Range(0,10)) = 2.5
```

5. We have now created another GUI element that allows us to visually interact with our Shader. This time we created a slider with the name **This is a Slider**, as shown in the following screenshot:

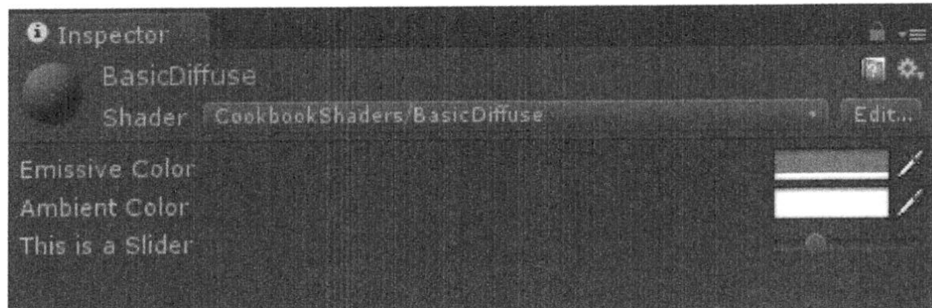

Properties allow you to create a visual way to tweak Shaders without having to change values in the Shader code itself.

How it works...

Every Unity Shader has a built-in structure it is looking for in its code. The properties block is one of those functions that is expected by Unity. The reason behind this is to give you, the Shader programmer, a means of quickly creating GUI elements that tie directly into your Shader code. These properties that you declare in the properties block can then be used in your Shader code to change values, colors, and textures.

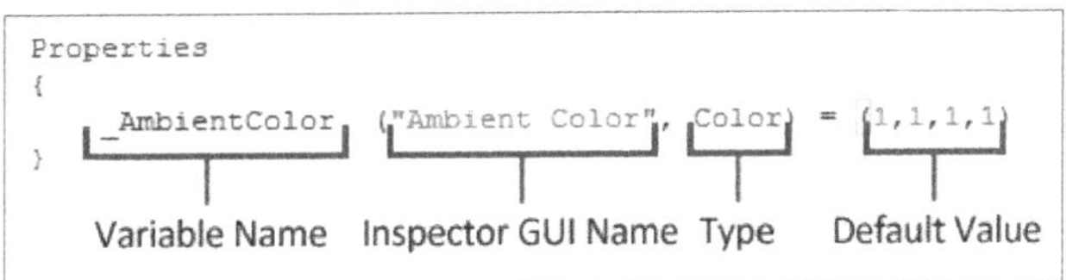

Let's take a look at what is going on underneath the hood here. When you first start writing a new property, you will need to give it a **Variable Name**. The variable name is going to be the name that your Shader code is going to use to get the value from the GUI element. This saves us a lot of time because we don't have to set up that system ourselves.

The next elements of a property are the **Inspector GUI Name** and the type of the property, which is contained within parentheses. The Inspector GUI Name is the name that is going to appear in the Material's **Inspector** tab when the user is interacting with and tweaking the Shader. The **Type** is the type of data that this property is going to control. There are many types that we can define for properties inside of Unity Shaders. The following table describes the types of variables we can have in our Shaders:

Surface Shader property types	
`Range (min, max)`	This creates a float property as a slider from the minimum value to the maximum value
`Color`	This creates a color swatch in the **Inspector** tab that opens up a color picker = (float,float,float,float)
`2D`	This creates a texture swatch that allows a user to drag a texture into the Shader
`Rect`	This creates a non-power-of-2 texture swatch and functions the same as the 2D GUI element
`Cube`	This creates a cube map swatch in **Inspector** and allows a user to drag-and-drop a cube map into the Shader
`Float`	This creates a float value in **Inspector** but without a slider
`Vector`	This creates a four-float property that allows you to create directions or colors

Finally, there is the default value. This simply sets the value of this property to the value you place in the code. So, in the example image, the default value for the property named `_AmbientColor`, which is of the type `Color`, is set to a value of `1,1,1,1`. Since this is a color property expecting a color, which is `RGBA` or a `float4`, or `r, g, b, a = x, y, z, w` this color property, when it is first created, is set to white.

See also

- The properties are documented in the Unity manual at `http://docs.unity3d.com/Documentation/Components/SL-Properties.html`

Using properties in a Surface Shader

Now that we have created some properties, let's actually hook them up to the Shader so we can use them as tweaks to our Shader and make the material process much more interactive.

We can use the properties' values from the Material's **Inspector** tab because we have attached a variable name to the property itself, but in the Shader code you have to set a couple things up before you can start calling the value by its variable name.

How to do it...

The following steps show you how to use the properties in a Surface Shader:

1. To begin, let's remove the following lines of code, as we deleted the property called **MainTex** in the *Creating a basic Surface Shader* recipe of this chapter:

```
sampler2D _MainTex;
half4 c = tex2D (_MainTex, IN.uv_MainTex);
```

2. Next, add the following lines of code to the Shader, below the `CGPROGRAM` line:

```
float4 _EmissiveColor;
float4 _AmbientColor;
float _MySliderValue;
```

3. With step 2 complete, we can now use the values from the properties in our Shader. Let's do this by adding the value from the `_EmissiveColor` property to the `_AmbientColor` property, and giving the result of that to the `o.Albedo` line of code. So, let's add the following code to the Shader inside the `surf` function:

```
void surf (Input IN, inout SurfaceOutput o)
{
  float4 c;
  c =  pow((_EmissiveColor + _AmbientColor),  _MySliderValue);

  o.Albedo = c.rgb;
  o.Alpha = c.a;
}
```

4. Finally, your Shader should look like the following Shader code. If you save your Shader in MonoDevelop and re-enter Unity, your Shader will compile. If there were no errors, you will now have the ability to change the ambient and emissive colors of the Material, as well as increase the saturation of the final color by using the slider value. Pretty neat, huh!

```
Shader "CookbookShaders/BasicDiffuse"
{
  //We define Properties in the properties block
  Properties
  {
    _EmissiveColor ("Emissive Color", Color) = (1,1,1,1)
    _AmbientColor  ("Ambient Color", Color) = (1,1,1,1)
    _MySliderValue ("This is a Slider", Range(0,10)) = 2.5
  }

  SubShader
```

```
    {
      Tags { "RenderType"="Opaque" }
      LOD 200

      CGPROGRAM
      #pragma surface surf Lambert

  //We need to declare the properties variable type inside of the
     CGPROGRAM so we can access its value from the properties block.
      float4 _EmissiveColor;
      float4 _AmbientColor;
      float _MySliderValue;

      struct Input
      {
        float2 uv_MainTex;
      };

      void surf (Input IN, inout SurfaceOutput o)
      {
        //We can then use the properties values in our shader
        float4 c;
        c =  pow((_EmissiveColor + _AmbientColor), _MySliderValue);

        o.Albedo = c.rgb;
        o.Alpha = c.a;
      }

      ENDCG
    }

    FallBack "Diffuse"
  }
```

The `pow(arg1, arg2)` is a built-in function that will perform the equivalent math function of power. So, argument 1 is the value we want to raise to a power, and argument 2 is the power we want to raise it to.

To find out more information about the `pow()` function, look to the Cg tutorial. It is a great free resource that you can use for learning more about shading and to get a glossary of all the functions available to you in the Cg shading language:

`http://http.developer.nvidia.com/CgTutorial/cg_tutorial_appendix_e.html`

The following screenshot demonstrates the result obtained by using our properties to control our Material's colors and saturation, from within the Material's **Inspector** tab:

How it works...

When you declare a new property in the property block, you are providing a way for the Shader to retrieve the tweaked value from the Material's **Inspector** tab. This value is stored in the variable name portion of the property. In this case, `_AmbientColor`, `_EmissiveColor`, and `_MySliderValue` are the variables in which we are storing the tweaked values. In order for you to be able to use the value in the `SubShader{}` block, you need to create three new variables with the same names as the property's variable name. This automatically sets up a link between these two so they know they have to work with the same data. Also, it declares the type of data we want to store in our subshader variables, which will come in handy when we look at optimizing Shaders in a later chapter.

Once you have created the subshader variables, you can then use the values in the `surf()` function. In this case we want to add the `_EmissiveColor` and `_AmbientColor` variables together and take it to a power of whatever the `_MySliderValue` variable is equal to in the Material's **Inspector** tab.

We have now created the foundation for any Shader you will create that requires a diffuse component.

Creating a custom diffuse lighting model

Using Unity's built-in lighting functions is all well and good, but you will quickly outgrow these and want to create a lot more custom lighting models. Speaking from experience, we have never worked on a project that has used just the built-in Unity lighting functions and called it good. We would create custom lighting models for just about everything. This would allow us to do things such as produce rim lighting effects, more Cubemap-based types of lightings, or even control over how your Shaders react to gameplay, as seen in Shaders that control force fields.

This recipe will focus on creating our own custom diffuse lighting model that we can use to modify and create a number of different effects.

How to do it...

Using the basic diffuse Shader we created in the last recipe, let's modify it again by performing the following steps:

1. Let's modify the `#pragma` statement to the following code:

   ```
   #pragma surface surf BasicDiffuse
   ```

2. Add the following code to the subshader:

   ```
   inline float4 LightingBasicDiffuse (SurfaceOutput s, fixed3
   lightDir, fixed atten)
   {
     float difLight = max(0, dot (s.Normal, lightDir));

     float4 col;
     col.rgb = s.Albedo * _LightColor0.rgb * (difLight * atten * 2);
     col.a = s.Alpha;
     return col;
   }
   ```

3. Save the Shader in MonoDevelop and return to Unity. The Shader will compile, and if everything went well, you will see that no real visible change has happened to our Material. What we have done is removed the connection to the built-in Unity diffuse lighting and created our own lighting model that we can customize.

How it works...

There are definitely a lot of elements working here, so let's try to break it down piece by piece and learn why this works in the way that it does:

- The `#pragma` surface directive tells the Shader which lighting model to use for its calculation. It worked when we first created the Shader because Lambert is a lighting model defined in the `Lighting.cginc` file. So it was able to use this on creation. We have now told the Shader to look for a lighting model by the name **BasicDiffuse**.
- Creating a new lighting model is done by declaring a new lighting model function. Once you have done that, you simply replace the function's name with a name of your choice. For example, `LightingName` becomes `Lighting<Your Chosen Name>`. There are three types of lighting model functions that you can use:
  - `half4 LightingName (SurfaceOutput s, half3 lightDir, half atten){}`

    This function is used for forward rendering when the view direction is not needed.

- `half4 LightingName (SurfaceOutput s, half3 lightDir, half3 viewDir, half atten){}`

  This function is used in forward rendering when a view direction is needed.

- `half4 LightingName_PrePass (SurfaceOutput s, half4 light){}`

  This function is used when you are using deferred rendering for your project.

- The dot product function is another built-in mathematical function in the Cg language. We can use it to compare the directions of two vectors in space. The dot product checks whether two vectors are either parallel to each other or perpendicular. By giving the dot product function, for two vectors you will get a float value in the range of `-1` to `1`; where `-1` is parallel and has the vector facing away from you, `1` is parallel and has the vector facing toward you, and 0 is completely perpendicular to you.

"The vector dot product (or inner product) of the normalized vectors N and L is a measure of the angle between the two vectors. The smaller the angle between the vectors, the greater the dot-product value will be, and the more incident light the surface will receive."

Reference:

`http://http.developer.nvidia.com/CgTutorial/cg_tutorial_chapter05.html`

- To complete the diffuse calculation, we need to multiply it with the data being provided to us by Unity and by the `SurfaceOutput` struct. For this we need to multiply the `s.Albedo` value (which comes from our `surf` function) with the incoming `_LightColor0.rgb` value (which Unity provides), and then multiply the result of that with `(difLight * atten)`. Then, finally, return that value as the color. See the following code:

```
inline float4 LightingBasicDiffuse (SurfaceOutput s, fixed3
lightDir, fixed atten)
{
  float difLight = max(0, dot (s.Normal, lightDir));

  float4 col;
col.rgb = s.Albedo * _LightColor0.rgb * (difLight * atten * 2);
  col.a = s.Alpha;
  return col;
}
```

The following screenshot demonstrates the result of our basic diffuse Shader:

There's more...

By using the built-in Cg function called `max`, we can clamp the values that get returned from the dot product function. The `max` function takes two arguments, `max(arg1, arg2)`. We are using it in our Shader to make sure the values we are using for our diffuse calculation are between 0 and the maximum of the dot product. This way we will never get a value below 0, especially not -1, which would create extremely black areas in your Shader that wouldn't play well with your Shader math later in the Shader process.

There is also the `saturate` function within the Cg function library. This helps us to clamp float values between 0 and 1 as well. The only difference between `max()` and `saturate()`, is that you simply feed your float value into `saturate`. The `max` function takes two arguments and returns the maximum value between the two.

See also

- You can find more information on the Surface Shader lighting model function arguments at `http://docs.unity3d.com/Documentation/Components/SL-SurfaceShaderLighting.html`

Creating a Half Lambert lighting model

Half Lambert was a technique created by Valve as a way of getting the lighting to show the surface of an object in low-light areas. It basically brightens up the diffuse lighting of the Material and wraps the diffuse light around an object's surface.

"Half Lambert" lighting is a technique first developed in the original Half-Life (https://developer.valvesoftware.com/wiki/Half-Life). It is designed to prevent the rear of an object losing its shape and looking too flat. Half Lambert is a completely nonphysical technique and gives a purely perceived visual enhancement. It is an example of a forgiving lighting model.

Reference:

https://developer.valvesoftware.com/wiki/Half_Lambert

How to do it...

Using the basic Shader that we created in the last recipe, let's update the diffuse calculation by following the next step:

- Modify the diffuse calculation by multiplying it by 0.5. So, you would add the following code to your lighting function:

```
inline float4 LightingBasicDiffuse (SurfaceOutput s, fixed3 lightDir, fixed atten)
{
    float difLight = dot (s.Normal, lightDir);
    float hLambert = difLight * 0.5 + 0.5;

    float4 col;
    col.rgb = s.Albedo * _LightColor0.rgb * (hLambert * atten * 2);
    col.a = s.Alpha;
    return col;
}
```

The following screenshot demonstrates the result of the implementation of the Half Lambert technique into our Shader's lighting model:

How it works...

The Half Lambert technique works by taking the range of values of the diffuse lighting, dividing it in half, and then adding 0.5 back to it. This basically means that if you have a value of 1 and you cut it in half, you will have 0.5. Then, if you add 0.5 back to it, you will have 1 again. If you did this same operation to a value of 0, you would end up with 0.5. So, we have taken a range of values from 0 to 1 and re-mapped it to be within a range of 0.5 to 1.0.

The following shows the diffuse value mapped to a function graph, showing the result of the Half Lambert calculation:

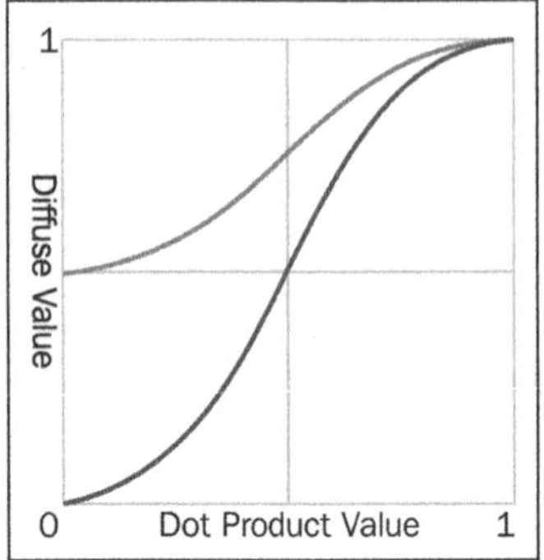

Creating a ramp texture to control diffuse shading

Another great tool in your Shader writing toolbox is the use of a ramp texture to drive the color of the diffuse lighting. This allows you to accentuate the surface's colors to fake the effects of more bounce light or a more advanced lighting setup. You see this technique used a lot more for cartoony games, where you need a more artist-driven look to your Shaders and not so much of a physically-accurate lighting model.

This technique became more popular with Team Fortress 2, where Valve came up with a unique approach to lighting their characters. They produced a very popular white paper on the subject, and you should definitely give it a read.

The Valve White Paper on Team Fortress 2 Lighting and shading available at `http://www.valvesoftware.com/publications/2007/NPAR07_IllustrativeRenderingInTeamFortress2.pdf`.

Getting ready

To get this started you will need to create a ramp texture in some image editing application. We used Photoshop for this particular demonstration, but any image editing application should be able to make a gradient:

How to do it...

Let's begin our Shader by entering the following code:

- Simply modify the lighting function so that it includes this new code:

```
inline float4 LightingBasicDiffuse (SurfaceOutput s, fixed3 lightDir, fixed atten)
{
    float difLight = dot (s.Normal, lightDir);
    float hLambert = difLight * 0.5 + 0.5;
    float3 ramp = tex2D(_RampTex, float2(hLambert)).rgb;

    float4 col;
    col.rgb = s.Albedo * _LightColor0.rgb * (ramp);
    col.a = s.Alpha;
    return col;
}
```

The following is the result you will see after running the code:

How it works...

This line of code is returning a set of colors, or a float3, which is also the same as r, g, b. These colors are being produced by a Cg function called `tex2D`. The `tex2D()` function takes two arguments. The first is the texture property we use for this operation. The second includes the UVs from the model that we want to map to the texture.

In this case we do not want to use any UVs from a vertex, but instead we want to use the diffuse float range to map the UVs of the ramp texture. This ultimately wraps the ramp texture around the surface of the object, based on the direction to the light being calculated.

We take the re-mapped diffuse values from the Half Lambert operation and pass them into `float2()` to create the lookup values for the texture. When a value of 0 is set as the `hLambert` variable, the `tex2D` function looks up the pixel value at the UV value of (0,0). In this case it's the subtle peach color from the ramps gradient. When a value of 1 is set for the `hLambert` variable, the `tex2D` function looks up the pixel at the UV value of (1,1), or the white color.

Now it is possible for the artist to have some custom control over how the light looks on the surface of an object. This is why this technique is more commonly seen on a project where you need more of an illustrative look.

Creating a faked BRDF using a 2D ramp texture

We can take the ramp diffuse recipe one step further by using the view direction, provided by the lighting functions, to create a more advanced visual look to our lighting. By utilizing the view direction, we will be able to generate some faked rim lighting.

If we look at the ramp diffuse technique, we are only using one value to place into the UV lookup of the ramp texture. This means that we will get a very linear type of lighting effect. In this recipe we will change our lighting function to take advantage of an additional argument, the **view direction**.

The view direction is the user's view of the object itself. It is a vector, pointing in a direction that we can use in conjunction with the normal and light direction. This view vector will provide us with the means to create a more advance texture lookup.

In the Cg industry this technique is often referred to as a **BRDF effect**. BRDF stands for **bidirectional reflectance distribution function**. While that is a mouthful, it simply means the way in which light is reflected off an opaque surface from both the view direction and the light direction. To see the effects of this BRDF Shader, let's continue by setting up our scene and writing the Shader.

Getting ready

Before starting, we will need a more embellished ramp texture this time. We need to include gradients for both dimensions of the texture.

1. Create a new texture with a size of 512 x 512.
2. Create a gradient, diagonally starting from the bottom left of the image, going to the top-right of the image.
3. Create another gradient from the top-left side, going until just before the middle of the image.
4. Finally, create another ramp from the bottom-right side to just before the middle of the image. You should end up with a texture shown in the following image:

How to do it...

Let's go through this recipe by following the next few steps, using the basic diffuse Shader as our starting point:

1. First we need to change our lighting function to include the `viewDir` variable that Unity provides us, to get the current view direction of the camera in the scene as it looks at our object. Modify your lighting function to look like the following code:

```
inline float4 LightingBasicDiffuse (SurfaceOutput s, fixed3 lightDir, half3 viewDir, fixed atten)
{
    float difLight = dot (s.Normal, lightDir);
    float hLambert = difLight * 0.5 + 0.5;
    float3 ramp = tex2D(_RampTex, float2(hLambert)).rgb;

    float4 col;
    col.rgb = s.Albedo * _LightColor0.rgb * (ramp);
    col.a = s.Alpha;
    return col;
}
```

2. We then need to calculate the dot product of the view direction and the surface normal (as shown in the following code). This will produce a falloff type effect that we can use to drive our BRDF texture.

```
inline float4 LightingBasicDiffuse (SurfaceOutput s, fixed3 lightDir, half3 viewDir, fixed atten)
{
    float difLight = dot (s.Normal, lightDir);
    float rimLight = dot(s.Normal, viewDir);
    float hLambert = difLight * 0.5 + 0.5;
    float3 ramp = tex2D(_RampTex, float2(hLambert)).rgb;

    float4 col;
    col.rgb = s.Albedo * _LightColor0.rgb * (ramp);
    col.a = s.Alpha;
    return col;
}
```

3. To complete the operation, we need to feed our dot product result into the `float2()` function of the `tex2D()` function. Modify your lighting function to the following code:

```
inline float4 LightingBasicDiffuse (SurfaceOutput s, fixed3 lightDir, half3 viewDir, fixed atten)
{
    float difLight = dot (s.Normal, lightDir);
    float rimLight = dot(s.Normal, viewDir);
    float hLambert = difLight * 0.5 + 0.5;
    float3 ramp = tex2D(_RampTex, float2(hLambert, rimLight)).rgb;

    float4 col;
    col.rgb = s.Albedo * _LightColor0.rgb * (ramp);
    col.a = s.Alpha;
    return col;
}
```

4. Save your Shader and re-enter Unity. Make sure you are using your new BRDF texture as the ramp texture in Unity. You should notice that your lighting now includes two rim light type effects: one for the bottom of the model and one for the top.

The following image demonstrates the results of using a BRDF ramp texture to drive the overall diffuse color. This technique is great for a production team as it makes it easy for an artist to update a texture, in Photoshop, rather than tweak lighting in the game:

How it works...

When using the view direction parameter, we can create a very simple falloff type effect. You can use this parameter to create a lot of different types of effects: a bubble type transparency, the start of a rim light effect, shield effects, or even the start of a toon outline effect.

The preceding image shows the dot product of the view direction and the surface normal. Consider if you were to look at the values being produce by taking the dot product of the view direction and the surface normal.

In this case we are using it as one of the components in the BRDF ramp texture lookup. Since the `diffLight` calculation and the `rimLight` calculation both produce a linear range of values from 0 to 1, we can use both the ranges to pick different areas of the ramp texture.

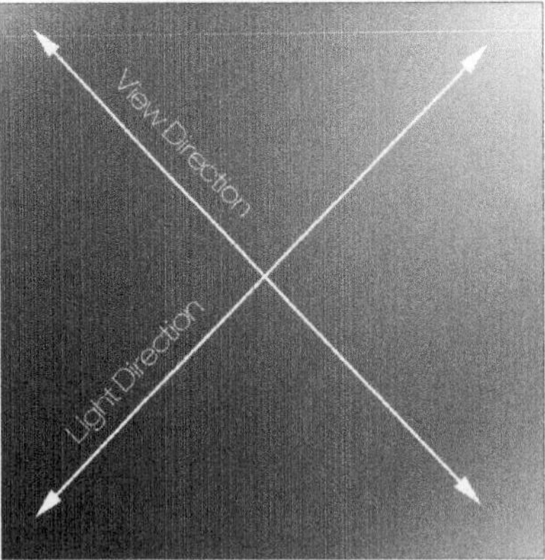

A visualization of what is happening inside the Shader code and how it is picking the color to put on the surface

So the key here is to understand what values we get from the dot product functions as well as how we can manipulate texture, inside of a lighting function, to wrap them around a surface in order to simulate a more complex lighting effect.

See also

- Refer to Polycount BRDF Map at `wiki.polycount.com/BrdfMap`

2

Using Textures for Effects

In this chapter we start looking at ways in which you can use textures to create different effects in your Shaders. As we saw in the previous chapter, textures can help us achieve more complex lighting effects. We can also use texture to animate, to blend and really, to drive any other property we want. In this chapter we learn about the following methods:

- Scrolling textures by modifying UV values
- Animating sprite sheets
- Packing and blending textures
- Normal mapping
- Creating procedural textures in the Unity editor
- Photoshop levels effect

Introduction

Textures can bring our Shaders to life, very quickly, in terms of achieving very realistic effects. Unfortunately, you have to be very careful about how many textures you use in your Shader as they can add up really quickly, and that will increasingly hit performance the more textures you add to your Shader. This is especially true for mobile solutions where you need to keep the amount of textures to a minimum, so that your application downloads faster and runs faster.

Textures themselves are images that are usually created in an image editing application, such as Photoshop, but can also be created inside of Unity itself. Textures themselves are mapped to the surface of an object by using the UVs of the object to create a relationship between the 2D point in the UVs, and the 3D point of a vertex. The pixel values are then interpolated between the vertices of the object to create the illusion of the 2D image being mapped on to the 3D surface.

We have already set up a texture property in the last chapter, so we won't have to cover that again, but if you would like to know more about the inner workings of how textures are mapped to a 3D surface, you can read the information available at `http://http.developer.nvidia.com/CgTutorial/cg_tutorial_chapter03.html`.

Let's start by taking a look at what we can do with textures and how they can make our real-time 3D visuals even more interesting and compelling. This chapter is going to start with some very basic textures effects, and then take you into the more advanced world of texturing for materials and Shaders.

Scrolling textures by modifying UV values

One of the most common texture techniques used in today's game industry is the process of allowing you to scroll their textures over the surface of an object. This allows you to create effects such as waterfalls, rivers, lava flows, and so on. It's also a technique that is the basis for creating animated sprite effects, but we will cover that in a subsequent recipe of this chapter. Let's first see how we will create a simple scrolling effect inside of a Surface Shader.

Getting ready

To begin this recipe, you will need to create a new Shader file and a new Material. This will set us up with a nice clean Shader that we can use to study the scrolling effect by itself.

How to do it...

To begin with, we will launch our new Shader file that we just created, and enter the code mentioned in the following steps:

1. The Shader will need two new properties that will allow us to control the speed of the texture scrolling. So let's add a speed property for the *X* direction and a speed property for the *Y* direction, as shown in the following code:

```
Properties
{
    _MainTint ("Diffuse Tint", Color) = (1,1,1,1)
    _MainTex ("Base (RGB)", 2D) = "white" {}
    _ScrollXSpeed ("X Scroll Speed", Range(0, 10)) = 2
    _ScrollYSpeed ("Y Scroll Speed", Range(0, 10)) = 2
}
```

2. Modify the Cg properties in the `CGPROGRAM` section and create new variables so that we can access the values from our properties:

```
fixed4 _MainTint;
fixed _ScrollXSpeed;
fixed _ScrollYSpeed;
sampler2D _MainTex;
```

3. Modify the surface function to change the UVs being given to the `tex2D()` function. Then use the built-in `_Time` variable to animate the UVs over time when **Play** is pressed in the editor:

```
void surf (Input IN, inout SurfaceOutput o)
{
    //Create a separate variable to store our uvs
    //before we pass them to the tex2D() function
    fixed2 scrolledUV = IN.uv_MainTex;

    //Create variables that store the individual x and y
    //components for the uvs scaled by time
    fixed xScrollValue = _ScrollXSpeed * _Time;
    fixed yScrollValue = _ScrollYSpeed * _Time;

    //Apply the final uv offset
    scrolledUV += fixed2(xScrollValue, yScrollValue);

    //Apply textures and tint
    half4 c = tex2D (_MainTex, scrolledUV);
    o.Albedo = c.rgb * _MainTint;
    o.Alpha = c.a;
}
```

The following image demonstrates the result of utilizing the scrolling UV system to create a simple river motion for your environments. It's hard to show something moving in a book, so you'll have to take my word for it.

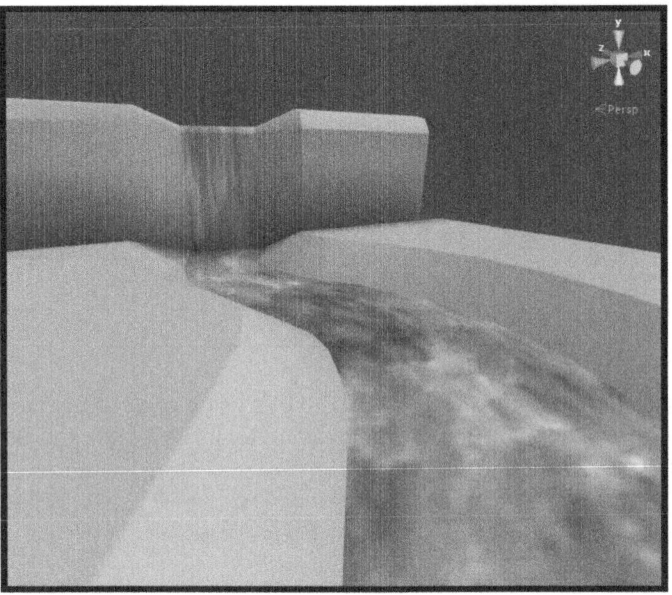

How it works...

The scrolling system starts with the declaration of a couple of properties, which will allow the user of this Shader to increase or decrease the speed of the scrolling effect itself. At their core they are float values being passed from the Material's **Inspector** tab to the surface function of the Shader. For more information on Shader properties, see *Chapter 1, Diffuse Shading*.

Once we have those float values from the Material's **Inspector** tab, we can use them to offset our UV values in the Shader.

To begin that process we first store the UVs in a separate variable called `scrolledUV`. This variable has to be a `float2 / fixed2` because the UV values are being passed to us from the `Input` structure:

```
struct Input
{
    float2 uv_MainTex;
};
```

Once we have access to the mesh's UVs, we can offset them using our scroll speed variables and the built-in `_Time` variable. This built-in variable returns a variable of type `float4`, meaning that each component of that variable contains different values of time, as it pertains to game time. A complete description of these individual time values are described at the following link:

http://docs.unity3d.com/Documentation/Components/SL-BuiltinValues.html

This `_Time` variable will give us an incremented float value based on Unity's game time clock. So, we can use that value to move our UVs in a UV direction and scale that time with our scroll speed variables:

```
//Create variables that store the individual x and y
//components for the uvs scaled by time
fixed xScrollValue = _ScrollXSpeed * _Time;
fixed yScrollValue = _ScrollYSpeed * _Time;
```

With the correct offset being calculated by time, we can add the new offset value back to the original UV position. This is why we are using the += operator in the next line. We want to take the original UV position, add on the new offset value, and then pass that to the `tex2D()` function as the texture's new UVs. This creates the effect of the texture moving on the surface. We are really manipulating the UVs so we are faking the effect of the texture moving.

```
//Apply the final uv offset
scrolledUV += fixed2(xScrollValue, yScrollValue);

//Apply textures and tint
half4 c = tex2D (_MainTex, scrolledUV);
```

Animating sprite sheets

Learning how to animate a sprite sheet will always come in handy. It can be used for particle effects, or for flip-book effects, and is most commonly seen in 2D side scroller games.

A sprite sheet, also referred to as a **sprite atlas**, if you aren't familiar with the term, is a big texture that has many smaller images embedded into it, and is sometimes referred to as an image sequence.

When you scroll over each of these smaller images in the sheet, you will get the effect of the content being animated. The concept is the same as making a flip book out of a sticky notepad or the frames on the film reel of a movie. If we cycle through each of the frames in our sprite sheet, we will create an animated effect.

This recipe will use a bit more math for the code, but no worries; we step through each new line of code and explain it thoroughly.

Getting ready

In order for us to be able to test our Shader code we will need some art content. We will have to either make a sprite sheet ourselves or find one on the Internet. The sprite sheet doesn't have to be complicated, it just needs a sequence of images to flip through. There is also this sprite sheet included in the book's support page located at `www.packtpub.com/support`.

Create a new Material and a new Shader. Then set up your Material by placing it onto a plane in the Scene view. Then place the sprite sheet into the texture swatch of the Material.

How to do it...

Let's get our sprite animation Shader working by entering the code in the following steps:

1. Create three new properties in the `Properties` block of the Shader. These will help us modify the system from the Materials **Inspector** without having to hardcode values:

```
Properties
{
    _MainTex ("Base (RGB)", 2D) = "white" {}

    //Create the properties below
    _TexWidth ("Sheet Width", float) = 0.0
    _CellAmount ("Cell Amount", float) = 0.0
    _Speed ("Speed", Range(0.01, 32)) = 12
}
```

2. Then store the input UVs into separate variables so that we can work with the values:

```
//Let's store our UVs in a separate variable
float2 spriteUV = IN.uv_MainTex;
```

3. Next we need to get the width of each cell. In the sprite sheet, this takes up a value in the range 0 to 1, so we need to produce a percentage value:

```
//Let's calculate the width of a singe cell in our
//sprite sheet and get a uv percentage that each cell takes up.
float cellPixelWidth = _TexWidth/_CellAmount;
float cellUVPercentage = cellPixelWidth/_TexWidth;
```

4. Next, we have to get the time component of our system that will give us the ability to move, or offset the UVs, from cell to cell:

```
//Let's get a stair step value out of time so we can increment
//the uv offset
float timeVal = fmod(_Time.y * _Speed, _CellAmount);
timeVal = ceil(timeVal);
```

5. Finally, we create the offset UVs that we can feed into the x direction of our sprite sheet. You should now have a Shader that creates a flip book for you.

```
//Animate the uvs forward by the width precentage of
//each cell
float xValue = spriteUV.x;
xValue += cellUVPercentage * timeVal * _CellAmount;
xValue *= cellUVPercentage;

spriteUV = float2(xValue, spriteUV.y);
```

The following is the result of offsetting the UVs of an object inside a Surface Shader. Again, you will have to take our word for it that the image is animated:

How it works...

The calculation starts by storing the UVs being passed from the `Input` struct into a separate variable. You don't necessarily have to do this, as it is more of a preference choice rather than a hard rule—it's just a way of reading code. In this case we called our new variable `spriteUV`, and declared it as a type `float2`. This is because we need to store the `x` and `y` values of our meshe's UVs in one variable.

The next step takes the width of our current texture and divides it up into smaller bits using the `_CellAmount` property declared in the property block. So if we have a texture that is 512 in width, and we divided it into 16 cells, we would get a value of 32. This represents the number of pixels that each cell has for its width, but we also need to know what percentage each cell takes up. This is because UV values are always calculated in a range of 0 to 1 or 0 percent to 100 percent. So we take the `cellPixelWidth` variable and divide it by the width of the texture itself. If we dive the cell width of 32 pixels by the texture width of 512 pixels, we end up with a value of 0.06, or 6 percent of the total width of the texture. This represents the value by which we need to offset the UVs in order to move to the next cell of the sprite sheet.

Next, we need to calculate some values that increase with time but are whole numbers. For instance, a value that increases as 0, 1, 2, 3, 4, and so on, until it reaches the total number of cells we have in our sprite sheet. To do this we can use the **CGFX** built-in function called `fmod()`.

Function	Description
`fmod(x , y)`	This returns the remainder of `x` / `y`, with the same sign as `x`. If `y` is 0, the result is defined by the implementation.

If we feed a value of `x` into the `fmod()` function and divide it by the value of `y`, we get the remainder of that operation returned to us. So, if we use the `_Time` value for `x` and use the `_CellAmount` property value for `y`, we will get a return value that increases with time, and it will repeat once it is equal to the `_CellAmount` value.

With that type of value generated, we then use the `ceil()` function to make sure that the value is a whole number, instead of some decimal. This basically works by taking a number such as 1.5 and forcing it to be 2. This creates the number pattern 0, 1, 2, 3, 4,... all the way to the `_CellAmount` property value. Once it reaches that cell amount value, it starts over at 0.

Function	Description
`ceil(x)`	Where the smallest integer is not less than `x`.

Finally, we get the current `x` value from the input UV and add the product of the cell percentage and the current time value multiplied by the total cell amount. This will move our UVs from cell to cell, but we have to also scale our UV value so that only one cell is visible at any one particular time. To accomplish this, we simply multiply the result of the offset UV by the cell percentage, and we have our final UV value. All that needs to be done is to pass that new UV value into the UV value of the `tex2D` function for the texture.

There's more...

You might have see it already, but you don't have to use only one of the offset directions. Just like we gave two directions to the offset in the previous scrolling UVs recipe, we can have a 2D animated sprite sheet. You simply need to add the `y` offset to the final offset value.

This is the same as the horizontal scrolling we set up, but now you can cycle through a larger sheet of images in multiple dimensions. While this shows just the number of things you can do on the Shader side of development, it might end up adding too many Shader instructions to your Shader. This means that it will eat up your application's performance.

To combat this, you can move the frame offset selection code to a C# script that talks to the Shader, and have the CPU drive that portion of the code. It really comes down to balancing your application when it's time to optimize, but it never hurts to think of elements that you may encounter in the future, and design your production around that. This book includes a C# script that demonstrates how a simple sprite animation system can be created using a script to pass data to a Shader. It basically does the time calculations for us, and passes only the time value to the Shader using the following code:

```
void FixedUpdate ()
{
    timeValue = Mathf.Ceil(Time.time % 16);
    transform.renderer.material.SetFloat("_TimeValue", timeValue);
}
```

See also

If you aren't up for creating a whole system for animating sprites yourself, there are many resources on the Asset Store that takes care of most, if not all, sprite animation needs. Here is a list of a few of those resources:

- **SpriteManager** (Free):

  `http://wiki.unity3d.com/index.php?title=SpriteManager`

- **2D ToolKit** (Asset Store / $65.00):

  `http://www.unikronsoftware.com/2dtoolkit/`

- **Sprite Manager 2** (Asset Store / $150.00):

  `http://anbsoft.com/middleware/sm2/`

If you are looking for a good application to help you make sprites, here is a list of a few of them:

- **TimelineFX** ($46.79):

  `http://www.rigzsoft.co.uk/`

- **Anime Studio Pro** ($199.99):

  `http://anime.smithmicro.com/index.html`

- **Adobe Flash Professional** ($699.00):

  `http://www.adobe.com/products/flash.html`

Packing and blending textures

Textures are also useful for storing loads of data, not just pixel colors as we generally tend to think of them, but for storing multiple sets of pixels in both the *x* and *y* directions and in the RGBA channels. We can actually pack multiple images into one single RGBA texture and use each of the R, G, B, and A components as individual textures themselves, by extracting each of those components in the Shader code.

The result of packing individual grayscale images into a single RGBA texture can be seen in the following image:

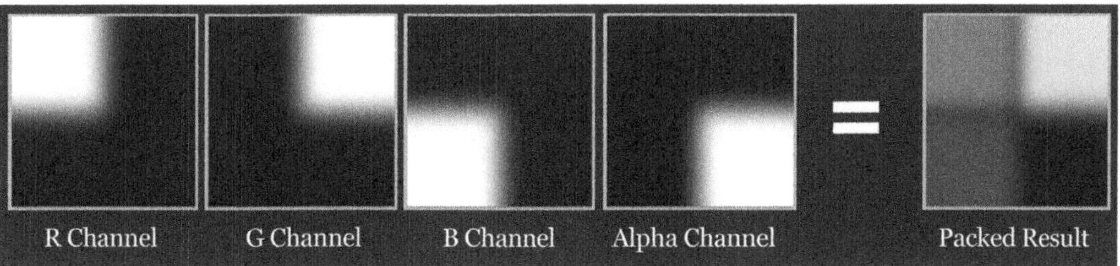

Why is this helpful? Well, in terms of the amount of actual memory your application takes up, textures are a large portion of your application's size. So, to begin reducing the size of your application, we can look at all of the images that we are using in our Shader and see if we can merge those textures into a single texture.

Any texture that is grayscale can be packed into one of the RGBA channels of another texture. This might sound a bit odd at first, but this recipe is going to demonstrate one of the uses for packing a texture and using those packed textures inside a Shader.

One example of using these packed textures is when you want to blend a set of textures together onto a single surface. You see this most often in terrain type Shaders, where you need to blend nicely into another texture using some sort of control texture, or the packed texture in this case. This recipe covers that technique and shows you how you can construct the beginnings of a nice four-texture blended terrain Shader.

Getting ready

Let's create a new Shader file in your Shader folder, and then create a new Material for this Shader. The naming convention is entirely up to you for your Shader and Material files, so try your best to keep them organized and easy to reference later on.

Once you have your Shader and Material ready, create a new scene in which we can test our Shader.

You will also need to gather up four textures that you would want to blend together. These can be anything, but for a nice terrain Shader, you will want a grass, dirt, rocky dirt, and a rock texture.

These are the color textures we will be using for this recipe, which are included with this book.

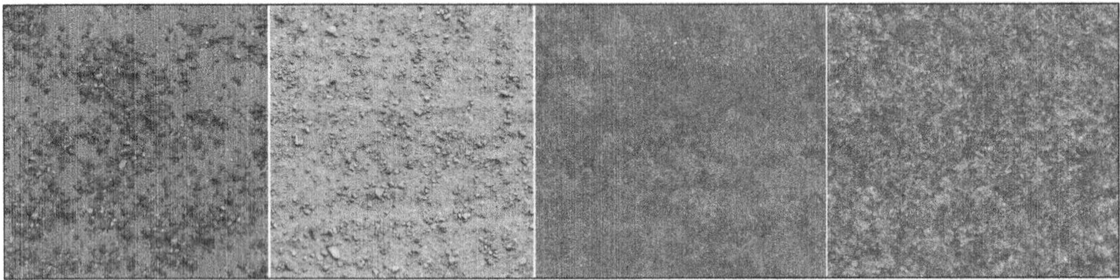

Finally, we will also need a blending texture that is packed with grayscale images. This will give us the four blending textures that we can use to direct how the color textures will be placed on the object surface.

We can use very intricate blending textures to create a very realistic distribution of terrain textures over a terrain mesh, as seen in the following image:

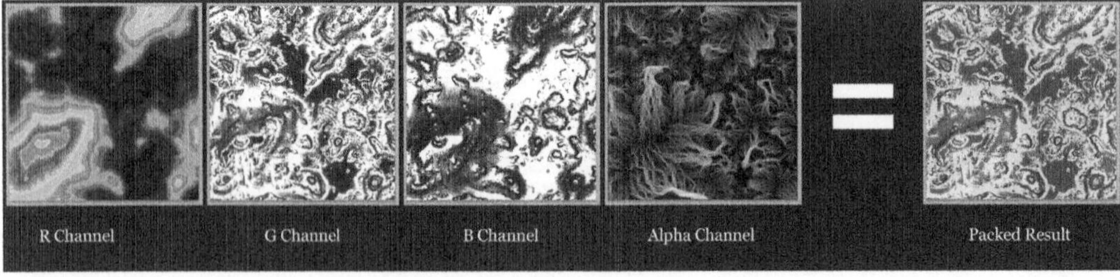

How to do it...

Let's learn how to use packed textures by entering the code shown in the following steps:

1. We need to add a few properties to our `Properties` block. We will need five `sampler2D` objects, or textures, and two color properties.

```
Properties
{
    _MainTint ("Diffuse Tint", Color) = (1,1,1,1)

    //Add the properties below so we can input all of our textures
    _ColorA ("Terrain Color A", Color) = (1,1,1,1)
    _ColorB ("Terrain Color B", Color) = (1,1,1,1)
    _RTexture ("Red Channel Texture", 2D) = ""{}
    _GTexture ("Green Channel Texture", 2D) = ""{}
    _BTexture ("Blue Channel Texture", 2D) = ""{}
    _ATexture ("Alpha Channel Texture", 2D) = ""{}
    _BlendTex ("Blend Texture", 2D) = ""{}
}
```

2. We then need to create the **SubShader** variables that will be our link to the data in the `Properties` block:

```
CGPROGRAM
#pragma surface surf Lambert

float4 _MainTint;
float4 _ColorA;
float4 _ColorB;
sampler2D _RTexture;
sampler2D _GTexture;
sampler2D _BTexture;
sampler2D _BlendTex;
sampler2D _ATexture;
```

3. So now we have our texture properties, and we are passing them into our `SubShader` function. In order to allow the user to change the tiling rates on a per-texture basis, we will need to modify our `Input` struct. This will allow us to use the tiling and offset parameters on each texture:

```
struct Input
{
    float2 uv_RTexture;
    float2 uv_GTexture;
    float2 uv_BTexture;
    float2 uv_ATexture;
    float2 uv_BlendTex;
};
```

4. In the `surf` function, get the texture information and store them into their own variables so we can work with the data in a clean, easy-to-understand way:

```
//Get the pixel data from the blend texture
//we need a float4 here because the texture
//will return R,G,B,and A or X,Y,Z, and W
float4 blendData = tex2D(_BlendTex, IN.uv_BlendTex);

//Get the data from the textures we want to blend
float4 rTexData = tex2D(_RTexture, IN.uv_RTexture);
float4 gTexData = tex2D(_GTexture, IN.uv_GTexture);
float4 bTexData = tex2D(_BTexture, IN.uv_BTexture);
float4 aTexData = tex2D(_ATexture, IN.uv_ATexture);
```

5. Let's blend each of our textures together using the `lerp()` function. It takes in three arguments, `lerp(value : a, value : b, blend: c)`. The `lerp` function takes in two textures and blends them with the float value given in the last argument:

```
//Now we need to contruct a new RGBA value and add all
//the different blended texture back together
float4 finalColor;
finalColor = lerp(rTexData, gTexData, blendData.g);
finalColor = lerp(finalColor, bTexData, blendData.b);
finalColor = lerp(finalColor, aTexData, blendData.a);
finalColor.a = 1.0;
```

6. Finally, we multiply our blended textures with the color tint values and use the red channel to determine where the two different terrain tint colors go:

```
//Add on our terrain tinting colors
float4 terrainLayers = lerp(_ColorA, _ColorB, blendData.r);
finalColor *= terrainLayers;
finalColor = saturate(finalColor);

o.Albedo = finalColor.rgb * _MainTint.rgb;
o.Alpha = finalColor.a;
```

The result of blending together four terrain textures and creating a terrain tinting technique can be seen in the following image:

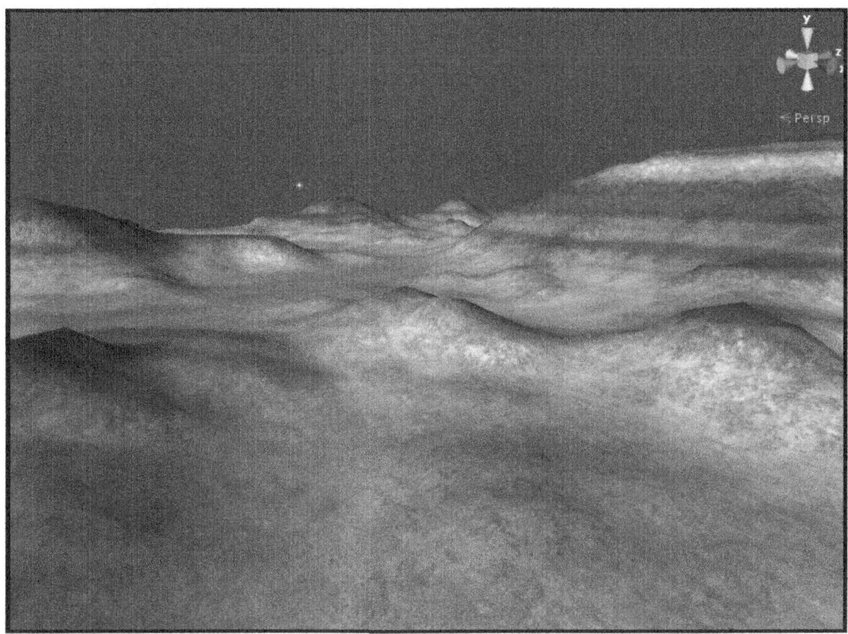

How it works...

This might seem like quite a few lines of code, but the concept behind blending is actually quite simple. For the technique to work we have to employ the `lerp()` built-in function from the CGFX standard library. This function allows us to pick a value between argument one and argument two by using argument three as the blend amount.

Function	Description
`lerp( a , b, f )`	Involves linear interpolation: `(1 - f )* a + b * f` Here, `a` and `b` are matching vector or scalar types. `f` can be either a scalar or a vector of the same type as `a` and `b`.

So, for example, if we wanted to find the mid-value between 1 and 2, we could feed the value 0.5 as the third argument to the `lerp()` function and it would return the value 1.5. This works perfectly for our blending needs as the values of an individual channel in an RGBA texture are single float values, usually in the range of 0 to 1.

In the Shader, we simply take one of the channels from our blend texture and use it to drive the color that is picked in a `lerp` function, for each pixel. For instance, we take our grass texture and our dirt texture and use the red channel from our blending texture, and feed that into a `lerp()` function. This will give us the correct blended color result for each pixel on the surface.

A more visual representation of what is happening when using the `lerp()` function is shown in the following image:

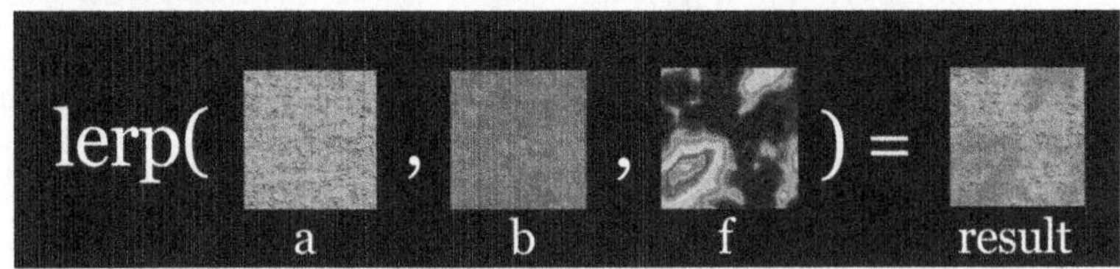

The Shader code simply uses the four channels of the blend texture, and all the color textures, to create a final blended texture. This final texture then becomes our color that we can multiply with our diffuse lighting.

See also

The terrain for this recipe was created with World Machine. This is a great way to produce very complex terrain blending textures and meshes.

- **World Machine** ($189.00):

  `http://www.world-machine.com/`

Normal mapping

One of the most common texture techniques used in today's game development pipelines is the use of **normal maps**. These give us the ability to fake the effect of high-resolution geometry on a low-resolution model. This is because instead of performing lighting calculations on a per-vertex level, we are using each pixel in the normal map as a normal on the model, giving us much more resolution on how the lighting should be, while still maintaining the low polygon count of our object.

> *In 3D computer graphics, normal mapping, or "Dot3 bump mapping", is a technique used for faking the lighting of bumps and dents – an implementation of Bump mapping. It is used to add details without using more polygons. A common use of this technique is to greatly enhance the appearance and details of a low polygon model by generating a normal map from a high polygon model or height map.*
>
> *Normal maps are commonly stored as regular RGB images where the RGB components corresponds to the X, Y, and Z coordinates, respectively, of the surface normal.*

The previous text is a quote from Wikipedia (`http://en.wikipedia.org/wiki/Normal_mapping`).

There are many ways to create normal maps these days. Some applications such as **CrazyBump** (`http://www.crazybump.com/`) and **N2DO** (`http://quixel.se/ndo/`) will take in 2D data and convert it to normal data for you. Other applications, such as **Zbrush** (`http://www.pixologic.com/`) and **Mudbox** (`http://usa.autodesk.com`), will take 3D sculpted data and create normal maps for you. The actual process of creating normal maps is definitely out of the scope of this book, but the links in the previous text should help you get started.

Unity makes the process of adding normals to your Shaders quite an easy process within the Surface Shader realm, using the `UnpackNormals()` function. Let's see how this is done.

Getting ready

Create a new Material and Shader and set them up on a new object in the Scene view. This will give us a clean workspace in which we can look at just the normal mapping technique.

You will need a normal map for this recipe, but there is also one included in the Unity project that is included with this book.

An example normal map included with this book's contents is shown here:

How to do it...

1. Let's get our `Properties` block set up to have a color tint and a texture:

```
Properties
{
    _MainTint ("Diffuse Tint", Color) = (1,1,1,1)
    _NormalTex ("Normal Map", 2D) = "bump" {}
}
```

2. Link the properties to the Cg program by declaring them inside the subshader below the `CGPROGRAM` statement:

```
CGPROGRAM
#pragma surface surf Lambert

//Link the property to the CG program
sampler2D _NormalTex;
float4 _MainTint;
```

3. We need to make sure that we update the `Input` struct with the proper variable name, so that we can use the model's UVs for the normal map texture.

```
//Make sure you get the uvs for the texture in the Struct
struct Input
{
    float2 uv_NormalTex;
};
```

4. Finally, we extract the normal information from the normal map texture by using the built-in `UnpackNormal()` function. Then you only have to apply those new normals to the output of the Surface Shader:

```
//Get the normal Data out of the normal map textures
//using the UnpackNormal() function.
float3 normalMap = UnpackNormal(tex2D(_NormalTex, IN.uv_NormalTex));

//Apply the new normals to the lighting model
o.Normal = normalMap.rgb;
```

The following image demonstrates the result of our normal map Shader:

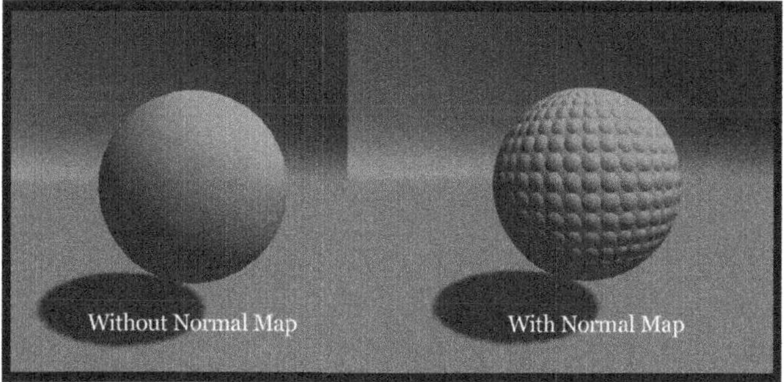

How it works...

The actual math to perform the normal mapping effect is definitely beyond the scope of this chapter, but Unity has done it all for us already anyway. They have created the functions for us, so that we don't have to keep doing it over and over again. This another reason why Surface Shaders are a really efficient way to write Shaders.

If you look inside the `UnityCG.cginc` file, found in the `Data` folder in your Unity install directory, you will find the definitions for the `UnpackNormal()` function. When you declare this function inside your Surface Shader, Unity takes the provided normal map and processes it for you, and gives you the correct type of data back to you so that you can use it in your per-pixel lighting function. It's a huge time saver!

Once you have processed the normal map with the `UnpackNormal()` function, you send it back to your `SurfaceOutput` struct, so that it can be used in the lighting function. This is done by the line `o.Normal = normalMap.rgb;`.

There's more...

You can also add some controls to your normal map Shader that lets a user adjust the intensity of the normal map. This is easily done by modifying the `x` and `y` components of the normal map variable, and then adding it all back together.

1. Add another property to the properties block and name it `_NormalMapIntensity`, as shown in the following code:

```
Properties
{
    //Add these Properties
    _MainTint ("Diffuse Tint", Color) = (1,1,1,1)
    _NormalTex ("Normal Map", 2D) = "bump" {}
    _NormalIntensity ("Normal Map Intensity", Range(0,2)) = 1
}
```

2. Make sure to declare that property inside the `SubShader` function:

```
//Link the property to the CG program
sampler2D _NormalTex;
float4 _MainTint;
float _NormalIntensity;
```

3. Multiply the `x` and `y` components of the unpacked normal map and re-apply that value back to the normal map variable. Now you can let a user adjust the intensity of the normal map in the Material **Inspector**:

```
//Get the normal Data out of the normal map textures
//using the UnpackNormal() function.
float3 normalMap = UnpackNormal(tex2D(_NormalTex, IN.uv_NormalTex));
normalMap = float3(normalMap.x * _NormalIntensity, normalMap.y * _NormalIntensity, normalMap.z);
```

The following image shows the result of modifying the normal map with our scalar values:

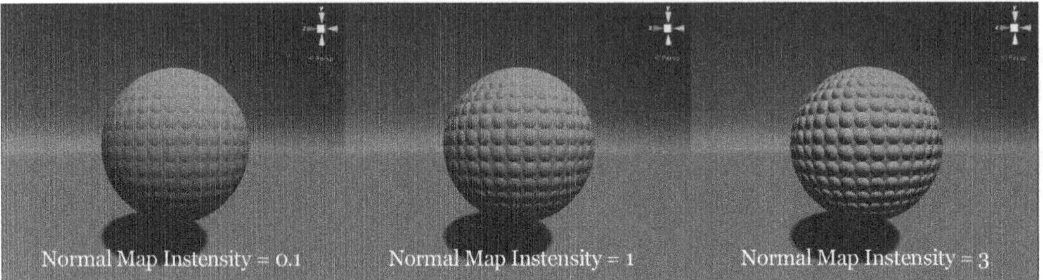

Creating procedural textures in the Unity editor

There are times when you want to dynamically create textures and modify their pixels at runtime, to produce different effects. These are usually called **procedural texture effects**. Instead of having to manually create some new texture inside an image editing application, you can create a set of pixels in a two-dimensional nature and apply that to a new texture. Then, take that new texture and pass it to the Shader itself to use in its calculations.

This technique can be very useful for painting onto an already-existing texture map, using a dynamically created texture map, to create some interaction between the gamer and the game environment. It can also be used as a decal type effect, or for creating procedural shapes used in the functions of the Shader. There are many situations in which you might want to create a new texture and fill it with some procedural pattern, and use it in your Shaders.

The process of creating dynamic textures does rely on creating a separate script that processes the texture for you, but it is something that you should know how to do, in terms of having a good set of techniques for your shading pipeline. Let's see how to set up a script that will send its dynamically-created texture to a Surface Shader.

Getting ready

You will need to prepare yourself for this recipe by carrying out the following steps:

1. Create a new C# script in your Unity project, and name it `ProceduralTexture`.
2. Create an empty GameObject in your scene, zero-out its **Position** values, and assign the `ProceduralTexture.cs` script to it.
3. Next, create a new Shader, a new Material, and a new object that will hold our Shader and Material. Make sure you name the Shader and Material, so that you can find them easily.
4. With all of that set up, we are ready to create the code that will generate a parabola type shape, apply it to the texture, and give that texture to the Shader. By the end of the recipe you will have created a texture that looks like the following image:

How to do it...

1. Create a variable to control the height and width of our texture, and a `Texture2D` variable to store our generated texture. We will also need some private variables to store some data while the script is working.

```
#region Public Variables
//These values will let us control the width/Height
//and see the generated texture
public int widthHeight = 512;
public Texture2D generatedTexture;
#endregion

#region Private Variables
//These variables will be internal to this
//script
private Material currentMaterial;
private Vector2 centerPosition;
#endregion
```

2. In the `Start ()` function of the script, we need to first check to see if the object, to which this script is attached does in fact have a Material assigned to it. If it does, we will call our custom function `GenerateParabola()` and pass its return value back to our `Texture2D` variable:

```
void Start ()
{
    //Simple check to make sure we have a material on this transform
    //This will determine if we can make a texture or not
    if(!currentMaterial)
    {
        currentMaterial = transform.renderer.sharedMaterial;
        if(!currentMaterial)
        {
            Debug.LogWarning("Cannot find a material on: " + transform.name);
        }
    }

    //generate the procedural texture
    if(currentMaterial)
    {
        //Generate the parabola texture
        centerPosition = new Vector2(0.5f, 0.5f);
        generatedTexture = GenerateParabola();

        //Assign it to this transforms material
        currentMaterial.SetTexture("_MainTex", generatedTexture);
    }

}
```

3. We then need to declare our custom function that will produce the desired effect for us:

```
private Texture2D GenerateParabola()
{

}
```

4. Finally, we fill our custom function with the algorithm that produces the parabola shape in the texture. Don't worry if this doesn't make sense yet; we will cover each line of code in the next section of this recipe.

```
private Texture2D GenerateParabola()
{
    //Create a new Texture2D
    Texture2D proceduralTexture = new Texture2D(widthHeight, widthHeight);

    //Get the center of the texture
    Vector2 centerPixelPosition = centerPosition * widthHeight;

    //loop through each pixel of the new texture and determine its
    //distance from the center and assign a pixel value based on that.
    for(int x = 0; x < widthHeight; x++)
    {
        for(int y = 0; y < widthHeight; y++)
        {
            //Get the distance from the center of the texture to
            //our currently selected pixel
            Vector2 currentPosition = new Vector2(x,y);
            float pixelDistance = Vector2.Distance(currentPosition, centerPixelPosition)/(widthHeight*0.5f);

            //Invert the values and make sure we dont get any negative values
            //or values above 1.
            pixelDistance = Mathf.Abs(1-Mathf.Clamp(pixelDistance, 0f,1f));

            //Create a new color value based off of our
            Color pixelColor = new Color(pixelDistance, pixelDistance, pixelDistance, 1.0f);
            proceduralTexture.SetPixel(x,y,pixelColor);
        }
    }
    //Finally force the application of the new pixels to the texture
    proceduralTexture.Apply();

    //return the texture to the main program.
    return proceduralTexture;
}
```

How it works...

The script starts out simply by checking to see if this particular object in the scene actually has a material on it that we can assign a texture to. If it does, we assign our `currentMaterial` variable the return value of `transform.renderer.sharedMaterial`, which returns a Material.

We then move to our next `if()` statement and check to see if we have a valid Material. If we do, we call the `GenerateParabola()` function, which will return a `Texture2D` for us.

Once the program has moved to the `GenerateParabola()` function, it begins by creating a new texture, using the new `Texture2D()` constructor, and passing in our `widthHeight` variables. The result of this action creates an empty texture that allows us to add in pixel colors for each pixel in `widthHeight` squared.

With the new texture, we calculate the center pixel position and store it in the `centerPixelPosition` variable.

We then start two `for` loops that will simply loop through each pixel in the new empty texture that we created. If you aren't familiar with the C# `for` loop, see `http://msdn.microsoft.com/en-us/library/ch45axte.aspx`.

Then, for each pixel at `Vector2(x,y)` currently selected in the loops, we measure its distance from the center pixel, using the `Vector2.Distance()` function. This function will return a float value for us. For instance, if the current pixel position in the loop is equal to `Vector2(32,32)`, we would get a distance value of 316.78, if we created a 512 x 512 texture. That is, the pixel distance is (32,32) from the center.

We will then need to re-map the pixel distance to be within a range of 0. 0 to 1.0, so it can be used as a color value (Unity uses values from 0.0 to 1.0 as color values). All we have to do in order to achieve this remapping is to divide the distance value by half the texture's width or height. So, in this case, we divide our distance by 256, since it is half the value 512. So, if we have a distance of 316.78, as we saw in the previous example, we would get a value of 1.23.

Now, we need to make sure we don't get any values above 1.0 or below 0.0, so we use the `Mathf.Clamp()` function, which allows us to clamp the value to limits that you pass in as arguments. We passed in 0 and 1 to make sure we get a normalized value.

Finally, we invert the color by subtracting the current value from 1, and then pass that final value into the channels of a new color variable. See the following image:

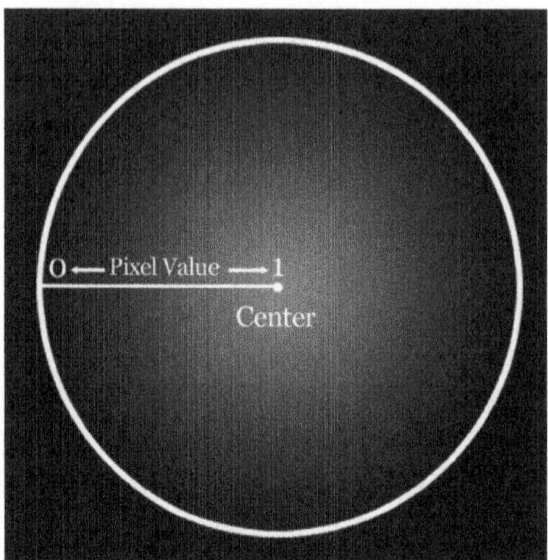

There's more...

Now that you have seen how to generate pixel values by using just a little bit of vector math, think of all the other types of data you can generate and store into a texture. The following code demonstrates other types of data you can generate, by looking at the dot product of a world vector and the pixel direction from the center of the image.

1. Here is the math to create rings around the center of the texture:

```
//Get the distance from the center of the texture to
//our currently selected pixel
Vector2 currentPosition = new Vector2(x,y);
float pixelDistance = Vector2.Distance(currentPosition, centerPixelPosition)/(widthHeight*0.5f);
pixelDistance = Mathf.Abs(1-Mathf.Clamp(pixelDistance, 0f,1f));
pixelDistance = (Mathf.Sin(pixelDistance * 30.0f) * pixelDistance);
```

2. The following is the math for creating the dot product of the pixel direction as compared with the right and up world vectors:

```
//you can also do some more advanced vector calculations to achieve
//other types of data about the model itself and its uvs and
//pixels
Vector2 pixelDirection = centerPixelPosition - currentPosition;
pixelDirection.Normalize();
float rightDirection = Vector2.Dot(pixelDirection, Vector3.right);
float leftDirection = Vector2.Dot(pixelDirection, Vector3.left);
float upDirection = Vector2.Dot(pixelDirection, Vector3.up);
```

3. The following is the math for creating the angle of the pixel direction as compared to world directions:

```
//you can also do some more advanced vector calculations to achieve
//other types of data about the model itself and its uvs and
//pixels
Vector2 pixelDirection = centerPixelPosition - currentPosition;
pixelDirection.Normalize();
float rightDirection = Vector2.Angle(pixelDirection, Vector3.right)/360;
float leftDirection = Vector2.Angle(pixelDirection, Vector3.left)/360;
float upDirection = Vector2.Angle(pixelDirection, Vector3.up)/360;
```

The different results of processing the pixels with different vector and angle calculations can be seen in the following image.

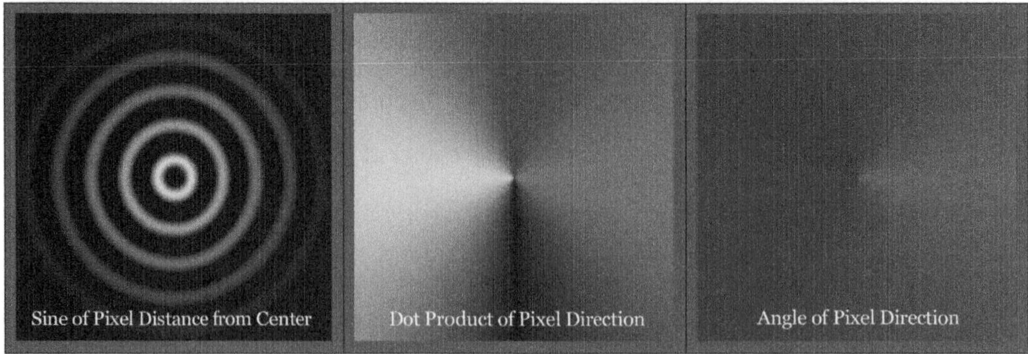

Photoshop levels effect

If you have ever done any sort of image editing, such as touching up a family photograph, making game textures, or digitally painting a picture, we are sure you understand the power of having levels to globally adjust your entire image. Well, it is completely possible to create Photoshop-like effects inside your Shaders as well.

All the different image editing tools and blending modes that you find in Photoshop are all described with a set of math operations. Ultimately, we are multiplying, adding, subtracting, and comparing pixel values with some other value, to finally get a return value. This return value then becomes the new pixel color in the image you're editing.

While we could write a whole book on just the different math recipes for the Photoshop effects, we are focusing on just levels here. We will cover more advanced blending modes in *Chapter 10, Screen Effects with Unity Render Textures*.

Getting ready

In order to complete this recipe, you will need to have a new Shader and Material created, and assign it to an object in a new Unity scene. You will also need a source texture with which to test out our level's code. You can also use the Materials that are included with this cookbook.

How to do it...

1. Add the following properties to the new Shader:

```
Properties
{
    _MainTex ("Base (RGB)", 2D) = "white" {}

    //Add the Input Levels Values
    _inBlack ("Input Black", Range(0, 255)) = 0
    _inGamma ("Input Gamma", Range(0, 2)) = 1.61
    _inWhite ("Input White", Range(0, 255)) = 255

    //Add the Output Levels
    _outWhite ("Output White", Range(0, 255)) = 255
    _outBlack ("Output Black", Range(0, 255)) = 0
}
```

2. Make sure to also declare those properties as variables in your `CGPROGRAM` statement:

```
    //Add these variables
    //to the CGPROGRAM
    float _inBlack;
    float _inGamma;
    float _inWhite;
    float _outWhite;
    float _outBlack;
```

3. Create a new variable to store only the red channel of our current `_MainTex` texture:

```
  //Create a variable to store
  //a pixel channel from our _MainTex texture
  float outRPixel;
```

4. Since the values that are given to us by the `tex2D()` function are in a range from 0.0 to 1.0, we need to re-map the range to 0.0 to 255.0.

```
    //remap 0 to 1 range to 0 to 255
    outRPixel = (c.r * 255.0);
```

5. We then subtract our input black colors to bring all pixels to black as you slide the slider towards 255.0:

```
//Subtract the black value given to us
//by the  inBlack property
outRPixel = max(0, outRPixel - _inBlack);
```

6. Then we increase the whites of all pixels as we slide the input white slider towards 0.0, and take the result to a power of input gamma:

```
//Increase white value of each pixel with inWhite
outRPixel = saturate(pow(outRPixel / (_inWhite - _inBlack), _inGamma));
```

7. Finally, we multiply the new pixel value by the output white minus the output black, and then re-map the new pixel value to a range from 0.0 to 1.0:

```
//Change final black point and white point and
//re-map from 0 to 255 to 0 to 1
outRPixel = (outRPixel * (_outWhite - _outBlack) + _outBlack)/255.0;
```

The following image demonstrates the final effect of applying a level's procedure to our texture, through a Shader:

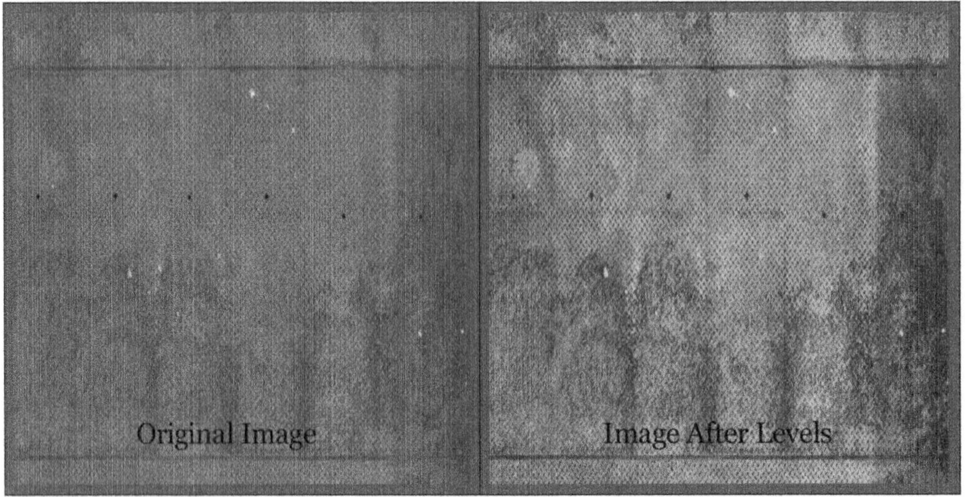

How it works...

The Shader's `surf` function starts by sampling a color texture using the `tex2D()` function and stores it in a variable called `c`. At this point, we want to start to work on the individual channels and modify each channel's pixels. To do this, we create a new variable called `outRPixel` and assign it the value of `c.r * 255.0`. This will take the value from the range 0.0 to 1.0 to a value of 0.0 to 255.0.

The program then takes the current pixel value and subtracts the `_inBlack` property value, in order to darken the pixels value. We also make sure that the value doesn't go below 0.0 after the subtraction, by using the `max()` function, which gives us the maximum of two values.

Function	Description
`max( a, b )`	This returns the maximum of a and b

We now want to take our modified pixel value and divide it by the new white point values. We can get the new white point value by subtracting the `_inBlack` value from the `_inWhite` value. This will simply raise the pixel value or make it brighter. This raised pixel value is then taken to a power of `_inGamma`, which basically allows you to move the midpoint value of the current pixel.

Finally, we modify the pixel again with the `_outWhite` and `_outBlack`, so you can have a final global control of what the minimum pixel value can be, as well as what the maximum pixel value can be. This result is then divided by 255.0, to get it back within the 0.0 to 1.0 range.

We take that final result and pass it to `o.Albedo` for our final diffuse color. When you play with the sliders in the Material's **Inspector** tab, you notice that you have a lot of control over the texture's contrast and brightness.

There's more...

We are sure you noticed, but we have a lot of duplicate code in our Shader. We can actually create a custom function within our Shader to clean our Shader code. This will help keep things clear and to make our Shader more efficient from a development standpoint. See the following custom function:

```
float GetPixelLevel(float pixelColor)
{
    float pixelResult;
    pixelResult = (pixelColor * 255.0);
    pixelResult = max(0, pixelResult - _inBlack);
    pixelResult = saturate(pow(pixelResult / (_inWhite - _inBlack), _inGamma));
    pixelResult = (pixelResult * (_outWhite - _outBlack) + _outBlack)/255.0;
    return pixelResult;
}
```

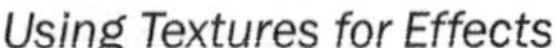

By using this new function inside our Shader to process the final pixel level, we reduced our `surf` function Shader code to only three lines for all channels, instead of 15. This greatly cleans up our code and we now only have to make code changes in a single place, rather than three.

See also

- More information on levels can be found at *GPU Gems* (`http://http.developer.nvidia.com/GPUGems/gpugems_ch22.html`)

3

Making Your Game Shine with Specular

Everybody loves games like Gears of War and Call of Duty, but what is it about these games that make them so visually compelling and very realistic? Well, it is a combination of things really, but one of the more key elements that these games employ in their Shader pipelines are different types of Specular. This chapter will introduce you to the basics of Specular and demonstrate some of the tricks that today's AAA games use every day in their Shader pipelines.

In this chapter, will learn the following:

- Utilizing Unity3D's built-in Specular type
- Creating a Phong Specular type
- Creating a BlinnPhong Specular type
- Masking Specular with textures
- Metallic versus soft Specular
- Creating an Anisotropic Specular type

Introduction

The specularity of an object surface simply describes how shiny it is. These types of effects are often referred to as view-dependent effects in the Shader world. This is because in order to achieve a realistic Specular effect in your Shaders, you need to include the direction the camera or user is facing the object's surface. Although Specular requires one more component to achieve its visual believability, which is the light direction. By combining these two directions or vectors, we end up with a hotspot or highlight on the surface of the object, half way between the view direction and the light direction. This half-way direction is called the half vector and is something new we are going to explore in this chapter, along with customizing our Specular effects to simulate metallic and cloth Specular surfaces.

Utilizing Unity3D's built-in Specular type

Unity has already provided us with a Specular function we can use for our Shaders. It is called the BlinnPhong Specular lighting model. It is one of the more basic and efficient forms of Specular, which you can find used in a lot of games even today. Since it is already built into the Unity Surface Shader language, we thought it is best to start with that first and build on it. You can also find an example in the Unity reference manual, but we will go into a bit more depth with it and explain where the data is coming from and why it is working the way it is. This will help you to get a nice grounding in setting up Specular, so that we can build on that knowledge in the future recipes in this chapter.

Getting ready

Let's start by carrying out the following:

1. Create a new Shader and give it a name.
2. Create a new Material, give it a name, and assign the new Shader to its shaper property.
3. Then create a sphere object and place it roughly at world center.
4. Finally, let's create a directional light to cast some light onto our object.

When your assets have been set up in Unity, you should have a scene that resembles the following screenshot:

How to do it...

1. Begin by adding the following properties to the Shader's `Properties` block:

```
Properties
{
    _MainTex ("Base (RGB)", 2D) = "white" {}
    _MainTint ("Diffuse Tint", Color) = (1,1,1,1)
    _SpecColor ("Specular Color", Color) = (1,1,1,1)
    _SpecPower ("Specular Power", Range(0,1)) = 0.5
}
```

2. We then need to make sure we add the variables to the `CGPROGRAM` block, so that we can use the data in our new properties inside our Shader's `CGPROGRAM` block. Notice that we don't need to declare the `_SpecColor` property as a variable. This is because Unity has already created this variable for us in the built-in Specular model. All we need to do is declare it in our Properties block and it will pass the data along to the `surf()` function.

```
sampler2D _MainTex;
float _SpecPower;
float4 _MainTint;
```

3. Our Shader now needs to be told which lighting model we want to use to light our model with. You have seen the Lambert lighting model and how to make your own lighting model, but we haven't seen the **BlinnPhong lighting model** yet. So, let's add `BlinnPhong` to our `#pragma` statement like so:

```
CGPROGRAM
#pragma surface surf BlinnPhong
```

4. We then need to modify our `surf()` function to look like the following:

```
void surf (Input IN, inout SurfaceOutput o)
{
    half4 c = tex2D (_MainTex, IN.uv_MainTex) * _MainTint;
    o.Specular = _SpecPower;
    o.Gloss = 1.0;
    o.Albedo = c.rgb;
    o.Alpha = c.a;
}
ENDCG
```

How it works...

This basic Specular is a great starting point when you are prototyping your Shaders, as you can get a lot accomplished in terms of writing the core functionality of the Shader, while not having to worry about the basic lighting functions.

Unity has provided us with a lighting model that has already taken the task of creating your Specular lighting for you. If you look into the `UnityCG.cginc` file found in your Unity's install directory under the `Data` folder, you will notice that you have Lambert and BlinnPhong lighting models available for you to use. The moment you compile your Shader with the `#pragma` surface surf BlinnPhong, you are telling the Shader to utilize the BlinnPhong lighting function in the `UnityCG.cginc` file, so that we don't have to write that code over and over again.

With your Shader compiled and no errors present, you should see a result similar to the following screenshot:

Creating a Phong Specular type

The most basic and performance-friendly Specular type is the **Phong** Specular effect. It is the calculation of the light direction reflecting off of the surface compared to the user's view direction. It is a very common Specular model used in many applications, from games to movies. While it isn't the most realistic in terms of accurately modeling the reflected Specular, it gives a great approximation that performs well in most situations. Plus, if your object is further away from the camera and the need for a very accurate Specular isn't needed, this is a great way to provide a Specular effect on your Shaders.

In this recipe, we will be covering how to implement the per vertex version of the and also see how to implement the per pixel version using some new parameters in the surface Shader's `Input` struct. We will see the difference and discuss when and why to use these two different implementations for different situations.

Getting ready

1. Create a new Shader, Material, and object, and give them appropriate names so that you can find them later.
2. Finally, attach the Shader to the Material and the Material to the object. To finish off your new scene, create a new directional light so that we can see our Specular effect as we code it.

How to do it...

1. You might be seeing a pattern at this point, but we always like to start out with our most basic part of the Shader writing process: the creation of properties. So, let's add the following properties to the Shader:

```
Properties
{
    _MainTint ("Diffuse Tint", Color) = (1,1,1,1)
    _MainTex ("Base (RGB)", 2D) = "white" {}
    _SpecularColor ("Specular Color", Color) = (1,1,1,1)
    _SpecPower ("Specular Power", Range(0,30)) = 1

}
```

2. We then have to make sure to add the corresponding variables to our `CGPROGRAM` block inside our `SubShader` block.

```
float4 _SpecularColor;
sampler2D _MainTex;
float4 _MainTint;
float _SpecPower;
```

3. Now we have to add our custom lighting model so that we can compute our own Phong Specular. Add the following code to the Shader's `SubShader()` function. Don't worry if it doesn't make sense at this point; we will cover each line of code in the next section:

```
inline fixed4 LightingPhong (SurfaceOutput s, fixed3 lightDir, half3 viewDir, fixed atten)
{
    //Calculate diffuse and the reflection vector
    float diff = dot(s.Normal, lightDir);
    float3 reflectionVector = normalize(2.0 * s.Normal * diff - lightDir);

    float spec = pow(max(0,dot(reflectionVector, viewDir)), _SpecPower);
    float3 finalSpec = _SpecularColor.rgb * spec;

    fixed4 c;
    c.rgb = (s.Albedo * _LightColor0.rgb * diff) + (_LightColor0.rgb * finalSpec);
    c.a = 1.0;
    return c;
}
```

4. Finally, we have to tell the `CGPROGRAM` block that it needs to use our custom lighting function instead of one of the built-in ones. We do this by changing the `#pragma` statement to the following:

```
CGPROGRAM
#pragma surface surf Phong
```

The following screenshot demonstrates the result of our custom Phong lighting model using our own custom reflection vector:

How it works...

Let's break down the lighting function by itself, as the rest of the Shader should be pretty familiar to you at this point.

We simply start by using the lighting function that gives us the view direction. Remember that Unity has given you a set of lighting functions that you can use, but in order to use them correctly you have to have the same arguments they provide. Refer to the following table, or go to `http://docs.unity3d.com/Documentation/Components/SL-SurfaceShaderLighting.html`:

Not view Dependent	`half4 Lighting Name You choose (SurfaceOutput s, half3 lightDir, half atten);`
View Dependent	`half4 Lighting Name You choose (SurfaceOutput s, half3 lightDir, half3 viewDir, half atten);`

In our case, we are doing a Specular Shader, so we need to have the view-dependent lighting function structure. So, we have to write:

```
CGPROGRAM
#pragma surface surf Phong

inline fixed4 LightingPhong (SurfaceOutput s, fixed3 lightDir, half3 viewDir, fixed atten)
{

}
```

This will tell the Shader that we want to create our own view-dependent Shader. Always make sure that your lighting function name is the same in your lighting function declaration and the `#pragma` statement, or Unity will not be able to find your lighting model.

The lighting function then begins by declaring the usual `Diffuse` component by dotting the vertex normal with the light direction or vector. This will give us a value of `1` when a normal on the model is facing towards the light, and a value of `-1` when facing away from the light direction.

We then calculate the reflection vector taking the vertex normal, scaling it by 2.0 and by the diff value, then subtracting the light direction from it. This has the effect of bending the normal towards the light; so as a vertex normal is pointing away from the light, it is forced to look at the light. Refer to the following screenshot for a more visual representation. The script that produces this debug effect is included at the book's support page at `www.packtpub.com/support`.

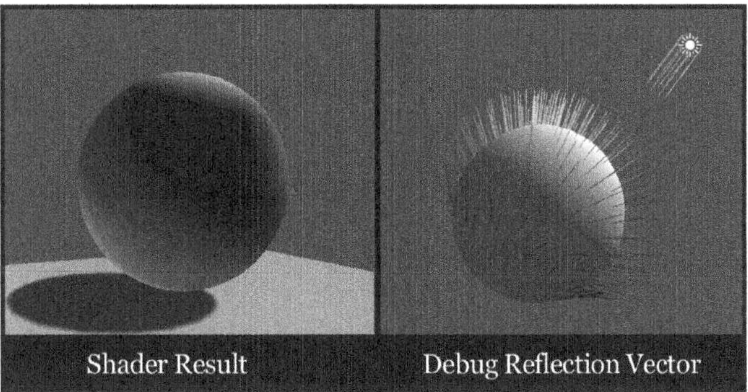

Then all we have left to do is to create the final spec's value and color. To do this, we dot the reflection vector with the view direction and take it to a power of `_SpecPower`. Finally, we just multiply the `_SpecularColor.rgb` value over the spec value to get our final Specular highlight.

The following screenshot displays the final result of our Phong Specular calculation isolated out in the Shader:

Creating a BlinnPhong Specular type

Blinn is another more efficient way of calculating and estimating specularity. It is done by getting the half vector from the view direction and the light direction. It was brought into the world of Cg by a man named Jim Blinn. He found that it was much more efficient to just get the half vector instead of calculating our own reflection vectors. It cut down on both code and processing time. If you actually look at the built-in BlinnPhong lighting model included in the `UnityCG.cginc` file, you will notice that it is using the half vector as well, hence the reason why it is named **BlinnPhong**. It is just a simpler version of the full Phong calculation.

Getting ready

1. This time, instead of creating a whole new scene, let's just use the objects and scene we have, and create a new Shader and Material and name them `BlinnPhong`.
2. Once you have a new Shader, double-click on it to launch MonoDevelop, so that we can start to edit our Shader.

How to do it...

1. First, we need to add our own properties to the `Properties` block, so that we can control the look of the Specular highlight.

```
Properties
{
    _MainTint ("Diffuse Tint", Color) = (1,1,1,1)
    _MainTex ("Base (RGB)", 2D) = "white" {}
    _SpecularColor ("Specular Color", Color) = (1,1,1,1)
    _SpecPower ("Specular Power", Range(0.1, 60)) = 3
}
```

2. Then, we need to make sure that we have created the corresponding variables inside our `CGPROGRAM` block, so that we can access the data from our `Properties` block, inside of our subshader.

```
sampler2D _MainTex;
float4 _MainTint;
float4 _SpecularColor;
float _SpecPower;
```

3. Now it's time to create our custom lighting model that will process our `Diffuse` and `Specular` calculations.

```
inline fixed4 LightingCustomBlinnPhong (SurfaceOutput s, fixed3 lightDir, half3 viewDir, fixed atten)
{
    float3 halfVector = normalize (lightDir + viewDir);

    float diff = max (0, dot (s.Normal, lightDir));

    float nh = max (0, dot (s.Normal, halfVector));
    float spec = pow (nh, _SpecPower) * _SpecularColor;

    float4 c;
    c.rgb = (s.Albedo * _LightColor0.rgb * diff) + (_LightColor0.rgb * _SpecularColor.rgb * spec) * (atten * 2);
    c.a = s.Alpha;
    return c;
}
```

4. To complete our Shader, we will need to tell our `CGPROGRAM` block to use our custom lighting model rather than a built-in one, by modifying the `#pragma` statement with the following code:

```
CGPROGRAM
#pragma surface surf CustomBlinnPhong
```

The following screenshot demonstrates the results of our BlinnPhong lighting model:

How it works...

The BlinnPhong Specular is almost exactly like the Phong Specular, except that it is more efficient because it uses less code to achieve almost the same effect. You will find this approach nine times out of ten in today's modern Shaders, as it is easier to code and lighter on the Shader performance.

Instead of calculating our own reflection vector, we are simply going to get the vector half way between the view direction and the light direction, basically simulating the reflection vector. It has actually been found that this approach is more physically accurate than the last approach, but we thought it is necessary to show you all the possibilities.

So to get the half vector, we simply need to add the view direction and the light direction together, as shown in the following code snippet:

```
float3 halfVector = normalize (lightDir + viewDir);
```

Then, we simply need to dot the vertex normal with that new half vector to get our main Specular value. After that, we just take it to a power of `_SpecPower` and multiply it by the Specular color variable. It's much lighter on the code and much lighter on the math, but still gives us a nice Specular highlight that will work for a lot of real-time situations.

Masking Specular with textures

Now that we have taken a look at how to create a Specular effect for our Shaders, let's start to take a look into the ways in which we can start to modify our Specular and give more artistic control over its final visual quality. In this next recipe, we will look at how we can use textures to drive our Specular and Specular power attributes.

The technique of using Specular textures is seen in most modern game development pipelines because it allows the 3D artists to control the final visual effect on a per-pixel basis. This provides us with a way in which we can have a mat-type surface and a shiny surface all in one Shader; or, we can drive the width of the Specular or the Specular power with another texture, to have one surface with a broad Specular highlight and another surface with a very sharp, tiny highlight.

There are many effects one can achieve by mixing his/her Shader calculations with textures, and giving artists the ability to control their Shader's final visual effect is key to an efficient pipeline. Let's see how we can use textures to drive our Specular lighting models. This recipe will introduce you to some new concepts, such as creating your own `Input` struct, and learning how the data is being passed around from the `output` struct, to the lighting function, to the `Input` struct, and to the `surf()` function. Understanding the flow of data between these core Surface Shader elements is core to a successful Shader pipeline.

Getting ready

- We will need a new Shader, Material, and another object to apply our Shader and Material on to.
- With the Shader and Material connected and assigned to your object in your scene, double-click the Shader to bring it up in MonoDevelop.
- We will also need a Specular texture to use. Any texture will do as long as it has some nice variation in colors and patterns. The following screenshot shows the textures we are using for this recipe:

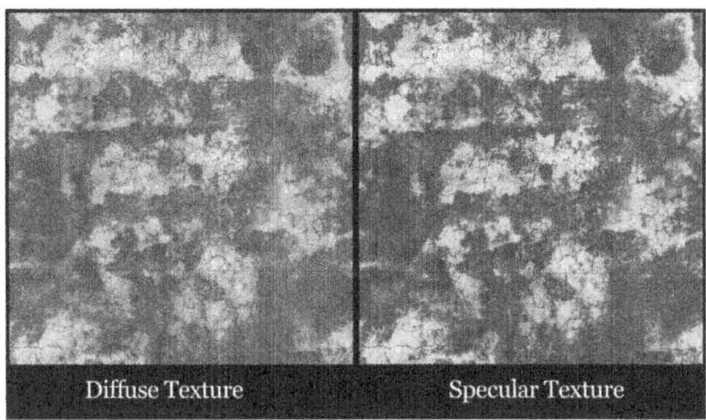

How to do it...

1. First, let's populate our `Properties` block with some new properties. Add the following code to your Shader's `Properties` block:

```
Properties
{
    //Set properties here so we can feed our shader information
    //from the inspector in the editor
    _MainTint ("Diffuse Tint", Color) = (1,1,1,1)
    _MainTex ("Base (RGB)", 2D) = "white" {}
    _SpecularColor ("Specular Tint", Color) = (1,1,1,1)
    _SpecularMask ("Specular Texture", 2D) = "white" {}
    _SpecPower ("Specular Power", Range(0.1, 120)) = 3
}
```

2. We then need to add the corresponding variables to the subshader, so that we can access the data from the properties in our `Properties` block. Add the following code, just after the `#pragma` statement:

```
//get the data from our properties block
sampler2D _MainTex;
sampler2D _SpecularMask;
float4 _MainTint;
float4 _SpecularColor;
float _SpecPower;
```

3. Now we have to add our own custom `Output` struct. This will allow us to store more data for use between our surf function and our lighting model. Don't worry if this doesn't make sense just yet. We will cover the finer details of this `Output` struct in the next section of the recipe. Place the following code just after the variables in the `SubShader` block:

```
//Create a custom Output Struct
struct SurfaceCustomOutput
{
    fixed3 Albedo;
    fixed3 Normal;
    fixed3 Emission;
    fixed3 SpecularColor;
    half Specular;
    fixed Gloss;
    fixed Alpha;
};
```

4. Just after the `Output` struct we just entered, we need to add our custom lighting model. In this case, we have a custom lighting model called `LightingCustomPhong`. Enter the following code just after the `Output` struct we just created:

```
inline fixed4 LightingCustomPhong (SurfaceCustomOutput s, fixed3 lightDir, half3 viewDir, fixed atten)
{
    //Calculate diffuse and the reflection vector
    float diff = dot(s.Normal, lightDir);
    float3 reflectionVector = normalize(2.0 * s.Normal * diff - lightDir);

    //Calculate the Phong specular
    float spec = pow(max(0.0f,dot(reflectionVector, viewDir)), _SpecPower) * s.Specular;
    float3 finalSpec = s.SpecularColor * spec * _SpecularColor.rgb;

    //Create final color
    fixed4 c;
    c.rgb = (s.Albedo * _LightColor0.rgb * diff) + (_LightColor0.rgb * finalSpec);
    c.a = s.Alpha;
    return c;
}
```

5. In order for our custom lighting model to work, we have to tell the `SubShader` block which lighting model we want to use. Enter the following code to the `#pragma` statement so that it loads our custom lighting model:

```
CGPROGRAM
#pragma surface surf CustomPhong
```

6. Since we are going to be using a texture to modify the values of our base Specular calculation, we need to store another set of UVs for that texture specifically. This is done inside the `Input` struct by placing the word `uv` in front of the variable's name that is holding the texture. Enter the following code just after your custom lighting model:

```
struct Input
{
    //Get uv information from the Input Struct
    float2 uv_MainTex;
    float2 uv_SpecularMask;
};
```

7. To finish off the Shader, we just need to modify our `surf()` function with the following code. This will let us pass the texture information to our lighting model function, so that we can use the pixel values of the texture to modify our Specular values in the lighting model function:

```
void surf (Input IN, inout SurfaceCustomOutput o)
{
    //Get the color information from the textures
    float4 c = tex2D (_MainTex, IN.uv_MainTex) * _MainTint;
    float4 specMask = tex2D(_SpecularMask, IN.uv_SpecularMask) * _SpecularColor;

    //Set the parameters in the Output Struct
    o.Albedo = c.rgb;
    o.Specular = specMask.r;
    o.SpecularColor = specMask.rgb;
    o.Alpha = c.a;
}
```

The following screenshot shows the result of masking our Specular calculations with a color texture and its channel information. We now have a nice variation in Specular over the entire surface, instead of just a global value for the Specular:

How it works...

This Shader is basically the same as Phong calculations, except that we are now going to modify our Specular with a per-pixel texture, giving our Specular much more visual interest and depth.

To do this, we need to be able to pass information from our surface function to our lighting functions. The reason is that we can't get the UVs of a surface within the lighting function. You can procedurally generate UVs in the lighting function but if you want to unpack a texture and get its pixel information, you have to use the `Input` struct, and the only way to access the data from the `Input` struct is to use the `surf()` function.

So to set up this data relationship, we have to create our own `SurfaceCustomOutput` struct. This struct is the container for all the final data in a Surface Shader and luckily for us, the lighting function and the `surf()` function can both access the data from it. So if we create our own, we can add more data to it. The following code is our `SurfaceCustomOutput` struct in our Shader:

```
//Create a custom Output Struct
struct SurfaceCustomOutput
{
    fixed3 Albedo;
    fixed3 Normal;
    fixed3 Emission;
    fixed3 SpecularColor;
    half Specular;
    fixed Gloss;
    fixed Alpha;
};
```

So, we add this to our Shader and we need to tell the `surf()` function and the lighting function that they should use this struct instead of the built-in one. This is done by the following code:

```
//Create a custom Output Struct
struct SurfaceCustomOutput
{
    fixed3 Albedo;
    fixed3 Normal;
    fixed3 Emission;
    fixed3 SpecularColor;
    half Specular;
    fixed Gloss;
    fixed Alpha;
};

inline fixed4 LightingCustomPhong (SurfaceCustomOutput s, fixed3 lightDir, half3 viewDir, fixed atten)
{
}

void surf (Input IN, inout SurfaceCustomOutput o)
{
}
ENDCG
```

Notice how the `surf()` function and the lighting function now have the struct `SurfaceCustomOutput` for one of their arguments. We have also added a new entry into our `SurfaceOutput` struct called `SpecularColor`. This will allow us to store the per-pixel information from our Specular color texture and use it in our lighting function, instead of just multiplying a single global color over our whole Specular value.

We simply use the `tex2D()` function to get our texture information, and then pass that into our `SurfaceCustomOutput` struct by assigning `o.SpecularColor` the return value of the `tex2D()` function. Once that is done, you can now access the texture information in the lighting function.

```
void surf (Input IN, inout SurfaceCustomOutput o)
{
    //Get the color information from the textures
    float4 c = tex2D (_MainTex, IN.uv_MainTex) * _MainTint;
    float4 specMask = tex2D(_SpecularMask, IN.uv_SpecularMask) * _SpecularColor;

    //Set the parameters in the Output Struct
    o.Albedo = c.rgb;
    o.Specular = specMask.r;
    o.SpecularColor = specMask.rgb;
    o.Alpha = c.a;
}
```

This technique is crucial for creating custom effects in your Shaders. Now you know how to access textures from the `surf()` function and use it in your lighting function. This allows you to create very high-quality, per-pixel effects in your Shader.

Metallic versus soft Specular

In this section, we are going to explore a way to create a Shader that gives us the versatility to have a soft Specular as well as a hard Specular. You will find in most productions that you will need to create a nice set of Shaders to perform many tasks. As managing too many Shaders can become overwhelming, it is common for Shader programmers to create a set of Shaders that can both be used for cloth and for metal in one Shader file. It's all about how the end user sets the properties on their model. Our goal in this recipe is to achieve this modularity with Specular, so that an end user can get a soft, shiny material and then using the same Shader, achieve a very hard metallic Shader.

To accomplish this flexibility, we are going to create a similar Specular lighting model to the Cook Torrance Shader, but we will give it our own touch so that it is a bit friendlier for the artist or end user using this Shader.

Getting ready

1. Create a fresh Unity scene and set up a simple sphere, plane, and directional light in the new scene. Make sure to save the scene with a name of your choice.
2. Create a new Shader and Material, and give them names that you decide on.
3. Finally, attach the Shader to the Material and attach the Material to the sphere object in your new scene.

4. We are also going to need to get some textures together that will allow an artist to refine the roughness of the Specular by defining how blurry and how sharp the Specular should be. Refer to the following screenshot for examples on how these textures look.

The following screenshot visually shows examples of different roughness textures used in this recipe:

How to do it...

1. First and foremost, we need to set up the properties we will need for our Shader. Enter the following code into the `Properties` block of your Shader:

```
Properties
{
    _MainTint ("Diffuse Tint", Color) = (1,1,1,1)
    _MainTex ("Base (RGB)", 2D) = "white" {}
    _RoughnessTex ("Roughness texture", 2D) = "" {}
    _Roughness ("Roughness", Range(0,1)) = 0.5
    _SpecularColor ("Specular Color", Color) = (1,1,1,1)
    _SpecPower ("Specular Power", Range(0,30)) = 2
    _Fresnel ("Fresnel Value", Range(0,1.0)) = 0.05
}
```

2. We then need to make sure that the property data is available to our `SubShader` block. Enter the following code just after the `#pragma` statement in your Shader:

```
sampler2D _MainTex;
sampler2D _RoughnessTex;
float _Roughness;
float _Fresnel;
float _SpecPower;
float4 _MainTint;
float4 _SpecularColor;
```

3. We now need to declare our new lighting model and tell the `#pragma` statement to look for it:

```
CGPROGRAM
#pragma surface surf MetallicSoft
#pragma target 3.0

inline fixed4 LightingMetallicSoft (SurfaceOutput s, fixed3 lightDir, half3 viewDir, fixed atten)
{

}
```

4. At this point we are ready to fill in our custom lighting model function with our lighting calculations. We are first going to want to generate all of our diffuse and view dependent vectors, as this lighting model is going to make use of them all.

```
//Compute simple diffuse and view direction values
float3 halfVector = normalize(lightDir + viewDir);
float NdotL = saturate(dot(s.Normal, normalize(lightDir)));
float NdotH_raw = dot(s.Normal, halfVector);
float NdotH = saturate(dot(s.Normal, halfVector));
float NdotV = saturate(dot(s.Normal, normalize(viewDir)));
float VdotH = saturate(dot(halfVector, normalize(viewDir)));
```

5. The next section of code in the Shader takes care of producing the roughness values for our Specular, by using a texture to define the Specular shape and to procedurally simulate micro bumps in the surface of the object. Enter the following code:

```
//Micro facets distribution
float geoEnum = 2.0*NdotH;
float3 G1 = (geoEnum * NdotV)/NdotH;
float3 G2 = (geoEnum * NdotL)/NdotH;
float3 G =  min(1.0f, min(G1, G2));

//Sample our Specular look up BRDF
float roughness = tex2D(_RoughnessTex, float2(NdotH_raw * 0.5 + 0.5, _Roughness)).r;
```

6. The last element we need for our Specular calculation is a **Fresnel** term. This will help us mask off the Specular when your view becomes very glancing to the object's surface.

```
//Create our custom fresnel value
float fresnel = pow(1.0-VdotH, 5.0);
fresnel *= (1.0 - _Fresnel);
fresnel += _Fresnel;
```

7. Now that we have all the components ready for our Specular, we just need to combine them together to generate our final Specular value.

```
//Create the final spec
float3 spec = float3(fresnel * G * roughness * roughness) * _SpecPower;
```

8. To complete the lighting model, we simply need to add our `Diffuse` terms and our `Specular` terms together:

```
float4 c;
c.rgb = (s.Albedo * _LightColor0.rgb * NdotL)+  (spec * _SpecularColor.rgb) * (atten * 2.0f);
c.a = s.Alpha;
return c;
```

With all the code entered into your Shader, return to the Unity editor to let the Shader compile. If no errors were reported, you should have a result similar to the following screenshot:

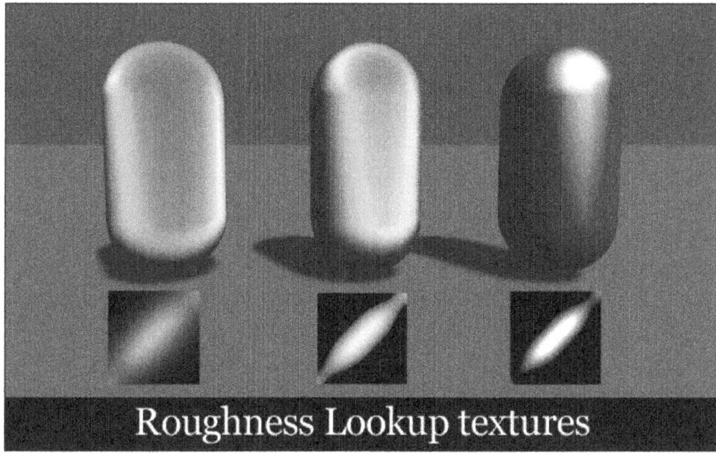

How it works...

Alright...that might seem like a lot of stuff going on there, but actually it is all pretty simple to understand. You can even debug each step of the Shader's code by assigning `c.rgb` with a `float3` value. Once you do that, you will see, in the editor view, that the Shader is now displaying the step of whichever calculation you are feeding it; always a good tip to keep in mind when debugging Shaders.

If we actually debug the first block of code, where we are calculating all of our Diffuse and view dependent vectors, you would see something very similar to the following screenshot:

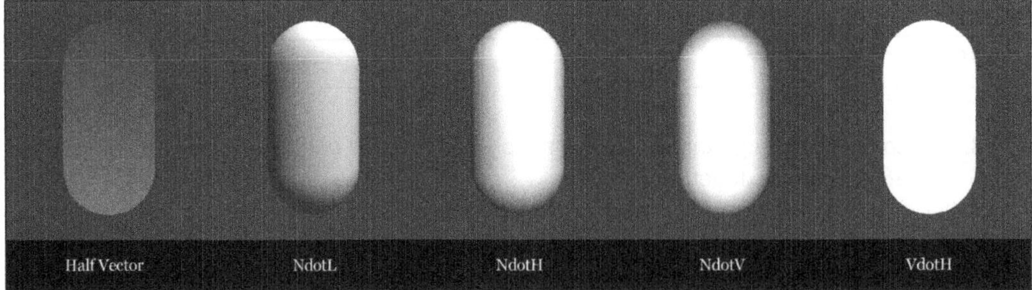

Once we have all of this data we need to start to work with it, almost like layers in Photoshop. We start this process by generating a procedural value that simulates small micro bumps in the surface of the object, to fake the effect of light bouncing around and distributing the light.

```
//Micro facets distribution
float geoEnum = 2.0*NdotH;
float3 G1 = (geoEnum * NdotV)/NdotH;
float3 G2 = (geoEnum * NdotL)/NdotH;
float3 G =  min(1.0f, min(G1, G2));
```

One of the more key aspects of this lighting model is the fact that we control the width of the Specular, or its roughness, by looking up a texture that has a baked-in Specular function. This will allow us to procedurally generate some UVs and pick a spot on the texture to use for our Specular. For this we want to use the `NdotH` or the dot product of the half vector and the vertex normal, and feed that into a `float2()` variable for the `tex2D()` function. This `float2()` variable will become our UV that we use to look up our texture. The second value is a property that we exposed in the **Inspector** tab. This allows the user to expand or contract the Specular highlight.

```
//Sample our Specular look up BRDF
float roughness = tex2D(_RoughnessTex, float2(NdotH_raw * 0.5 + 0.5, _Roughness)).r;
```

We then need to create our Fresnel effect, so that when we look in the opposite direction the light is pointing we get an increase in Specular intensity.

```
//Create our custom fresnel value
float fresnel = pow(1.0-VdotH, 5.0);
fresnel *= (1.0 - _Fresnel);
fresnel += _Fresnel;
```

With all of these components completed, we simply want to multiply them together to achieve our final Specular value. In this case, we have also multiplied another property called _SpecPower to give one more level of intensity control over the final Specular value.

```
//Create the final spec
float3 spec = float3(fresnel * G * roughness * roughness) * _SpecPower;
```

The last step is to combine our Specular with the Diffuse component and return the final color to the Surface Shader. Hopefully, you can see the level of modifications you can make to a simple system just by using other types of vectors and textures.

See also

- To find out more about the Cook Torrance Specular model, refer to the following links:

  http://en.wikipedia.org/wiki/Specular_highlight#Cook.E2.80.93Torrance_model

  http://content.gpwiki.org/index.php/D3DBook:%28Lighting%29_Cook-Torrance

  http://forum.unity3d.com/threads/158589-Cook-Torrance

Creating an Anisotropic Specular type

Anisotropic is a type of Specular or reflection that simulates the directionality of grooves in a surface, and modifies/stretches the Specular in the perpendicular direction. It is very useful when you want to simulate brushed metals, not a metal with a clear, smooth, polished surface. Imagine the Specular you see when you look at the data side of a CD or DVD, or the way Specular is shaped at the bottom of a pot or pan. You will notice that if you carefully examine the surface, you will see that there is a direction to the grooves in the surface, usually the way the metal was brushed. When you apply a Specular to that surface, you get a Specular stretched in the perpendicular direction.

This recipe will introduce you to the concept of augmenting your Specular highlights to achieve different types of brushed surfaces. In future recipes, we will look at ways in which we can use the concepts of this recipe to achieve other effects, such as stretched reflections and hair, but here we are going to learn the fundamentals of the technique first. We will be using this Shader as our reference for our own custom Anisotropic Shader:

http://wiki.unity3d.com/index.php?title=Anisotropic_Highlight_Shader

The following screenshot shows examples of different types of Specular effects one can achieve by using Anisotropic Shaders in Unity:

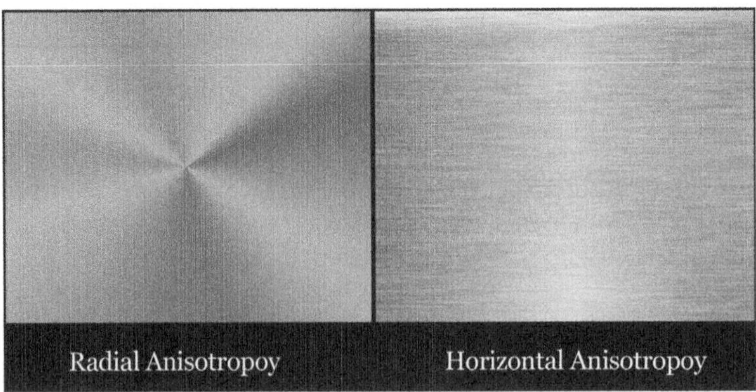

Getting ready

1. Create a new scene with some objects and lights, so that we can visually debug our Shader.
2. Then, create a new Shader and Material, and hook them up to our objects.
3. Lastly, we will need some sort of normal map that will indicate the directionality of our Anisotropic Specular highlight.

The following screenshot shows the Anisotropic normal map we will be using for this recipe. It is available from the book's support page at `www.packtpub.com/support`:

How to do it...

1. We first need to add the properties we are going to need for our Shader. These will allow a lot of artistic control over the final appearance of the surface:

```
Properties
{
    _MainTint ("Diffuse Tint", Color) = (1,1,1,1)
    _MainTex ("Base (RGB)", 2D) = "white" {}
    _SpecularColor ("specular Color", Color) = (1,1,1,1)
    _Specular ("Specular Amount", Range(0,1)) = 0.5
    _SpecPower ("Specular Power", Range(0,1)) = 0.5
    _AnisoDir ("Anisotropic Direction", 2D) = "" {}
    _AnisoOffset ("Anisotropic Offset", Range(-1,1)) = -0.2
}
```

2. We then need to make the connection between our `Properties` block and our `SubShader` block, so that we can use the data being provided by the `Properties` block:

```
    sampler2D _MainTex;
    sampler2D _AnisoDir;
    float4 _MainTint;
    float4 _SpecularColor;
    float _AnisoOffset;
    float _Specular;
    float _SpecPower;
```

3. Now we can create our lighting function that will produce the correct Anisotropic effect on our surface:

```
inline fixed4 LightingAnisotropic (SurfaceAnisoOutput s, fixed3 lightDir, half3 viewDir, fixed atten)
{
    fixed3 halfVector = normalize(normalize(lightDir) + normalize(viewDir));
    float NdotL = saturate(dot(s.Normal, lightDir));

    fixed HdotA = dot(normalize(s.Normal + s.AnisoDirection), halfVector);
    float aniso = max(0, sin(radians((HdotA + _AnisoOffset) * 180f)));

    float spec = saturate(pow(aniso, s.Gloss * 128) * s.Specular);

    fixed4 c;
    c.rgb = ((s.Albedo * _LightColor0.rgb * NdotL) + (_LightColor0.rgb * _SpecularColor.rgb * spec)) * (atten * 2);
    c.a = 1.0;
    return c;
}
```

4. In order to use this new lighting function, we need to tell the subshader's `#pragma` statement to look for it instead of using one of the built-in lighting functions. We are also telling the Shader to target Shader model 3.0, so that we can have more space for textures in our program:

```
CGPROGRAM
#pragma surface surf Anisotropic
#pragma target 3.0
```

5. We have also given the Anisotropic normal map its own UVs by declaring the following code in the `Input` struct. This isn't entirely necessary as we could just use the UVs from the main texture, but this gives us independent control over the tiling of our brushed metal effect, so that we can scale it to any size we want.

```
struct Input
{
    float2 uv_MainTex;
    float2 uv_AnisoDir;
};
```

6. Finally, we need to use the `surf()` function to pass the correct data to our lighting function. So we get the per-pixel information from our Anisotropic normal map and set our Specular parameters.

```
void surf (Input IN, inout SurfaceAnisoOutput o)
{
    half4 c = tex2D (_MainTex, IN.uv_MainTex) * _MainTint;
    float3 anisoTex = UnpackNormal(tex2D(_AnisoDir, IN.uv_AnisoDir));

    o.AnisoDirection = anisoTex;
    o.Specular = _Specular;
    o.Gloss = _SpecPower;
    o.Albedo = c.rgb;
    o.Alpha = c.a;
}
```

The following screenshot demonstrates the result of our Anisotropic Shader. The Anisotropic normal map allows us to give the surface direction and helps us disperse the Specular highlight around the surface:

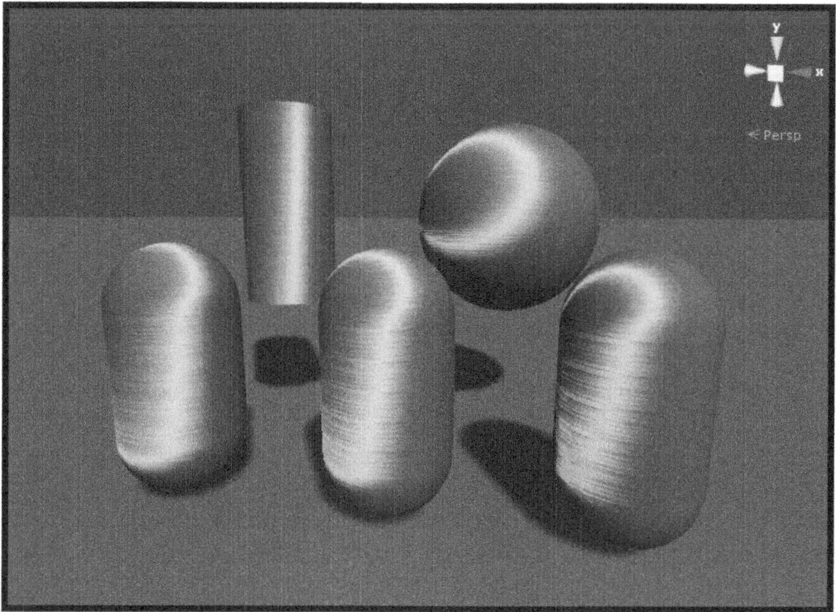

How it works...

Let's break this Shader down into its core components and explain why we are getting the effect we are getting. We will mostly be covering the custom lighting function here, as the rest of the Shader should be pretty self-explanatory at this point.

We first start by declaring our own `SurfaceCustomOutput` struct. We need to do this in order to get the per-pixel information from the Anisotropic normal map, and the only way we can do that in a Surface Shader, is to use a `tex2D()` function inside the `surf()` function.

```
struct SurfaceAnisoOutput
{
    fixed3 Albedo;
    fixed3 Normal;
    fixed3 Emission;
    fixed3 AnisoDirection;
    half Specular;
    fixed Gloss;
    fixed Alpha;
};
```

We can use the `SurfaceOutput` struct as a way of interacting between the lighting function and the surface function. In our case, we are storing the per-pixel texture information in the variable called `anisoTex` in our `surf()` function, and then passing that data to the `SurfaceAnisoOutput` struct by storing it in the `AnisoDirection` variable. Once we have that, we can use that per-pixel information in the lighting function, by using `s.AnisoDirection`.

With that data connection set up, we can move on to our actual lighting calculations. This begins by getting the usual out of the way, the half vector, so that we don't have to do the full reflection calculation and the diffuse lighting, which is the vertex normal dotted with the light vector or direction.

```
fixed3 halfVector = normalize(normalize(lightDir) + normalize(viewDir));
float NdotL = saturate(dot(s.Normal, lightDir));
```

Then we start the actual modification to the Specular to get the right look. We first dot the normalized sum of the vertex normal and the per-pixel vectors from our Anisotropic normal map with the `halfVector` calculated in the previous step. This gives us a float value that gives a value of `1` as the surface normal, modified by the Anisotropic normal map, as it becomes parallel with the `halfVector` and `0` as it is perpendicular. Finally, we modify this value with a `sin()` function so that we can basically get a darker middle highlight and ultimately a ring effect based off of the `halfVector`.

```
fixed HdotA = dot(normalize(s.Normal + s.AnisoDirection), halfVector);
float aniso = max(0, sin(radians((HdotA + _AnisoOffset) * 180)));
```

Finally, we scale the effect of the `aniso` value by taking it to a power of `s.Gloss`, and then globally decrease its strength by multiplying it by `s.Specular`.

```
float spec = saturate(pow(aniso, s.Gloss * 128) * s.Specular);
```

This effect is great for creating more advanced metal type surfaces, especially ones that are brushed and seem to have directionality to them. It also works well for hair or any sort of soft surface with directionality to it. The following screenshot shows the result of just displaying the final Anisotropic lighting calculation:

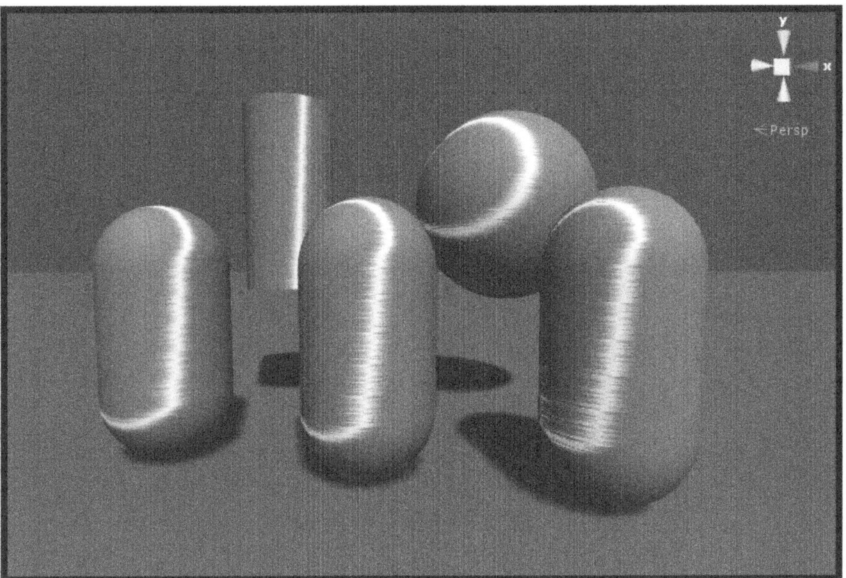

4

Reflecting Your World

Reflection is key nowadays to make your Shaders really punch from a visual standpoint. It is the process of using the world around you and letting the Shader reflect that world's information to simulate the environment reflecting on the surface of the Shader. This is in part because we are able to use a new kind of texture called a Cubemap. This type of texture is made up of six textures and uses these six textures to surround the current surface in a cube-like fashion. So imagine a cube and each face of that cube has one of the six textures on the face of it. This allows us to capture our environment and bake it into textures.

We will see how to generate our own Cubemaps from our own environments, and we are going to look at different ways in which we can use these generated Cubemaps to create reflection effects in our Shaders. This is great for simulating metal, car paint, and even plastics. So in this chapter we are going to learn the following:

- Creating Cubemaps in Unity3D
- Simple Cubemap reflection in Unity3D
- Masking reflections in Unity3D
- Normal maps and Reflections in Unity3D
- Fresnel reflections in Unity3D
- Creating a simple dynamic Cubemap system in Unity3D

Creating Cubemaps in Unity3D

In order for us to start to learn how to create reflection effects for our Shaders, we are going to have to learn how to create our own **Cubemaps**. You can find Cubemaps online, but you will quickly find out that you will want to produce your own, as the ones found online don't actually reflect your own game world. Any Cubemap found online is great for testing purposes only. Once you get into production, creating your own Cubemaps, which reflect your game world, is key to creating realistic reflection effects. We are going to cover a couple of ways in which you can do this directly in the Unity editor. In addition, we will take a look at standalone applications that will let you create your own Cubemaps. This will arm you with the knowledge to move onto the next chapters, as the generation of Cubemaps and understating them is crucial to this entire chapter.

So, this first recipe is going to arm us with a few different techniques for creating Cubemaps for your Shaders.

Getting ready

Unity has provided us with the code in JavaScript to be able to create a Cubemap from the environment we have created. So let's take a look at that. Here is the link to the script reference for it: `www.packtpub.com/support`. This will serve as a basis for our script. We are going to translate this to C#. In the last recipe in this chapter, we will cover how to create a simple system for generating Cubemaps at multiple positions and use that data to swap between these reflection maps as a character moves through an environment, ultimately giving us a semi-real-time reflection system.

For this recipe we will just learn how the creation of a single Cubemap works, which will prepare us for a dynamic reflection system that can be used for your game.

1. We will need to create some elements for our scene that will act as lights in our reflection Cubemap. So, we need to create some geometric planes in our scene. You can do this either in a modeling application, like Maya or Max, or you can use the default Unity plane. Either way, it doesn't really matter. Your scene should look similar to the following screenshot:

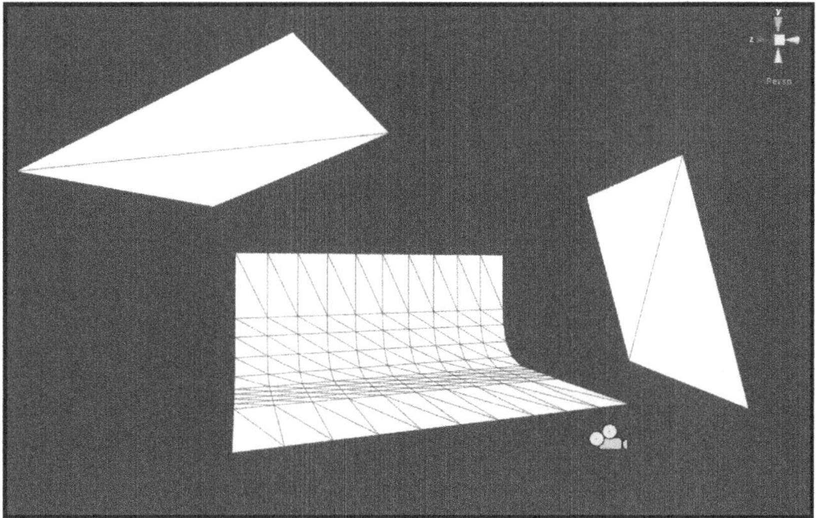

2. Now, we need to create some textures that will simulate the effect of different types of lights. So, we need to create some textures that will simulate the falloff and intensity of lights in our environment. Refer to the following screenshot:

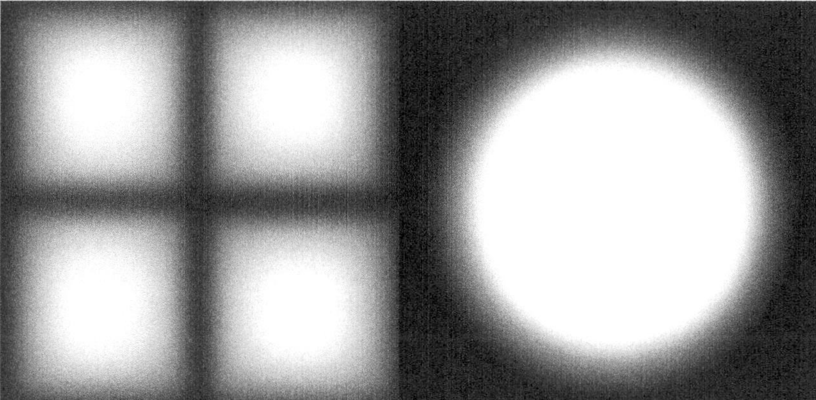

3. Now, we need to use one of the built-in Shaders Unity has provided us so that we can use our plane geometry and textures as lights in our Cubemap. It is suggested that we use the unlit/transparent shader, so that we get the full intensity of the textures that are simulating the lights. Once completed, your scene should look similar to the following:

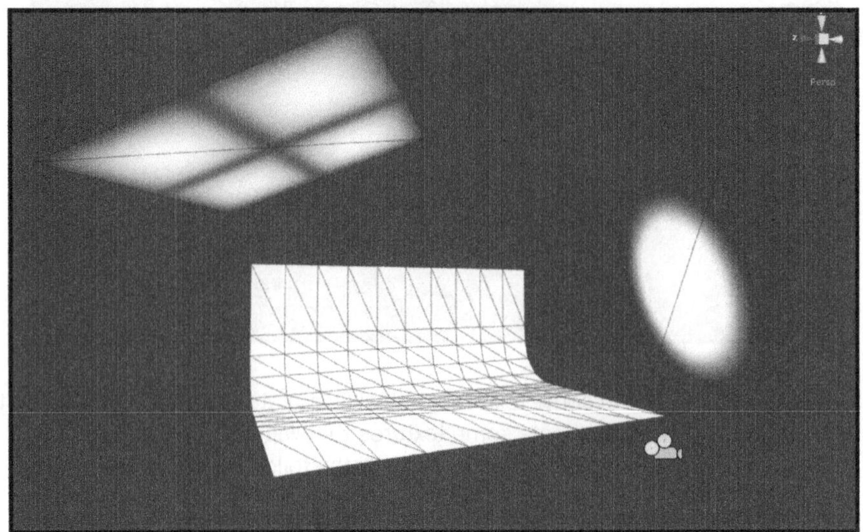

How to do it...

Let's begin writing our Shader by following the next few steps:

1. We first need to create a new script, but since this is going to be a pop-up editor window, we must put this script in a folder called `Editor`. Create that folder now in your `Project` panel, and then create a C# script in that folder called `GenerateStaticCubemap`. Once it is created, double-click on the new script to launch it in MonoDevelop.

2. With the script open in MonoDevelop, we need to start to edit our script to perform the functions we need. To start with, we need to make a new `using` directive so that we are using the `UnityEditor` namespace.

```
using UnityEngine;
using UnityEditor;
using System.Collections;
```

3. In order for this script to be considered a pop-up type editor window, we need to make the `GenerateStaticCubemap` script inherit from the `ScriptableWizard` class. This will provide us with some nice low-level functions we can use in our script.

```
public class GenerateStaticCubemap : ScriptableWizard
{
```

4. We then need to add a few public variables so that we can store our new Cubemap and the position of our Cubemap. Add the following code to the start of the class:

```
    public Transform renderPosition;
    public Cubemap cubemap;
```

5. Our first function in this script is a built-in function called `OnWizardUpdate()`. This function is called when the wizard is first opened, or whenever the GUI is changed by the user. So, this is a good place to check and to make sure that the user has supplied the wizard some assets to work with. If we don't have a Cubemap or a transform in the variables, we need to set the `isValid` Boolean to `false` and not allow the future functions.

```
void OnWizardUpdate ()
{
    helpString = "Select transform to render" +
        "from and cubemap to render into";
    if(renderPosition != null && cubemap != null)
    {
        isValid = true;
    }
    else
    {
        isValid = false;
    }
}
```

6. If the `isValid` Boolean is equal to `true`, the wizard will call the `OnWizardCreate()` function. This will produce a new camera for us; then position it using our provided transform, and use the `RenderToCubemap()` function to return a Cubemap.

```
void OnWizardCreate()
{
    //Create a temp camera for rendering
    GameObject go = new GameObject("CubeCam", typeof(Camera));

    //place it onto our render position
    go.transform.position = renderPosition.position;
    go.transform.rotation = Quaternion.identity;

    //render the Cubemap
    go.camera.RenderToCubemap(cubemap);

    //Destroy the temp camera
    DestroyImmediate(go);
}
```

7. Finally, we need to call this wizard to activate it from a menu option in the Unity editor menu. Enter the following code to your `GenerateStaticCubemap` class:

```
[MenuItem("CookBook/Render Cubemap")]
static void RenderCubemap()
{
    ScriptableWizard.DisplayWizard("Render CubeMap",
                    typeof(GenerateStaticCubemap), "Render!");
}
```

How it works...

We begin by creating a new script and declaring its class as inheriting from a scriptable wizard. This tells Unity3D that we intend to make a new pop-up window type custom editor for Unity. This is why we have to put this script into a folder named `Editor`. If we don't, Unity won't recognize it as a custom editor type script.

The variables that we declare in the next step give us a way to store the position we want to create the Cubemap from, and a way to store a new Cubemap `GameObject` constructor created in the **Project** tab. Having these variables will let us generate our new Cubemap.

We then have the `OnWizardUpdate()` function that is a function provided to us by the `ScriptableWizard` class. It is called when the wizard is first opened and when any of the wizard's GUI elements change. So, we can use it to do some verification that the user has in fact entered a transform and a new Cubemap. If they have, we set the `isValid` variable to `true`; if they haven't, we set `isValid` to `false`. The `isValid` variable is a built-in variable, which is given to us by the `ScriptableWizard` class. It simply lets you turn on and off the **Create** button found at the bottom of the wizard. This prevents anyone from running the next function with an empty transform or Cubemap.

Once we have made sure that the user has given us the right data to work with, we can then move on to the `OnWizardCreate()` function. This is where the guts of the Cubemap creation happens. It starts by creating a new `GameObject` constructor and making sure that it is created as a `Camera` type. We then position it using the provided transform's position.

At this point, we have a new camera and have positioned it. All that needs to be done is to call the `RenderToCubeMap()` function and pass to it the user-provided Cubemap. Once this function runs, the six images for our Cubemap will be created and assembled into the Cubemap object the user has provided.

Finally, we create a menu option for our wizard, so that we can let users access this tool from Unity's top menu bar. With that menu item, we call upon the wizard's `Static` function, which actually displays the menu. This completes the process of creating a small tool to generate Cubemaps directly in the Unity editor.

See also

Let's take a look at other applications that can generate Cubemaps as well. This will give you a nice list of resources that you can use to create your own reflection pipeline or workflow:

- **ATI CubeMapGen**: `http://developer.amd.com/resources/archive/archived-tools/gpu-tools-archive/cubemapgen/`
- **HDR Light Studio Pro**: `http://www.hdrlightstudio.com/`

Simple Cubemap reflection in Unity3D

Now that we know how to create our own custom Cubemaps, we can now look at how we use this new texture type to simulate reflections in our Shaders. The concept of using Cubemaps for reflections is pretty simple actually, but provides a very powerful tool for your Shader effects. It works by using the normal from each vertex on the surface of the model to look up a position on the Cubemap textures. This lookup will return a color value that simulates the effect of the Cubemap being reflected on the surface of your object. That is the basic idea.

This particular recipe will take the first step into using Cubemaps for reflections. Unity actually provides us with ways to get the reflection vector automatically, so we don't have to calculate it ourselves. This is done inside the `Input` struct by using the built-in **worldRefl** vector. This will help us in the lookup operation for our **Cubemap** texture. So, this first step will give us the most bare-bones way of creating a reflection effect for your Surface Shaders.

Getting ready

Before we begin our Shader code, we need to set up a simple scene by creating a few assets.

1. Create a new scene, Material, and Shader. Make sure to give your new assets a name that easily identifies them.
2. Attach the new Shader to your new Material, and then assign your Material to your object.
3. Finally, create or gather a Cubemap that you can use for the Shader.

The following screenshot shows the Cubemap we are using for this recipe. Yours could be different, but we just wanted to show what we are using to remove any confusion.

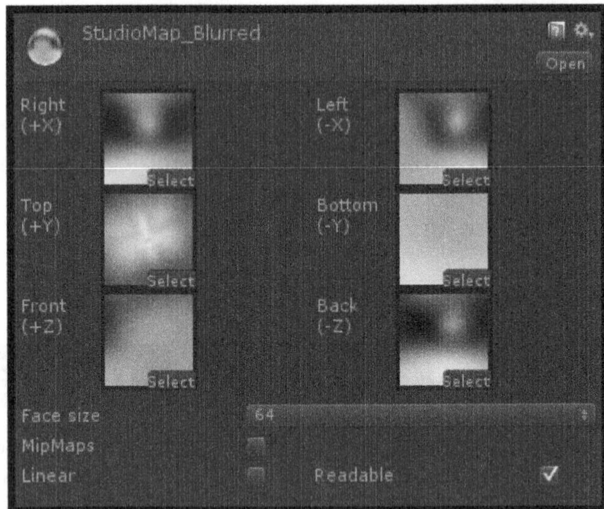

How to do it...

Let's begin to code our Shader by following the next few steps.

1. First let's create some new properties in the `Properties` block. We will need a place to get our Cubemap texture and to control the amount of reflection:

```
Properties
{
    _MainTint ("Diffuse Tint", Color) = (1,1,1,1)
    _MainTex ("Base (RGB)", 2D) = "white" {}
    _Cubemap ("CubeMap", CUBE) = ""{}
    _ReflAmount ("Reflection Amount", Range(0.01, 1)) = 0.5
}
```

2. We then need to make sure we create the connection to the properties inside our `SubShader` block. This will allow us to access the data from our `Properties` block.

```
sampler2D _MainTex;
samplerCUBE _Cubemap;
float4 _MainTint;
float _ReflAmount;
```

3. In order for us to simulate the correct reflection angle to the surface, we will need to get some sort of vector data that will provide us with the proper world reflection directions. To do this, we can use another built-in feature of Unity's Surface Shaders. Inside the `Input` struct, the following code will give us a world reflection vector we can use in our Shader:

```
struct Input
{
    float2 uv_MainTex;
    float3 worldRefl;
};
```

4. Finally, we just need to get the texture information from our Cubemap, using the `texCUBE()` function and our new world reflection vector, given to us by the `Input` struct. Add the following code to your `surf()` function:

```
void surf (Input IN, inout SurfaceOutput o)
{
    half4 c = tex2D (_MainTex, IN.uv_MainTex) * _MainTint;
    o.Emission = texCUBE(_Cubemap, IN.worldRefl).rgb * _ReflAmount;
    o.Albedo = c.rgb;
    o.Alpha = c.a;
}
```

A result of creating our own custom Cubemap is shown in the following screenshot:

How it works...

If all went well, you should see your Cubemap being reflected onto your object such that it samples the Cubemap just as a real reflective object would. This is all made possible because Unity3D has a built-in property for its Surface Shader's `Input` struct. The `worldRefl` property gives us the reflection vector we need to correctly sample our Cubemap. Just by simply using the `worldRefl` property inside our `texCube()` function, we can easily sample the correct reflection view for our Cubemap.

The following screenshot shows an example of what the reflection data, being passed to the Shader, looks like when viewed with a debug script:

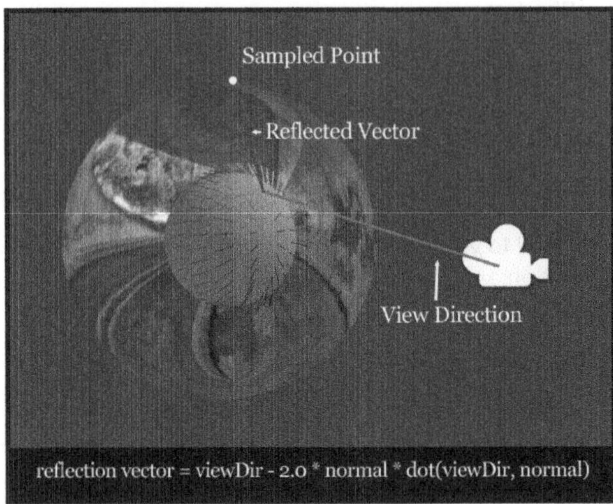

Masking reflections in Unity3D

Having a reflection is nice, but we aren't going to want to make reflective spheres all the time. Just about everything reflects a certain amount of its environment, and hence, we need some sort of per pixel control over the reflection effect.

In this recipe, we are going to look at a technique that lets us drive the reflection amount, by using a texture as a mask. Basically, we can use the gray scale values of a texture to say how reflective the surface is, meaning that a black value in the texture is going to produce a non-reflective surface and a white value is going to produce a fully reflective surface. This allows for a level of artistic control that is seen in just about every game production pipeline these days. So, let's take a look at how to do it in Unity using Surface Shaders.

Getting ready

Let's get our new scene ready for our new masked reflection Shader.

1. We will need to have a Cubemap ready for our Shader, you can generate a new one or just use the one from the previous recipe. The Cubemap we will be using for this recipe, which is included in the sample code for this book, is shown here:

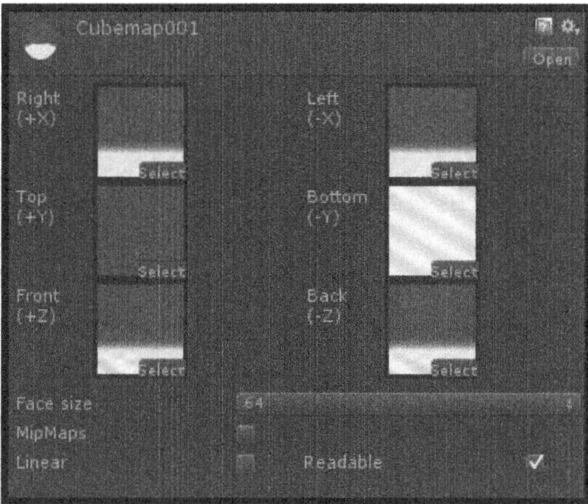

2. We will also need a texture that will describe where the surface of our object is reflective and where it is not. Remember, black will represent zero reflectivity and white will represent full reflectivity, with all the gray scale in between providing a certain amount of reflectivity. See the following texture for the one we are using in this recipe:

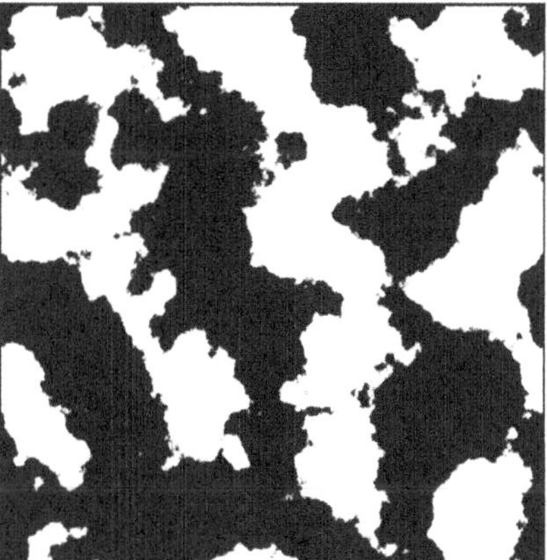

3. Finally, create a new scene with an object, ground, and a directional light so that we can see our Shader in all its reflectiveness!

How to do it...

With our scene set up, we can now begin to write the code necessary to produce our reflection effect.

1. Add the following properties to your Shader. This will let us assign our own custom Cubemap and reflection masks to our Shader:

```
Properties
{
     _MainTint ("Diffuse Tint", Color) = (1,1,1,1)
     _MainTex ("Base (RGB)", 2D) = "white" {}
     _ReflAmount ("Reflection Amount", Range(0, 1)) = 1
     _Cubemap ("Cubemap", CUBE) = ""{}
     _ReflMask ("Reflection Mask", 2D) = ""{}
}
```

2. We then need to make sure we add the same properties as variables to our `SubShader` block.

```
    sampler2D _MainTex;
    sampler2D _ReflMask;
    samplerCUBE _Cubemap;
    float4 _MainTint;
    float _ReflAmount;
```

3. In order for us to properly simulate the reflection from the Cubemap, we are going to need to declare the `worldRefl` property in the `Input` struct. We can use this data as the lookup parameter in the `texCUBE()` function.

```
struct Input
{
     float2 uv_MainTex;
     float3 worldRefl;
};
```

4. Lastly, we need to update our `surf()` function with the following code. This will be explained in the next section of this recipe:

```
void surf (Input IN, inout SurfaceOutput o)
{
    half4 c = tex2D (_MainTex, IN.uv_MainTex);
    float3 reflection = texCUBE(_Cubemap, IN.worldRefl).rgb;
    float4 reflMask = tex2D(_ReflMask, IN.uv_MainTex);

    o.Albedo = c.rgb * _MainTint;
    o.Emission = (reflection * reflMask.r) * _ReflAmount;
    o.Alpha = c.a;
}
```

The following screenshot shows the result of masking the reflection component with a texture in a Unity3D Surface Shader:

How it works...

This Shader works quite simply by first sampling the Cubemap using the `texCUBE()` function. This function is built-in to the CGFX language. It provides us with the sampled Cubemap colors that we can then apply to the surface of our Shader. Unity helps us in this endeavor by providing us with the `worldRefl` property in the Input struct. As explained in the last recipe, this property will pass in for us the reflection vector from our camera view.

Once we have the reflection element, we then need to sample our reflection mask texture. This is simply done by using the `tex2D()` built-in function, which we have seen before in *Chapter 2, Using Textures for Effects*.

With both texture types sampled and stored into a variable in our `surf()` function, we simply have to multiply the Cubemap colors with the reflection texture colors and pass that into the `o.Emission` parameter of our surface's `Output` struct. Finally, to globally control the overall reflection intensity, we multiply the result of the reflection masking by our `_ReflectionAmount` property. This will let us control the overall amount of reflection over the whole surface.

The following screenshot shows the different results by controlling the overall reflection with the `_ReflectionAmount` property:

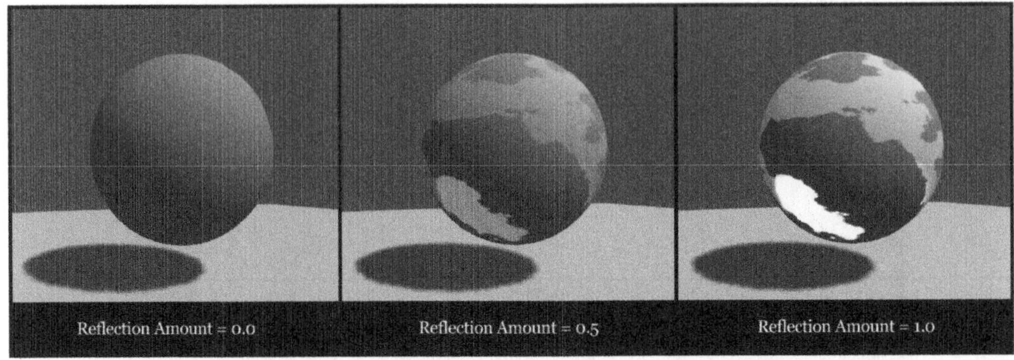

Normal maps and reflections in Unity3D

There are situations where you are going to want to have the normal also perturb the reflected Cubemap. Let's say you want to simulate a surface like frosted glass, or the surface of an ice cube. You couldn't model in all the details of the surface and expect it to run at 60 fps in your game. We have to use normal maps to fake the effects of higher resolution details, so we need to learn how to pass the normal map information to the reflection effect.

To accomplish this task, we are going to look at another built-in parameter to the Input struct that will pass in the modified surface normal, generated by the normal mapping technique. So, let's see how we need to modify the `Input` struct to produce this effect.

Getting ready

Let's create a new, fresh scene by following the next few steps.

1. Again, we will need a Cubemap to produce our reflection effects. So you can either use the Cubemap from the previous recipes, or generate a new one. The Cubemap we will be using for this recipe, which is included in the sample code for this book, is shown here:

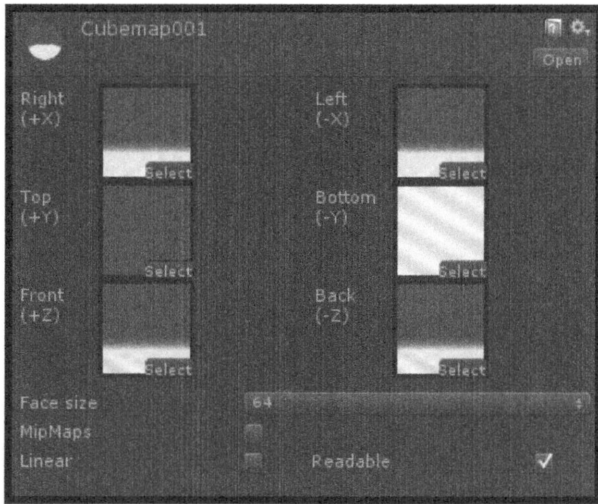

2. We will also need a normal map to produce our normal-mapped reflections.

3. Finally, create a new scene with an object, a ground plane, and a directional light, and the create a new Shader and Material. This will allow us to see our Shader and validate that it is working.

How to do it...

Now, let's write our Shader code so that we can learn how to add normal maps to a reflective Shader.

1. Let's add the properties that we will need to give us the ability to add our own custom Cubemap and normal map. This step should start to seem pretty familiar to you now. You always want to set yourself up with the appropriate properties to let you develop your Shaders. Add the following code to your `Properties` block in your new Shader:

```
Properties
{
    _MainTint ("Diffuse Tint", Color) = (1,1,1,1)
    _MainTex ("Base (RGB)", 2D) = "white" {}
    _NormalMap ("Normal Map", 2D) = "bump" {}
    _Cubemap ("Cubemap", CUBE) = ""{}
    _ReflAmount ("Reflection Amount", Range(0,1)) = 0.5
}
```

2. We then need to declare the properties in the `SubShader` block so that we can access the data from our `Properties` block.

```
    samplerCUBE _Cubemap;
    sampler2D _MainTex;
    sampler2D _NormalMap;
    float4 _MainTint;
    float _ReflAmount;
```

3. The `Input` struct then needs to be updated to include the following code. This is where the real magic of normal-mapped reflections happens. By using the `INTERNAL_DATA` statement, we can access the surface normal after it has been modified by the normal map:

```
    struct Input
    {
        float2 uv_MainTex;
        float2 uv_NormalMap;
        float3 worldRefl;
        INTERNAL_DATA
    };
```

4. Finally, we need to modify our `surf()` function with the following code to get our normal-mapped reflection:

```
void surf (Input IN, inout SurfaceOutput o)
{
    half4 c = tex2D (_MainTex, IN.uv_MainTex);
    float3 normals = UnpackNormal(tex2D(_NormalMap, IN.uv_NormalMap)).rgb;

    o.Normal = normals;
    o.Emission = texCUBE (_Cubemap, WorldReflectionVector (IN, o.Normal)).rgb * _ReflAmount;
    o.Albedo = c.rgb * _MainTint;
    o.Alpha = c.a;
}
```

The following screenshot shows the result of using a normal map to affect the reflection effect:

How it works...

You will notice that this Shader looks very similar to the last Shader we wrote, with one very important difference. We want to use a per-pixel normal map to modify our reflected Cubemap. In order to do this, you have to have the surface normal of the object after the normal map has been applied to the Shader. This means that after the lines of code, we need to write:

```
float3 normals = UnpackNormal(tex2D(_NormalMap, IN.uv_NormalMap)).rgb;
o.Normal = normals;
```

Once those lines of code in the Shader have been calculated, the normal on the surface of the model will have been modified; hence, we need to use it to perturb our reflection. We can access this modified normal by declaring `INTERNAL_DATA` in our `Input` struct, and then using `WorldReflectionVector(IN, o.Normal)` as the look-up information for our Cubemap. This is another built-in function that Unity has provided for us, so that we don't have to do the laborious coding ourselves. We can concentrate on just writing the meat of the Shader that produces our desired effects.

There's more...

There are quite a few other built-in functions we can access in our `Input` struct, and we will most assuredly use them in future chapters; but the following table describes what each of these built-in functions does and how to use them. You can also go to `http://docs.unity3d.com/Documentation/Components/SL-SurfaceShaders.html` to get more information about these built-in functions:

`float3 viewDir`	Will contain view direction, for computing Parallax effects, rim lighting, and so on.
`float4 COLOR`	Will contain interpolated per-vertex color.
`float4 screenPos`	Will contain screen-space position for reflection effects. Used by WetStreet shader in Dark Unity, for example.
`float3 worldPos`	Will contain world space position.
`float3 worldRefl`	Will contain world reflection vector if Surface Shader does not write to `o.Normal`. See Reflect-Diffuse shader for example.
`float3 worldNormal`	Will contain world normal vector if Surface Shader does not write to `o.Normal`.
`float3 worldRef; INTERNAL_DATA`	Will contain world reflection vector if Surface Shader writes to `o.Normal`. To get the reflection vector based on per-pixel normal map, use `WorldReflectionVector (IN, o.Normal)`. See Reflect-Bumped shader for example.
`float3 worldNormal; INTERNAL_DATA`	Will contain world normal vector if Surface Shader writes to `o.Normal`. To get the normal vector based on per-pixel normal map, use `WorldNormalVector (IN, o.Normal)`.

Fresnel reflections in Unity3D

One of the most used types of reflections is the **Fresnel** reflection. This will basically increase the amount of reflection as your view of the surface of an object. You will see this in almost any type of surface, but one of the most used surfaces of this type of effect is the body of a car. We can see that the surface is reflective, but as the surface of the car body becomes more glancing to your view, you'll notice that the reflections and Specular become more intense and create a nice rim-light-type effect.

Not all surfaces have the same amount of Fresnel reflection, though. Some surfaces, like a car body's surface, have a high intensity of Fresnel reflection, whereas something like a piece of plastic has a more dull Fresnel intensity.

This recipe will give you the basic implementation of a Fresnel reflection, as in the real world a Fresnel reflection is the calculation of reflection and refraction as compared to the viewer's angle of view to the surface of an object. But since we haven't covered any sort of refraction techniques, let's take a look at what most game productions implement and how we can modify it to create a very visually appealing reflection effect.

Getting ready

Again, let's create a new scene and fill it with some assets so that we can focus on the Shader we are coding.

1. We are going to need to have a Cubemap to produce our Fresnel effect. So you can either generate a new one, or use one from the previous recipes. The following screenshot shows the Cubemap we will be using for this recipe, which is included in the book's support page at `www.packtpub.com/support`.

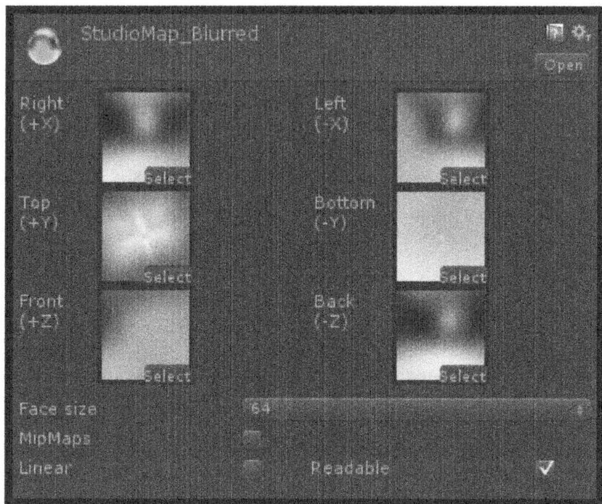

2. Create a new scene, an object, a ground plane, a new Shader, and a new Material.
3. Finally, create a directional light so that we have some light information as well.

How to do it...

Now let's code up our Shader and get the Fresnel effect working.

1. First, we need to set up our properties in our `Properties` block. This time we are going to utilize the built-in BlinnPhong lighting model, so we will need to declare some properties to use the Specular component of the lighting model.

```
Properties
{
    _MainTint("Diffuse Tint", Color) = (1,1,1,1)
    _MainTex ("Base (RGB)", 2D) = "white" {}
    _Cubemap ("Cubemap", CUBE) = ""{}
    _ReflectionAmount ("Reflection Amount", Range(0,1)) = 1
    _RimPower ("Fresnel Falloff", Range(0.1, 3)) = 2
    _SpecColor ("Specular Color", Color) = (1,1,1,1)
    _SpecPower ("Specular Power", Range(0,1)) = 0.5
}
```

2. For this Shader we will need to utilize Shader model 3.0, so that we have enough registers to bring all the data into the `surf()` function. So we need to add the `#pragma` statement to the definitions in the `SubShader` block.

```
CGPROGRAM
#pragma surface surf BlinnPhong
#pragma target 3.0
```

3. We then need to make sure that we create connections between our new properties and the `SubShader` block, so we need to declare our variables as follows:

```
samplerCUBE _Cubemap;
sampler2D _MainTex;
float4 _MainTint;
float _ReflectionAmount;
float _RimPower;
float _SpecPower;
```

4. To get our reflection to work, we need to declare the `worldRefl` parameter in the `Input` struct as well as the `viewDir` parameter.

```
struct Input
{
    float2 uv_MainTex;
    float3 worldRefl;
    float3 viewDir;
};
```

5. Then, we need to calculate the rim effect in the `surf()` function to create our simple Fresnel reflection effect.

```
void surf (Input IN, inout SurfaceOutput o)
{
    half4 c = tex2D (_MainTex, IN.uv_MainTex);

    float rim = 1.0 - saturate(dot(o.Normal, normalize(IN.viewDir)));
    rim = pow(rim, _RimPower);

    o.Albedo = c.rgb * _MainTint;
    o.Emission = (texCUBE(_Cubemap, IN.worldRefl).rgb * _ReflectionAmount) * rim;
    o.Specular = _SpecPower;
    o.Gloss = 1.0;
    o.Alpha = c.a;
}
```

The following screenshot demonstrates the final result of our simple Frensel effect Shader. It could also be used as the basis for a simple car Shader:

How it works...

In this example we are simply creating a falloff value that we can use to mask off where the surface is more reflective and less reflective. By using the view direction compared to the surface normal, we can compute a camera facing falloff value. We then invert that value to achieve a mask that is whiter at the edges of the surface, and blacker when the surface is facing more towards the viewer. Refer to the following screenshot for reference:

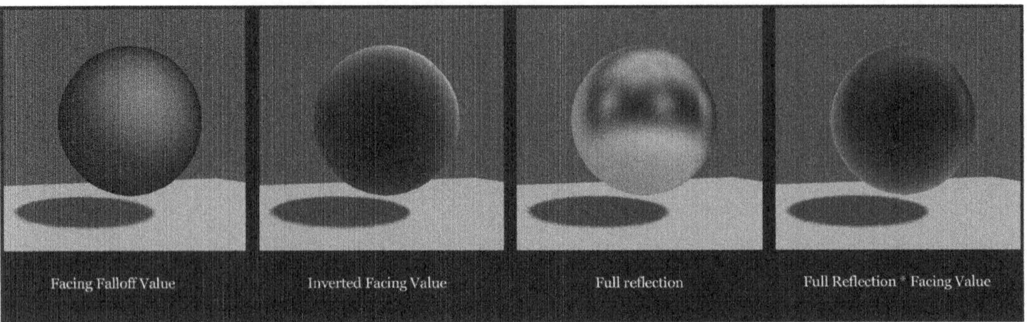

We then complete the Shader by adding in our Specular value and our `Diffuse` values to achieve the final Fresnel reflection Shader.

Creating a simple dynamic Cubemap system

We have learned a lot of great information so far, but our reflections don't really reflect the proper world as an object moves around the environment. For example, if you have an environment composed of multiple rooms and hallways, we couldn't bake out a Cubemap for the whole level and put it in a single Cubemap. That wouldn't reflect the proper environment from room to room. We would get a very static, uninteresting reflection.

There are a couple ways in which this can be solved such that the reflection of one room is different than that of the second room. The first and most basic way is to swap the Cubemap based off of positions in the rooms. So as you move from room to room, the Cubemap would swap out for the correct Cubemap for that room. The second way is to update the Cubemap in real time as the character moves about the environment, ultimately getting a new Cubemap every frame the game progresses. While the second option sounds more visually appealing, since you would see a pop between Cubemaps, it is rather expensive and so needs to be weighed against all the other resources your game will need.

This recipe is going to cover the first option and show you how you can set up a very simple system to swap between two Cubemaps based off of set positions in the environment. There is more information on creating a real-time reflection system in the last section of this recipe, so if you are interested and want to see the differences between these two techniques, then there you go!

Getting ready

1. We need to create a new scene and place a ground plane and a sphere in the world. Plus, add a directional light to get some lighting for our Shader.
2. Continue by adding two empty `GameObject` constructors to the scene and name them `pos001` and `pos002` respectively.
3. Let's then assign a new material to our sphere and attach the Fresnel Shader, which we just created in the last recipe, to our new Material. Your scene should now look like the next screenshot.
4. Finally, let's create a script and name it `SwapCubemaps.cs`.

The following screenshot shows the result of our prepared scene that is ready for our dynamic reflection system:

How to do it...

Once your scene is ready to go, we can begin to code up our reflection system by following the next few steps.

1. Let's begin by adding `[ExecuteInEditMode]` just before we declare our class.

```
[ExecuteInEditMode]
public class SwapCubemaps : MonoBehaviour
{
```

2. Then, we need to declare a few variables to store all the data in our system. We will explain these in the next section of this recipe.

```
public Cubemap cubeA;
public Cubemap cubeB;

public Transform posA;
public Transform posB;

private Material curMat;
private Cubemap curCube;
```

3. In order for us to visually see where our Cubemap positions are in space, we need to take advantage of the awesome **gizmos** features that Unity3D provides for us. So let's add the following code to the bottom of our script:

```
void OnDrawGizmos()
{
    Gizmos.color = Color.green;

    if(posA)
    {
        Gizmos.DrawWireSphere(posA.position, 0.5f);
    }

    if(posB)
    {
        Gizmos.DrawWireSphere(posB.position, 0.5f);
    }
}
```

4. Now, we need to create a new function that will determine which Cubemap we should be using based off of the distance between each of the positions we have set up:

```
private Cubemap CheckProbeDistance()
{
    float distA = Vector3.Distance(transform.position, posA.position);
    float distB = Vector3.Distance(transform.position, posB.position);

    if(distA < distB)
    {
        return cubeA;
    }
    else if(distB < distA)
    {
        return cubeB;
    }
    else
    {
        return cubeA;
    }

}
```

5. Finally, we just need to check every frame to see what the distance is between each of the positions in our environment and swap out the appropriate Cubemap in our Material:

```
void Update ()
{
    curMat = renderer.sharedMaterial;
    if(curMat)
    {
        curCube = CheckProbeDistance();
        curMat.SetTexture("_Cubemap", curCube);

    }
}
```

Once you save the Shader, return to the Unity editor and let the Shader compile. When done, hit **Play** and move the sphere back and forth. You should see a result similar to the following screenshot:

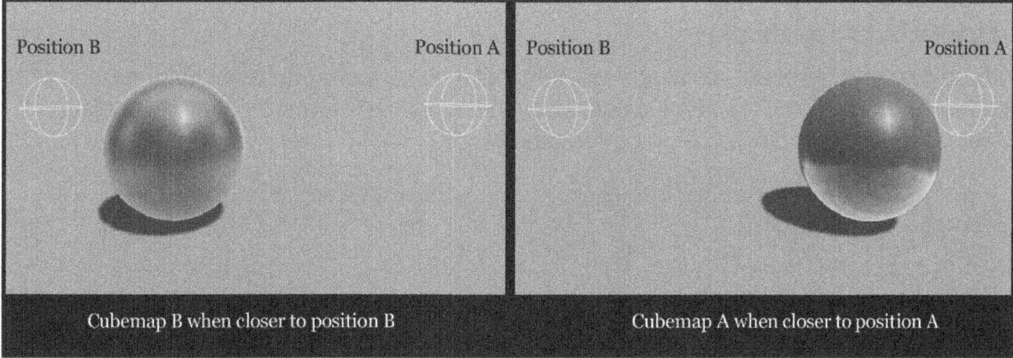

How it works...

We simply start out this script by declaring the `[ExecuteInEditMode]` property for our class. This will tell Unity that we want to run our Cubemap swapping script while it is in the editor, not just when we hit **Play**. This will allow us to test out our Cubemap swapping without having to hit **Play**—much faster workflow.

The script then has a few variables that we use to allow someone to input two Cubemaps and two positions, which we use to compare distances. Lastly, we have two private variables with which we keep track of the current material and the Cubemap while the program is running.

With our variables in place, we can then use the `OnDrawGizmos()` built-in function to actually display the positions of our transforms we let the users input. These positions will command the script as to when to swap out our Cubemaps.

We then get to the real meat of this program. We declare our own function/method that will calculate the distance our sphere is away from either of the two transforms we have, using `Vector3.Distance()`. It then checks to see which distance is smaller and returns a Cubemap for that position.

Finally, in the `Update()` function we get the current material from our sphere, or the object that this script is attached to, and simply assign the currently-selected Cubemap returned from our custom function.

This is just a very simple script to illustrate the concept, but it could be expanded into a complete system, where you have multiple Cubemaps per room. The system can autogenerate all the Cubemaps for us at runtime, which would really be useful for games that can't afford a full-real-time reflection system.

There's more...

You can also take a shot at creating a real-time reflection system, where a Cubemap is updated for every frame the game progresses. This is definitely a more visually appealing system, but does come at a cost to performance:

`http://docs.unity3d.com/Documentation/ScriptReference/Camera.RenderToCubemap.html`

5
Lighting Models

In this chapter, you will learn how to create the following lighting models:

- The Lit Sphere lighting model
- The diffuse convolution lighting model
- A vehicle paint lighting model
- The skin shader
- The cloth shader

Introduction

Throughout the last few chapters we have been looking at ways in which we can use different components of the Surface Shading language to construct Shaders and lighting models. In this chapter, we are going to take advantage of our new-found knowledge to create our own complete Shaders for different effects.

We are going to look at some common types of Shaders that are needed for many games in the industry. This will arm us with the workflows to produce our own Shaders and learn more about trying to tackle new Shaders when a game production calls for a custom Material. We will also discuss some of the ways in which you can create more efficiency when working within a team and how the artists on that team can use your Shaders.

The Lit Sphere lighting model

The Lit Sphere lighting model is a really interesting use of Image based lighting. We can actually use a 2D texture to completely bake in our lighting. It's the same effect as what you see in Zbrush. If you are familiar with Zbrush's MatCaps, the Lit Sphere works in the same way. We can create a texture that literally bakes in the way that the diffuse, the Specular, the reflection, and the rim lighting look, and use it to light our Shader. The only catch with this Shader is that since we have baked the lighting completely in, the lighting never changes, unless you swap to different textures throughout your environment, like we saw in the *Simple Cubemap reflection in Unity3D* recipe in *Chapter 4, Reflecting Your World*. So this Shader will not react to the lights in your environment, nor will it change as you move your view around your model. An example of a Lit Sphere texture lookup, usually referred to as a Sphere Map, is shown in the following screenshot:

This means that this Shader is good for creating nice diorama scenes or even to use in your game's cinematics where a camera is locked off and you need really complex lighting for your characters and environment.

So, let's take a look at how this type of lighting model is created and can be used inside Unity using Surface Shaders.

Getting ready

To begin this Shader, we need to learn how to create the textures that will become our lighting in our Shader. To do this we can use Photoshop, but it is much easier to use a little free tool, called MaCrea, found on the web at: `http://www.taron.de/macrea`; this is a great program offered for free to help you create these Lit Sphere maps. I would recommend watching the videos on Vimeo to get you acquainted with the MaCrea interface and workflows.

An introduction to MaCrea is available at `http://vimeo.com/14030320`.

Once you have become familiar with the process of creating these Sphere maps, we can move on to the rest of this recipe. The following screenshot shows shows the MaCrea interface and a completed Lit Sphere created with the program:

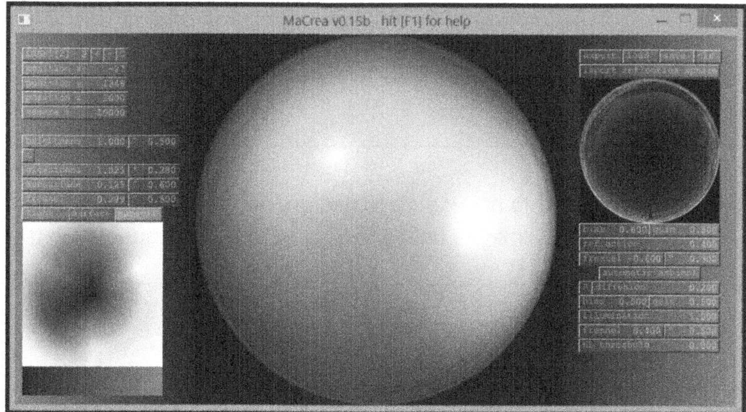

1. Create a new scene with a couple of objects, a plane, and a light.
2. Create a new Shader and Material. Then assign your Shader to your Material.

How to do it...

With our scene assets created and our Shader ready to go in MonoDevelop, we can start to create our Lit Sphere shading model.

1. As always, we need to set up our properties for our Surface Shader so that we can let the user of this Shader input different textures and change values. So, let's add the following code to our `Properties` block:

```
Properties
{
    _MainTint ("Diffuse Tint", Color) = (1,1,1,1)
    _MainTex ("Base (RGB)", 2D) = "white" {}
    _NormalMap ("Normal Map", 2D) = "bump" {}
}
```

2. Since this Shader is solely using the sphere map to light our model, we will not need the `Lambert` lighting function, but we will need to declare our own `Unlit` lighting function. We will also need to write a little bit of a vertex function in order for this Shader to work:

```
CGPROGRAM
#pragma surface surf Unlit vertex:vert
```

3. Then as always, we need to make sure to declare our properties inside our `SubShader` block in order for us to utilize the user-given data from the **Inspector** in the Unity editor.

```
sampler2D _MainTex;
sampler2D _NormalMap;
float4 _MainTint;
```

4. At this point, we can create our new `Lighting` function that will produce for us an Unlit lighting model. We have to do this, as in this case we do not want the lights to affect our Shader. We just want to cast the shadow from the object. So, we need to add the following `Lighting` function to our Shader:

```
inline fixed4 LightingUnlit (SurfaceOutput s, fixed3 lightDir, fixed atten)
{
    fixed4 c = fixed4(1,1,1,1);
    c.rgb = c * s.Albedo;
    c.a = s.Alpha;
    return c;
}
```

5. We now need to populate our `Input` struct with some extra properties so that we can pass the information from our `vertex()` function to our `surf()` function:

```
struct Input
{
    float2 uv_MainTex;
    float2 uv_NormalMap;
    float3 tan1;
    float3 tan2;
};
```

6. In order for us to look up the Sphere map correctly, we will need to multiply the tangent rotation matrix with the inverse transpose model view of the current model. This will give us the proper vectors with which we can apply the Sphere map texture. Don't worry if you don't understand what is happening here in the vertex shader, we will explain it more in the next section.

```
void vert (inout appdata_full v, out Input o)
{
    UNITY_INITIALIZE_OUTPUT(Input,o);

    TANGENT_SPACE_ROTATION;
    o.tan1 = mul(rotation, UNITY_MATRIX_IT_MV[0].xyz);
    o.tan2 = mul(rotation, UNITY_MATRIX_IT_MV[1].xyz);

}
```

7. Finally, we can fill out our `surf()` function with the appropriate calculations to produce the proper lookup values for our Sphere map texture and feed these into our `SurfaceOutput` struct. Again, the guts of this function will be explained in the next section:

```
void surf (Input IN, inout SurfaceOutput o)
{
    float3 normals = UnpackNormal(tex2D(_NormalMap, IN.uv_NormalMap));
    o.Normal = normals;

    float2 litSphereUV;
    litSphereUV.x = dot(IN.tan1, o.Normal);
    litSphereUV.y = dot(IN.tan2, o.Normal);

    half4 c = tex2D (_MainTex, litSphereUV*0.5+0.5);
    o.Albedo = c.rgb * _MainTint;
    o.Alpha = c.a;
}
```

The following screenshot is the result of our Shader using a sphere map, or as Zbrush calls them, MatCaps:

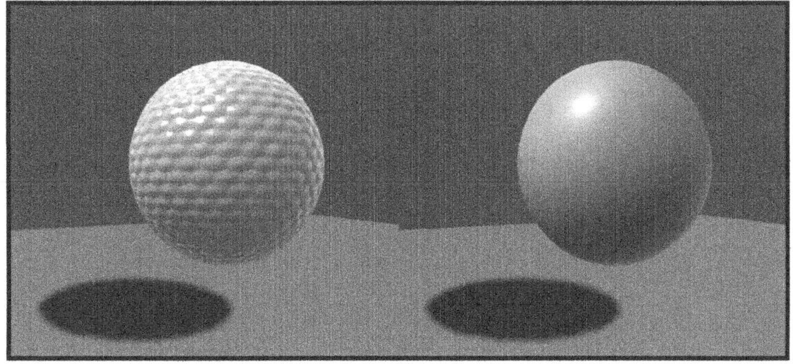

How it works...

The real magic of this lighting model is actually happening inside the `vert()` function, when we assign `o.tan1` and `o.tan2` a new vector by multiplying the rotated tangent vector with the inverse transpose model view matrix. This calculation is actually bending the vectors such that they look up the sphere map in the correct way. So where does the inverse transpose model view matrix come from? It is yet another built-in value that Unity provides us, so we don't have to do the calculations for ourselves.

Unity has actually provided us with the most common transformation matrices that are usually seen in standard CGFX shaders. This is one of the benefits of using Surface Shaders, we don't have to write these position transformations ourselves. We simply call the built-in parameter.

But why do we need to use this particular transformation of the vertices? Understanding how these matrices work is definitely beyond the scope of this book, as this isn't meant to be a book about the heavy math of why objects render to screen in a real-time engine, but the simple explanation is that we need to take the vertices in object space and convert them to world space, so we can then map the sphere map on to our surface accordingly. Try to think of it as changing your spatial relationship to the model.

The vectors being produced by the multiplication of the inverse transpose mode view and the rotated tangent normal are shown in the following screenshot. We use these vectors to look up values in our Sphere map texture:

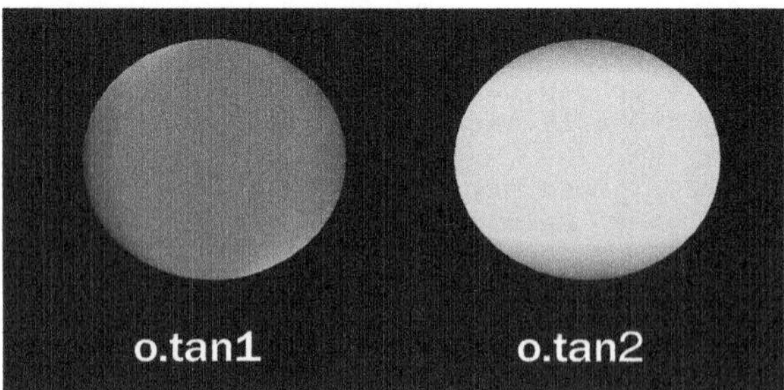

Finally, we complete our Shader by simply using the values `IN.tan1` and `IN.tan2` as the UV values for our sphere map texture lookup. We can use these values from the `Input` structure because we populated them with data from the `vert()` function.

This is a simple yet visually appealing way to achieve complex lighting situations. The only downside to using this technique is that the lighting doesn't update according to real lights. The lighting is always locked to the facing view direction of the camera, almost as if the texture is being projected on to the object in view.

See also

As always, the Internet is a great resource to find out more information on many topics. We have included a few links that will give you more information and training on sphere maps and the Lit Sphere shading model.

- There is a great explanation in the Cg tutorial online book here: `http://http.developer.nvidia.com/CgTutorial/cg_tutorial_chapter04.html`.
- You can find more information on all the built-in transformation matrices here: `http://docs.unity3d.com/Documentation/Components/SL-BuiltinStateInPrograms.html`.
- Information on reflections in MaCrea can be found at: `http://vimeo.com/14189456`.
- Information on cell shading in MaCrea can be found at: `http://vimeo.com/14033777`.

The diffuse convolution lighting model

Diffuse convolution is the process of blurring a Cubemap such that the overall intensity of the lighting in the Cubemap is retained but the details are blurred out. This type of technique is really useful when you want to achieve a more globally-lit surface. You can fake the effects of global illumination by capturing a Cubemap of your scene and running it through a diffuse convolution algorithm, and then lighting your model with the convolved Cubemap.

We are going to look at how we can use this technique inside Unity using Surface Shaders. We will also utilize CubeMapGen to produce our diffuse convolved Cubemap.

Getting ready

In order for us to achieve this technique, we need to be able to create a Cubemap that has been convolved. There are a few ways to do this, but we will focus on using CubeMapGen from ATI. You can download this tool from their site using this link: `http://developer.amd.com/resources/archive/archived-tools/gpu-tools-archive/cubemapgen/`.

The following image shows the CubeMapGen user interface as well as a Cubemap loaded into the program:

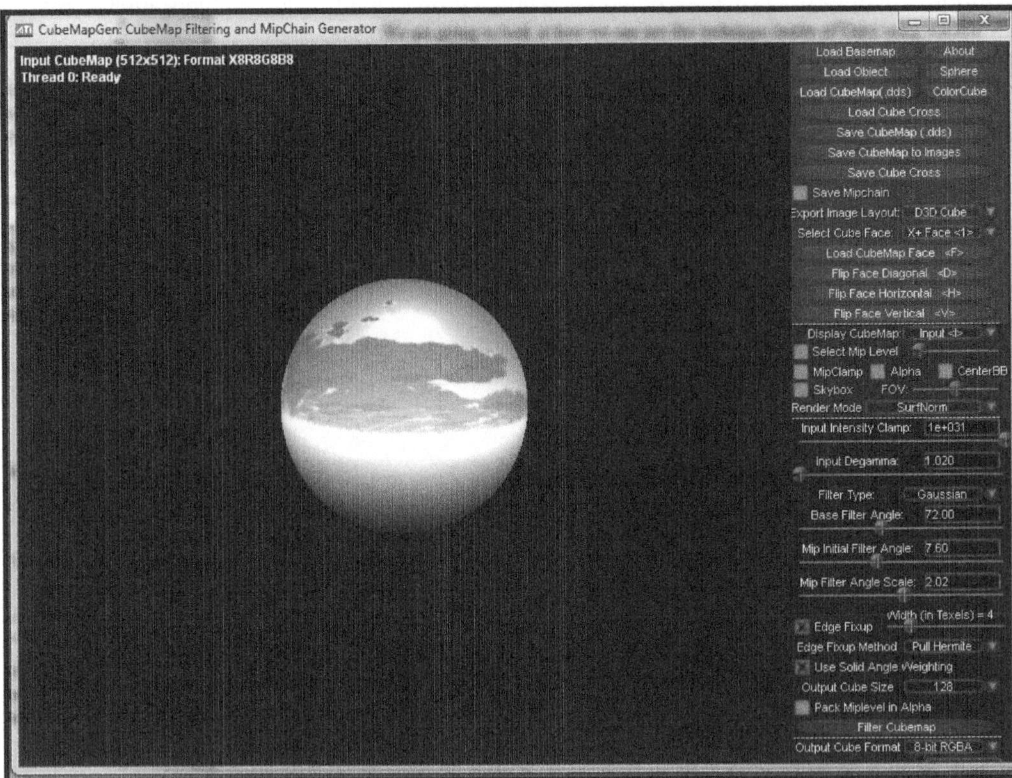

Let's walk through the process of creating a convolved Cubemap:

1. Launch CubeMapGen and load one of the Cubemaps that comes with the application. They will be located in the install directory of CubeMapGen.
2. Once you have loaded a Cubemap into the tool, we need to filter it, which means to convolve it or blur it with intelligence. So, we need to go into the blue section of the user interface and set **Filter Type** to **Gaussian**, **Base Filter Angle** to `72.00`, **Mip Initial Filter Angle** to `7.60`, **Mip Filter Angle Scale** to `2.02`, and **Edge fix up** to **4**. Then hit the **Filter Cubemap** button at the bottom of the blue section of the interface. This will take a little while, but you should end up with something like the following screenshot:

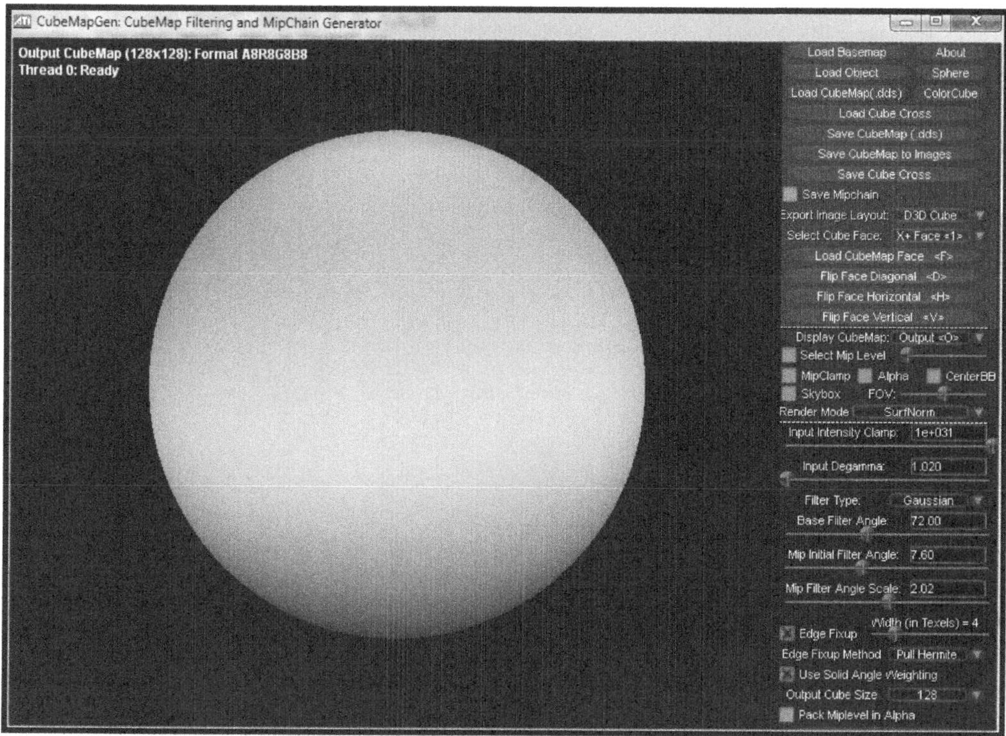

3. Once CubeMapGen has completed its filter process, you can then save your Cubemap into separate faces by hitting the **Save Cubemap to Images** button in the green section of the user interface. This will create each of the sides of the Cubemap for you. We can then take these images and construct a new Cubemap inside of Unity.
4. Now that we have completed the Cubemap creation, we need to set up a scene to create our Shader with. So, create a new scene and place some objects in the scene with one directional light. We will also need a new Material and a new Shader.

How to do it...

With all of our assets generated, we can now walk through the process of creating our Shader to utilize our convolved Cubemap.

1. As usual, let's create the properties that will let an artist interact with our Shader so that they can tune it how they see fit.

```
Properties
{
    _MainTint ("Global Tint", Color) = (1,1,1,1)
    _BumpMap ("Normal Map", 2D) = "bump" {}
    _AOMap ("Ambient Occlusion Map", 2D) = "white" {}
    _CubeMap ("Diffuse Convolution Cubemap", Cube) = ""{}
    _SpecIntensity ("Specular Intensity", Range(0, 1)) = 0.4
    _SpecWidth ("Specular Width", Range(0, 1)) = 0.2
}
```

2. We then need to declare our `#pragma` statements. In this case, we are going to create a new lighting model, as we want our Cubemap to light our model and not the lights themselves. We are also going to need to declare the 3.0 target shading model so that we don't run into a texture interpolation error.

```
CGPROGRAM
#pragma surface surf DiffuseConvolution
#pragma target 3.0
```

3. In order for us to be able to access the data coming in from our properties, we need to create the link between the `Properties` block and the `SubShader` block by declaring a corresponding variable for each of our properties. Enter the following code to create this link:

```
samplerCUBE _CubeMap;
sampler2D _BumpMap;
sampler2D _AOMap;
float4 _MainTint;
float _SpecIntensity;
float _SpecWidth;
```

4. Our `Input` struct is going to be pretty simple this time around, as all we need is the world normal from our model. We will need the `INTERNAL_DATA` statement, as we will be including a normal map in our Shader and this will give us the modified normal.

```
struct Input
{
    float2 uv_AOMap;
    float3 worldNormal;
    INTERNAL_DATA
};
```

5. Our next task is to create the structure for our lighting model. We will want to include the view direction, as we are going to be creating a simple specular for our Shader as well.

```
inline fixed4 LightingDiffuseConvolution (SurfaceOutput s, fixed3 lightDir, fixed3 viewDir, fixed atten)
{

}
```

6. Our lighting function is no good if we don't actually fill it with stuff that calculates our lighting. So, let's start that by getting all of our lighting vectors in order:

```
//Get all vectors for lighting
viewDir = normalize ( viewDir );
lightDir = normalize ( lightDir );
s.Normal = normalize ( s.Normal );
float NdotL = dot ( s.Normal, lightDir );
float3 halfVec = normalize ( lightDir + viewDir );
```

7. Then we need to take care of our Specular component.

```
//Calculate the Specular
float spec = pow (dot(s.Normal, halfVec), s.Specular*128.0) * s.Gloss;
```

8. Finally, we combine all of our calculations together to form our lighting model:

```
fixed4 c;
c.rgb = (s.Albedo * atten) + spec;
c.a = 1.0f;
return c;
```

9. With our lighting model completed we can now simply process our textures, sample our convolved Cubemap with the world normal of the model, and pass the result to the `SurfaceOutput` struct:

```
void surf (Input IN, inout SurfaceOutput o)
{
    half4 c = tex2D (_AOMap, IN.uv_AOMap);
    float3 normals = UnpackNormal(tex2D(_BumpMap, IN.uv_AOMap)).rgb;
    o.Normal = normals;

    float3 diffuseVal = texCUBE(_CubeMap, WorldNormalVector(IN, o.Normal)).rgb;

    o.Albedo = (c.rgb * diffuseVal) * _MainTint;
    o.Specular = _SpecWidth;
    o.Gloss = _SpecIntensity * c.rgb;
    o.Alpha = c.a;
}
```

Using the world normal, we can look up a color in a convolved Cubemap to give our models a very realistic look.

The result of our diffuse convolution shader can be seen in the following screenshot:

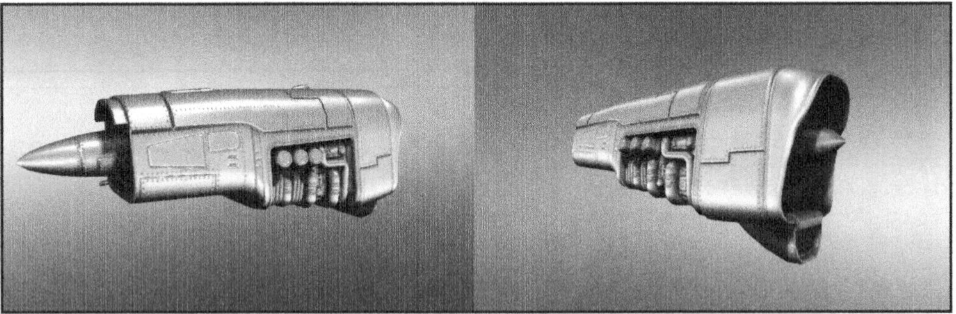

How it works...

Another simple yet visually stunning technique is the diffuse convolution technique. While it is a bit more interactive than the sphere map approach, the lighting is still locked off to a single Cubemap. You could update the Cubemap in real time to sample the environment around you, but the process of convolving the Cubemap would be too computationally expensive to do in real time. Not to worry though. This is why Unity has provided us with the light probe technique. It allows us to place points in an environment and sample the convolved ambient light coming into each point. This is commonly referred to as **ambient cube shading**.

This Shader, though, is great for setting up small scenes in which there isn't too much motion or interactivity with lights. This is commonly referred to as Image based lighting, as we are using the Cubemap images to light our model and not a light itself. This technique is great for cinematics in your game, or even a vehicle customization screen.

This simply works by taking the world normals of the model after they have been modified by the normal map, and using that data to look up a position in the Cubemap to retrieve its pixel color. This is why we have to declare `float3`, `worldNormal`, and the `INTERNAL_DATA` parameters in our Input struct. We then have to use the `WorldNormalVector()` function provided to us by Unity to get the final normal vector for our `texCUBE()` lookup. The rest of the Shader is pretty familiar to us by now.

In the following screenshot, we can see how the world normal looks up which color it should be from the Cubemap surrounding it:

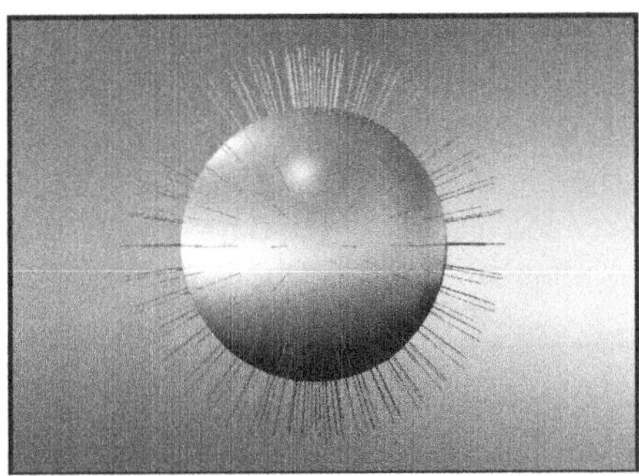

There's more...

For more information on using light probes within Unity to get Ambient Cubemaps. refer to `http://docs.unity3d.com/Documentation/Manual/LightProbes.html`.

See also

Remember to reference the *Creating Cubemaps in Unity3D* recipe in *Chapter 4, Reflecting Your World*, if you need a refresher.

Creating a vehicle paint lighting model

One of the most used Shader effects is the car shader or vehicle shader. This includes many of the techniques we have covered so far in the previous chapters, but now we are going to put all our new-found knowledge to the test. We will create the foundation for a real production-ready Shader that can be used on any of your vehicle models. This will definitely be one of the more advanced Shaders we have written as well as one of the longest, but we will step through it and I'll explain each element.

Getting ready

Let's get a new scene prepared with a few assets in it so that we can create our vehicle paint lighting model.

1. We will first need something to shade, so we need to create a new object in a new scene. It's nice to have a plane to act as a ground plane to catch shadows of our object we are shading. So we recommend placing one in the scene as well.
2. In order to write a Shader, we need to have a new Shader and a new Material. So, let's create those now and hook them up to our main object, in this case a sphere.
3. In order to achieve this particular vehicle shader, we will need to create a BRDF texture as well. If you remember from the BRDF section we just need to create a texture that has some variation in color, which represents the different viewing directions on the model. Simply put, we need a color for the diffuse light, and the view direction light. The following screenshot is an example of a texture used in this vehicle shader:

4. Our final step in preparing for the Shader is the creation of a Cubemap. Remember from *Chapter 4, Reflecting Your World* that we can use the generate Cubemap script to produce a Cubemap from our scene in unity. Let's do that now.

How to do it...

With all our assets ready we can start to construct our Shader. We will first run through the code in this Shader, and then break it out and describe each individual component. So let's create our Shader!

1. Our first step is to create the properties we are going to need. There are quite a few in this Shader, but we will explain what each one is doing in the next section. Some are pretty familiar to us by now, but they will still be explained.

```
Properties
{
    _MainTint ("Diffuse Tint", Color) = (1,1,1,1)
    _MainTex ("Base (RGB)", 2D) = "white" {}
    _SpecularColor ("Specular Color", Color) = (1,1,1,1)
    _SpecPower ("Specular Power", Range(0.01, 30)) = 3
    _ReflCube ("Reflection Cube", CUBE) = "" {}
    _BRDFTex ("BRDF Texture", 2D) = "white" {}
    _DiffusePower ("Diffuse Power", Range(0.01, 10)) = 0.5
    _FalloffPower ("Falloff Spread", Range(0.01, 10)) = 3
    _ReflAmount ("Reflection Amount", Range(0.01, 1.0)) = 0.5
    _ReflPower ("Reflection Power", Range(0.01, 3.0)) = 2.0
}
```

2. For this Shader we will be creating our own lighting model called `CarPaint`, so we need to first declare that in our Shader's `#pragma` statement:

```
CGPROGRAM
#pragma surface surf CarPaint
```

3. In order for us to access all the data from our properties, we need to declare them inside of our `SubShader` block as well. See the following code snippet:

```
sampler2D _MainTex;
sampler2D _BRDFTex;
fixed4 _MainTint;
fixed4 _SpecularColor;
fixed _SpecPower;
fixed _DiffusePower;
fixed _FalloffPower;
fixed _ReflAmount;
fixed _ReflPower;
samplerCUBE _ReflCube;
```

4. At this point we can start to work on our lighting model. For this Shader we will need to create a lot of data, so read through the following code snippet a couple of times, before actually inserting it into your Shader to absorb the information:

```
inline fixed4 LightingCarPaint (SurfaceOutput s, fixed3 lightDir, half3 viewDir, fixed atten)
{
    half3 h = normalize (lightDir + viewDir);
    fixed diff = max (0, dot (s.Normal, lightDir));

    float ahdn = 1-dot(h, normalize(s.Normal));
    ahdn = pow(clamp(ahdn, 0.0, 1.0), _DiffusePower);
    half4 brdf = tex2D(_BRDFTex, float2(diff, 1-ahdn));

    float nh = max (0, dot (s.Normal, h));
    float spec = pow (nh, s.Specular * _SpecPower) * s.Gloss;

    fixed4 c;
    c.rgb = (s.Albedo * _LightColor0.rgb * brdf.rgb + _LightColor0.rgb * _SpecularColor.rgb * spec)* (atten * 2);
    c.a = s.Alpha + _LightColor0.a * _SpecularColor.a * spec * atten;
    return c;
}
```

5. Let's turn our attention to the `Input` struct in our Shader and add the following code. This will let us produce the Fresnel effect you saw in the previous chapter.

```
struct Input
{
    float2 uv_MainTex;
    float3 worldRefl;
    float3 viewDir;
};
```

6. Finally, we have our `surf()` function that does most of the per pixel calculations. Here we will create the final effects for our car paint shader:

```
void surf (Input IN, inout SurfaceOutput o)
{
    half4 c = tex2D (_MainTex, IN.uv_MainTex);

    fixed falloff = saturate(1-dot(normalize(IN.viewDir), o.Normal));
    falloff = pow(falloff, _FalloffPower);

    o.Albedo = c.rgb * _MainTint;
    o.Emission = pow((texCUBE(_ReflCube, IN.worldRefl).rgb * falloff), _ReflPower) * _ReflAmount;
    o.Specular = c.r;
    o.Gloss = 1.0;
    o.Alpha = c.a;
}
```

The following screenshot shows the result of our car paint shader on a sphere in Unity3D:

How it works...

Our car paint shader is actually quite simple when you break it into its components, and we have actually already covered each of the components in *Chapter 1, Diffuse Shading* and *Chapter 3, Making Your Game Shine with Specular*. So hopefully, it should all be sinking in by now, but let's go over the broad concept.

We utilize the BRDF technique, seen in *Chapter 1, Diffuse Shading* to create the two-toned look of car paint. Now, not every vehicle will have this so it is up to you, the Shader programmer, to decide whether you are going to use a BRDF texture or some other form of diffuse component.

Finally, we simply calculate a Fresnel term and a fall-off component that drives the amount of reflectivity seen on the surface of the vehicle. All these lighting components are driven by the properties in the `Properties` block; so an artist can have ultimate control over the final look of their Shader for their vehicle.

There's more...

There are also car paint shaders for sale in the Unity Asset Store. Here is a link to one of them: `http://u3d.as/content/ravel-tammeleht/mo-dy-en-car-paint-shader-pack/2Xe`.

Skin shader

Skin shaders are always in high demand during the course of a game production, that is if your game production has characters with some sort of organic skin. This section is going to look at a skin shader approach that can be used in production. It isn't by any means the most accurate, but it does the trick and can produce some really nice effects.

Before we begin though, we need to understand what our skin surface has to do. This information will arm us with the knowledge we can use to break our Shader into its components, so that we can program in the different effects.

We can break the skin into four different components. This isn't the law of the land but you can get a very nice skin effect by concentrating on these four. They are as follows:

- **Sub-surface scattering**: This is the effect of the skin becoming very thin or very clear, such that the light behind it is creating a coloring effect. For skin this is usually a reddish hue to simulate the blood vessels being exposed. Here, we are going to learn how to calculate the curvature of a surface using its normal map.
- **Diffuse**: As you can imagine the effects of diffuse is not just a simple gray scale value when it comes to skin. We will still use the technique of dotting the light vector with the normal vector, but we need to utilize our BRDF technique to give more artistic control over how the light is affected while being distributed over the surface.
- **Specular**: Specular for skin is pretty tricky, as it is being controlled by how oily the surface is. We can still utilize the Specular tricks we have learned so far, but we want to add in our Fresnel and rim lighting techniques to control where the Specular is placed. This will distribute the Specular in a more realistic fashion. We could also use a lookup texture to control how the Specular is shaped, but we are going to implement a basic Specular for this recipe as we have covered how to do a Specular lookup in the previous chapter.
- **Blurred normals**: The reason a lot of skin shaders for games don't look that realistic or too plastic is because the normals of the normal map are reading at a very high-detail level and that is great when it comes to the Specular component, as we want to capture all that detail. But when we are talking about the diffuse component of the skin, we need a nice soft transition of colors.

Getting ready

So, now let's get our scene prepared and gather some assets so that we can have them ready as we implement the different components of our Shader.

1. Create a new scene, Shader, and Material. Make sure to attach the Shader to the Material and assign the material to your object. It would be best if you can have a model of a head, but if not, that's okay, you can still use a sphere, as we have been using for the previous chapters.

2. We will also need a BRDF texture to calculate our diffuse colors. There is a BRDF texture that comes with this book, located on the book's support page at `http://www.packtpub.com/support`. Your BRDF texture will need to simulate the coloring of skin for the different tones of the skin. Here, we will be simulating a Caucasian skin so that our BRDF texture looks like the following:

How to do it...

Now let's take a look at how we construct our Shader. We are going to step through each of the blocks of code, and then explain the key concepts in the next section.

1. To begin with, we need to fill our `Properties` block to get our different tweakable properties set up and give us a way to pass our textures to the Shader. We are now starting to get a lot of properties in our Shaders. This is the point in which you would want to speak with your artists and see if you can pack textures so that you don't need to have a bunch of sliders, but for our purposes this will suffice.

```
Properties
{
    _MainTint ("Global Tint", Color) = (1,1,1,1)
    _MainTex ("Base (RGB)", 2D) = "white" {}
    _BumpMap ("Normal Map", 2D) = "bump" {}
    _CurveScale ("Curvature Scale", Range(0.001, 0.09)) = 0.01
    _CurveAmount ("Curvature Amount", Range(0, 1)) = 0.5
    _BumpBias ("Normal Map Blur", Range(0, 5)) = 2.0
    _BRDF ("BRDF Ramp", 2D) = "white" {}
    _FresnelVal ("Fresnel Amount", Range(0.01, 0.3)) = 0.05
    _RimPower ("Rim Falloff", Range(0, 5)) = 2
    _RimColor ("Rim Color", Color) = (1,1,1,1)
    _SpecIntensity ("Specular Intensity", Range(0, 1)) = 0.4
    _SpecWidth ("Specular Width", Range(0, 1)) = 0.2
}
```

2. We then need to declare a few `#pragma` statements, as this Shader requires quite a bit of processing and specific features of CGFX. So we need to enter in the following into our `SubShader` block, in order to remove any unwanted compiling errors. These will be explained in the next section:

```
CGPROGRAM
#pragma surface surf SkinShader
#pragma target 3.0
#pragma only_renderers d3d9
```

3. Our Shader needs to have access to the data being passed into our properties so that we can use the values that a user of this Shader will set. So we need to declare the corresponding property name in our `SubShader` block.

```
    sampler2D _MainTex;
    sampler2D _BumpMap;
    sampler2D _BRDF;
    float4 _MainTint;
    float4 _RimColor;
    float _CurveScale;
    float _BumpBias;
    float _CurveAmount;
    float _FresnelVal;
    float _RimPower;
    float _SpecIntensity;
    float _SpecWidth;
```

4. In order for us to completely take advantage of the power of Surface Shaders, we will need to declare our own `SurfaceOutput` struct. This lets us pass data back and forth between our custom lighting function and our surface function. If we were to use just the built-in `SurfaceOutput` struct, we wouldn't be able to pass the blurred normals out to our lighting function, as well as the curvature value, which we are calculating on a per-pixel level.

```
struct SurfaceOutputSkin
{
    fixed3 Albedo;
    fixed3 Normal;
    fixed3 Emission;
    fixed3 Specular;
    fixed Gloss;
    fixed Alpha;
    float Curvature;
    fixed3 BlurredNormals;
};
```

5. To complete the base structure of our Shader, we need to declare our `Input` struct and fill it with some useful built-in data. In this case, we will need the world position of each vertex of our model as well as the world normals and as we are using a normal map for this Shader, we have to declare the `INTERNAL_DATA` line so that we can get the normals after the normal map has been applied to the surface.

```
struct Input
{
    float2 uv_MainTex;
    float3 worldPos;
    float3 worldNormal;
    INTERNAL_DATA
};
```

6. With all the data set up, we can now begin to write our custom lighting function. We do this by first declaring the lighting models function called `LightingSkinShader()`.

```
inline fixed4 LightingSkinShader (SurfaceOutputSkin s, fixed3 lightDir, fixed3 viewDir, fixed atten)
{

}
```

7. We can now fill our lighting model with the appropriate calculations to produce our skin lighting. To start it, we will get all of our vectors in order and normalized so that we are dealing with unit vectors. Make sure this code goes inside the lighting model function.

```
//Get all vectors for lighting
viewDir = normalize ( viewDir );
lightDir = normalize ( lightDir );
s.Normal = normalize ( s.Normal );
float NdotL = dot ( s.BlurredNormals, lightDir );
float3 halfVec = normalize ( lightDir + viewDir );
```

8. With the vectors ready, we can produce the values for our BRDF texture lookup.

```
//Create BRDF and Faked SSS
float3 brdf = tex2D(_BRDF, float2((NdotL * 0.5 + 0.5)* atten, s.Curvature)).rgb;
```

9. Next up is our Fresnel and rim lighting components.

```
//Create Fresnel and Rim lighting
float fresnel = saturate(pow(1-dot(viewDir, halfVec),5.0));
fresnel += _FresnelVal * (1 - fresnel);
float rim = saturate(pow(1-dot(viewDir, s.BlurredNormals),_RimPower)) * fresnel;
```

10. Then, we create our Specular component just as we had done it in *Chapter 3, Making Your Game Shine with Specular*.

```
//Create Spec
float specBase = max(0,dot(s.Normal, halfVec));
float spec = pow (specBase, s.Specular*128.0) * s.Gloss;
```

11. With all our calculations done for our lighting model, we can now combine them up and pass the result over to the surface function.

```
//Final Color
fixed4 c;
c.rgb = (s.Albedo * brdf * _LightColor0.rgb * atten) + (spec + (rim * _RimColor));
c.a = 1.0f;
return c;
```

12. Finally, we get to our `surf()` function where we get all of our texture information, calculate the blurred normals, and produce the curvature value for our model based off of the normal map.

```
void surf (Input IN, inout SurfaceOutputSkin o)
{
    //Get our texture information
    half4 c = tex2D (_MainTex, IN.uv_MainTex);
    fixed3 normals = UnpackNormal(tex2D(_BumpMap, IN.uv_MainTex));
    float3 normalBlur = UnpackNormal ( tex2Dbias ( _BumpMap, float4 ( IN.uv_MainTex, 0.0, _BumpBias ) ) );

    //Calculate Curvature
    float curvature = length ( fwidth ( WorldNormalVector ( IN, normalBlur ) ) )
                      / length ( fwidth ( IN.worldPos ) ) * _CurveScale;

    //apply all our information to our SurfaceOutput
    o.Normal = normals;
    o.BlurredNormals = normalBlur;
    o.Albedo = c.rgb * _MainTint;
    o.Curvature = curvature;
    o.Specular = _SpecWidth;
    o.Gloss = _SpecIntensity;
    o.Alpha = c.a;
}
```

With all the components combined in our Surface Shader, our skin shader should look like the following screenshot:

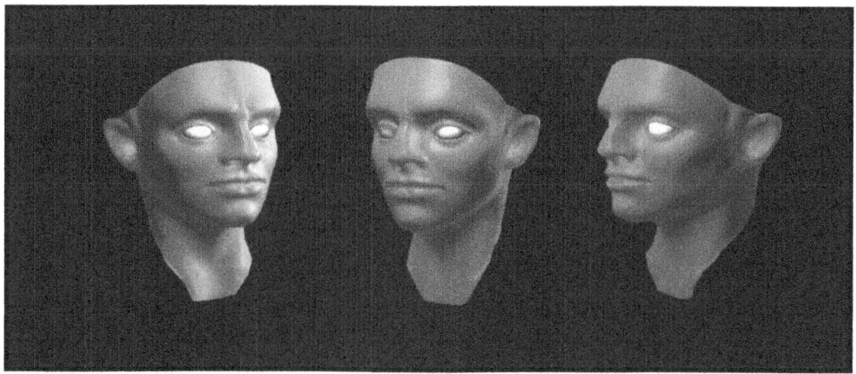

How it works...

For most of the Shader we have already seen how to implement its components, but there are a few components that are new to us. To begin with, we have declared a new type of struct called `SurfaceOutputSkin`, while we have seen this before, we will cover it here once more here.

The `SurfaceOutputSkin` struct is our own custom struct that both the lighting function and the surf() function can use as a means of passing data from the surf() function to the lighting function. Think of it like a transport. When we assign values to the struct inside of the `surf()` function, they get stored in the variables inside that struct. We can then use that data inside the lighting function to perform more per-pixel lighting.

The next component that is new to us is the curvature calculation. We are basically measuring the amount of change between the normals of the surface. So as the curvature of the surface changes, so does the angle between the normals on that surface. We can use this data to find the areas of highest curvature and get a black and white value from the calculation.

This calculation introduces two new built-in CGFX functions that will return for us the necessary data to find this change in the surface curvature. The first is the `fwidth()` function. In our Shader, you will notice that we are sending in a vector as the argument to the `fwidth()` function. This will return for us how quickly the vector is changing over the surface of the object. So, we end up with a vector that represents the curvature of the surface. Here is the link to the Cg standard library description: `http://http.developer.nvidia.com/Cg/fwidth.html`.

Using the `fwidth()` function from the Cg standard functions, we can get information about the curvature of the surface of our model.

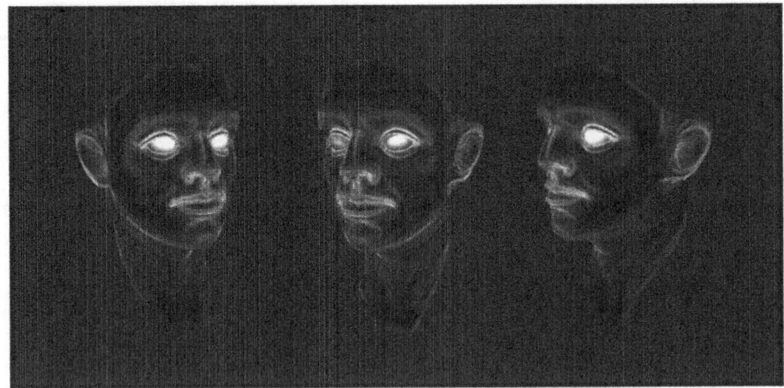

We then don't need the complete vector; we just want to find its magnitude on a per-pixel basis. So, we can use the `length()` function as this will return for us the length of the vector as a float value. Here is the description of the length function from the Cg standard library: `http://http.developer.nvidia.com/Cg/length.html`.

Using the `length()` function, we can find out the magnitude of the per-pixel curvature vector and get a float value that will drive how we look up our BRDF texture.

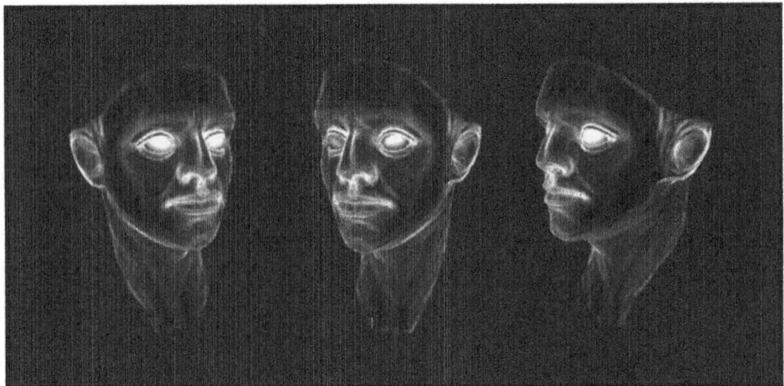

With that data processed, we simply divide the two floats and multiply the result by another float value, passed to us from our `CurveScale` property, to give control over how intense the curvature effect is.

The final result of our complete curvature calculation in our skin shader is shown in the following screenshot:

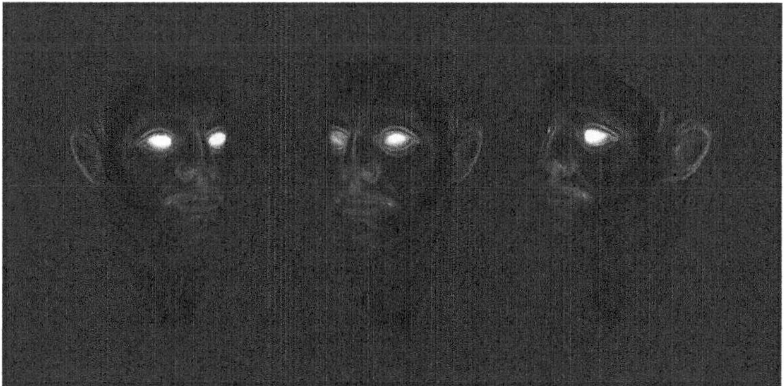

Finally, our last new function that we are utilizing to get a nice soft diffuse lighting on our skin is the `tex2Dbias()` function. This allows us to offset or move the current mip level to a lower or higher mip level using a property to allow control over how blurry the texture is. It's not that we are blurring the texture pixel for pixel, we are actually just selecting a lower mip level from our texture. For more information on mip maps and generating them, see this link to the Unity reference: `http://docs.unity3d.com/Documentation/Manual/Textures.html`.

There's more...

This particular implementation of a skin shader was inspired by a couple of Shaders found on the web. So we thought it proper to mention them here:

- **Unity forums**: `http://forum.unity3d.com/threads/131626-Gritty-realistic-skin-shader`.
- **Skin Shader 3**: `http://wiki.unity3d.com/index.php?title=Skin_Shader_3`.

Cloth shading

Cloth is another very common shading task that needs to be achieved in the process of making games or shading real-time interactive experiences. It involves understanding how the fibers of the cloth disperse the lighting over the surface to produce the look of cloth. It is also very view-dependent and so we will look at some new tricks we can employ to fake the effects of light glancing over the surface of the cloth, and the tiny fibers producing a very distinctive rim lighting effect.

This Shader will introduce us to the concept of detail normal maps and detail textures. By combining two normal maps together, we can actually achieve a higher level of detail that you could store in a 2048 x 2048 texture. This technique will help us simulate the micro level of bumps in the surface that will allow us to disperse the specular component over a wide surface.

Here, we can see the final cloth shader we are going to make in this recipe:

Getting ready

This Shader is going to require that we gather three different types of textures in order to simulate a cloth-like surface.

- We are going to need a Detail Normal map. This map will be tiled over the surface to simulate the micro stitching in the cloth.
- We will need a Normal Variation map that will give us a nice variation in the stitching to make it feel less uniform and more like it has been worn over the years.
- Finally, we need a Detail Diffuse map that we can multiply over the base color in order to give the diffuse a bit more depth and realism, and to emphasize the stitching in the cloth.

The following screenshot shows the three textures we will be using for this recipe. They are also included on this book's support page located at `www.packtpub.com/support`:

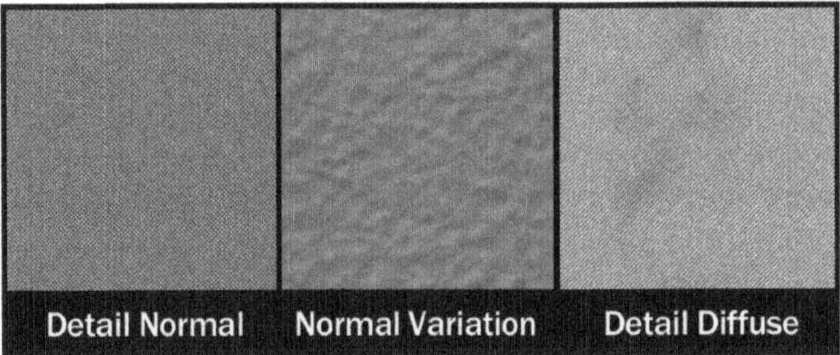

To complete the setup, we need to create a scene with an object and a directional light. Then finally, create a new Shader and Material to assign to our main object.

How to do it...

Let's get our Shader started by filling in our `Properties` block.

1. Our Shader is going to take just a few properties here to control which textures we use and how the falloff of our Fresnel and specular components look.

```
Properties
{
    _MainTint ("Global Tint", Color) = (1,1,1,1)
    _BumpMap ("Normal Map", 2D) = "bump" {}
    _DetailBump ("Detail Normal Map", 2D) = "bump" {}
    _DetailTex ("Fabric Weave", 2D) = "white" {}
    _FresnelColor ("Fresnel Color", Color) = (1,1,1,1)
    _FresnelPower ("Fresnel Power", Range(0, 12)) = 3
    _RimPower ("Rim FallOff", Range(0, 12)) = 3
    _SpecIntesity ("Specular Intensiity", Range(0, 1)) = 0.2
    _SpecWidth ("Specular Width", Range(0, 1)) = 0.2

}
```

2. As we want to have full control over how the lighting reacts to the surface of our cloth, we are going to declare a new lighting model in our `#pragma` statements, as well as setting this Shader to use Shader model 3.0. In order for us to create our own custom lighting model, we have to declare the name of our lighting model in the `#pragma` statements.

```
CGPROGRAM
#pragma surface surf Velvet
#pragma target 3.0
```

3. Now, we have to make the connection between the `Properties` block and the `SubShader` block. In order to use the data coming in from our `Properties` block, we have to declare the same named variables in our `SubShader` block.

```
sampler2D _BumpMap;
sampler2D _DetailBump;
sampler2D _DetailTex;
float4 _MainTint;
float4 _FresnelColor;
float _FresnelPower;
float _RimPower;
float _SpecIntesity;
float _SpecWidth;
```

4. To control the tiling rates of our detail textures independently, we need to declare the UV parameters in the `Input` struct. The UV information will be connected if you put `uv` in front of the same name of the texture. Connect the texture's tiling rates within the `Input` struct:

```
struct Input
{
    float2 uv_BumpMap;
    float2 uv_DetailBump;
    float2 uv_DetailTex;
};
```

5. Now, we need to build the function that will become our lighting model. Create the lighting function structure to start the process of creating a custom lighting model. We are going to need the `viewDir` lighting function structure for this Shader, as the cloth surface has view-dependent components.

```
inline fixed4 LightingVelvet (SurfaceOutput s, fixed3 lightDir, half3 viewDir, fixed atten)
{

}
```

It's always a good idea to take care of all your lighting vectors at the beginning of your lighting function. This frees you up to worry about other parts of the lighting calculation, instead of always having to normalize your vectors. Let's add our lighting vectors to the beginning of our lighting model:

```
//Create lighting vectors here
viewDir = normalize(viewDir);
lightDir = normalize(lightDir);
half3 halfVec = normalize (lightDir + viewDir);
fixed NdotL = max (0, dot (s.Normal, lightDir));
```

6. Our next task is to calculate our Specular component. Add the following code just after the lighting vectors:

```
//Create Specular
float NdotH = max (0, dot (s.Normal, halfVec));
float spec = pow (NdotH, s.Specular*128.0) * s.Gloss;
```

The shading of cloth is very dependent on how you are looking at its surface. The more glancing the surface of the cloth, the more the fibers catch the light behind it and amplify the intensity of the Specular component.

```
//Create Fresnel
float HdotV = pow(1-max(0, dot(halfVec, viewDir)), _FresnelPower);
float NdotE = pow(1-max(0, dot(s.Normal, viewDir)), _RimPower);
float finalSpecMask = NdotE * HdotV;
```

7. With all our main lighting calculations completed, we just need to output the final color. Complete the lighting model by entering the following code, just beneath the Fresnel calculation:

```
//Output the final color
fixed4 c;
c.rgb = (s.Albedo * NdotL * _LightColor0.rgb)
        + (spec * (finalSpecMask * _FresnelColor)) * (atten * 2);
c.a = 1.0;
return c;
```

8. Finally, we finish our Shader by filing in our `surf()` function. Here, we just need to unpack our normal maps, and send all the data to our `SurfaceOuput` struct. Let's complete the Shader by sampling our textures:

```
void surf (Input IN, inout SurfaceOutput o)
{
    half4 c = tex2D (_DetailTex, IN.uv_DetailTex);
    fixed3 normals = UnpackNormal(tex2D(_BumpMap, IN.uv_BumpMap)).rgb;
    fixed3 detailNormals = UnpackNormal(tex2D(_DetailBump, IN.uv_DetailBump)).rgb;
    fixed3 finalNormals = float3(normals.x + detailNormals.x,
                                  normals.y + detailNormals.y,
                                  normals.z + detailNormals.z);

    o.Normal = normalize(finalNormals);
    o.Specular = _SpecWidth;
    o.Gloss = _SpecIntesity;
    o.Albedo = c.rgb * _MainTint;
    o.Alpha = c.a;
}
```

The following screenshot demonstrates the result of using this cloth surface shader on a cloth-like model:

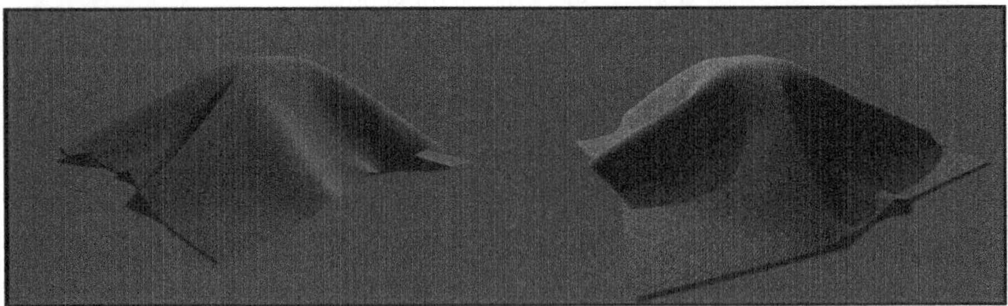

How it works...

Overall our cloth shader isn't that complicated really. We are doing some very basic lighting operations, but sometimes that's all you need for your Shaders. When writing Shaders you want to really look at the surface you are trying to simulate and break it into its components, and then program them one at a time. The real magic comes in how you end up combining the different calculations, much like blending layers in Photoshop.

The new technique demonstrated in our cloth shader is the process of combining two normal maps with different tiling rates. Our basic linear algebra will show that we can in fact add two vectors together to result in a new position. So we can do just that with our normal maps. We take our Variation Normal map, which provides us a vector by using the `UnpackNormal()` function, and add the normal vector from the Detail Normal map. This will basically result in a new normal map. We then need to normalize our final vector, so that it is back in the `0` to `1` range. If we don't, our normal map will look very bruised and visually wrong.

Finally, the combination of the Fresnel and the Specular calculation allows us to create the effect of the tiny fibers of cloth to catch the light at glancing angles to the surface of our object.

6
Transparency

In this chapter, you will learn about:

- Creating transparency with alpha
- Transparent cutoff shader
- Depth sorting with render queues
- GUI and transparency

Introduction

Transparency and graphics cards can be a little tricky at first when writing Shaders. By utilizing Unity's Surface Shaders we can quite easily start to build Shaders that can have full transparency for surfaces like glass, or partial transparency for surfaces like hair and foliage.

We are going to look at how to first construct a very simple Shader using transparency, build our knowledge set to include Shaders such as hair, and understand how transparency affects the order in which your objects are drawn.

Creating transparency with alpha

Our first step in understanding how to write a transparent Surface Shader is to understand what code we need to include in our Shader to allow for transparency to be enabled. Unity again has provided us with a few new built-in parameters that we can include in our Shaders to get transparency working quickly.

It is simply a process of using the alpha parameter in our `#pragma` statement in our Shader. This basically tells Unity that we are going to be using transparency in the Shader. There are a few things one has to be aware of though when creating transparent Shaders, since drawing order becomes an element in our code. We will cover the basics in this recipe, just so we can get a transparent object in our Unity scene. We will then begin to cover other means of transparency in the following recipes.

Getting ready

To begin this recipe, we will need to gather a few resources and set up a new scene in the Unity editor. Let's take the following steps to prepare for our Shader writing process:

1. Create a new scene in Unity and populate it with a sphere, a plane, and a simple directional light.
2. We then need to create a new Shader and a new Material. The Shader should be assigned to the Material and the Material to the sphere in your scene.
3. Finally, we need to gather a texture to act as the driving factor as to what is transparent and what is not on our object in the scene.

The following diagram is an example of the texture we are going to be using for this recipe. Since its colors are pure RGB and white, we can use the individual channels of the texture to act as a transparency value of 0 or 1, meaning white is opaque and black is completely transparent.

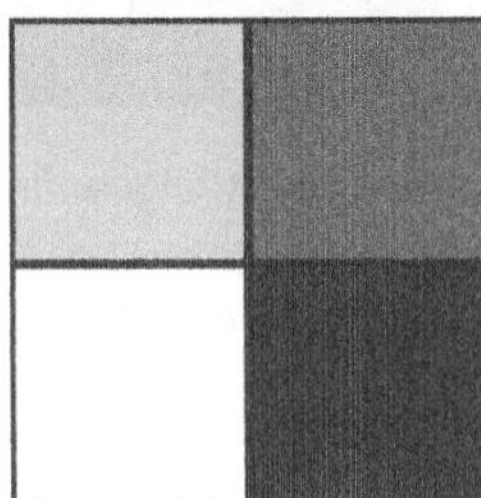

How to do it...

With our assets ready to go, we can start the process of filling in our Surface Shader to create our first transparent Shader.

1. Let's populate our `Properties` block with a new property that will give us a global control over our Shader:

```
Properties
{
    _MainTex ("Base (RGB)", 2D) = "white" {}
    _TransVal ("Transparency Value", Range(0,1)) = 0.5
}
```

2. We then need to modify our `#pragma` statement with a new parameter we haven't seen yet, the `alpha` parameter.

```
CGPROGRAM
#pragma surface surf Lambert alpha
```

3. Finally, we complete the Shader by adding the `o.Alpha` line to our `surf()` function:

```
void surf (Input IN, inout SurfaceOutput o)
{
    half4 c = tex2D (_MainTex, IN.uv_MainTex);

    o.Albedo = c.rgb;
    o.Alpha = c.r * _TransVal;
}
```

The following screenshot is the result of our transparent Shader in the Unity editor:

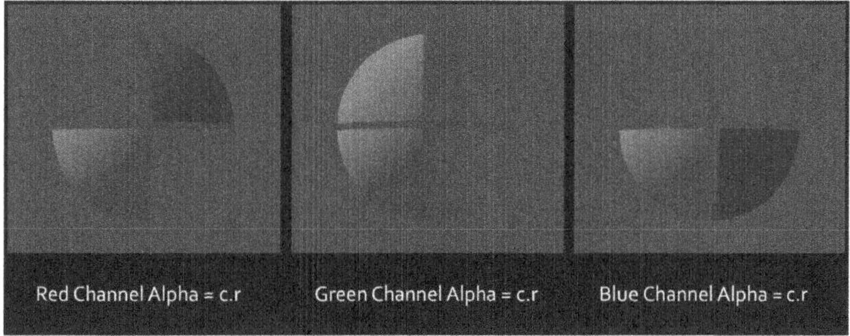

How it works...

As you can see, it is very easy to get a transparent Shader up and running using Unity's Surface Shaders. The Shader relies on two elements to be present when writing a transparent Shader, the `alpha` parameter for the `#pragma` statement and the value to be used for the `alpha` value in the `SurfaceOutput` struct.

Once we declare the parameter `alpha` in our `#pragma` statement, this tells Unity to allow for a transparent surface to be rendered to the screen. All that is needed to be done is to feed the `o.Alpha` value of our `SurfaceOuput` struct (the built-in one in this case) with a value of 0 or 1 on a per-pixel basis. In color terms, a value of white, or 1, gives us a completely opaque surface, while a value of black, or 0, gives us a completely transparent surface.

While there comes many items, we have to keep in mind when using transparent Shaders that this is the most basic implementation. As we move through this chapter, we will start to discuss the issues that arise when using alpha or semi-transparent Shaders in a real-time renderer such as Unity.

Transparent cutoff shader

Unity actually provides us with another type of parameter for our `#pragma` statement that will give us the ability to create a simpler transparent effect, called the cutoff transparency. This type of transparency uses a value to simply not draw certain pixels to the screen, thereby giving us a way to have either a completely opaque or completely transparent Shader, while in the last recipe our Shader gave us the ability to use the full range of gray scale to affect the transparency, otherwise called a semi-transparent shader.

Let's continue and see how to construct this type of Shader in Unity.

Getting ready

Let's start our Shader writing process by getting a few items together.

1. First, create a new scene and populate it with a simple sphere and a directional light.
2. Let's then create a new Shader and a new material.
3. Finally, assign the Shader to the Material and the Material to the sphere in our scene.
4. We are going to need a new texture this time. It would be best if you could find a texture with gray scale values, so we can see the effect of the cutoff value in action.

The following screenshot shows the texture we will be using for this recipe. We created this texture simply by using the Render Difference Clouds filter in Photoshop. The texture we created is also available from the book's support page at `www.packtpub.com/support`.

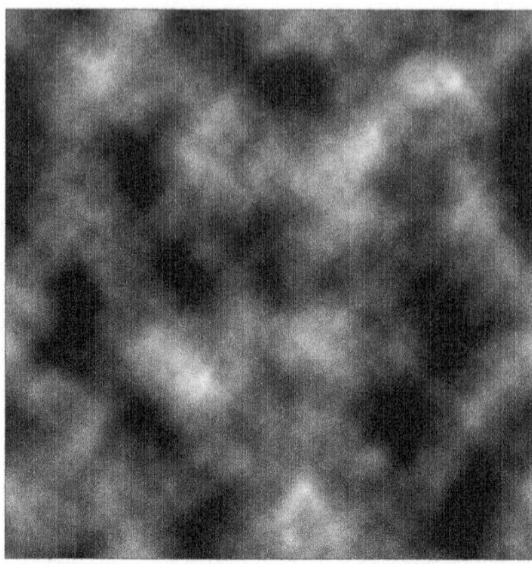

How to do it...

Now that we have our new scene and our assets gathered, let's take a look at what we have to write, in terms of code, in our new Shader.

1. To begin with, let's fill in our `Properties` block with a float value that will let us pick the cutoff value we want to use in our Shader:

   ```
   Properties
   {
       _MainTex ("Base (RGB)", 2D) = "white" {}
       _Cutoff ("Cutoff Value", Range(0,1)) = 0.5
   }
   ```

2. Then, we need to tell our Shader that we are going to be setting this Shader to a cutoff type Shader:

   ```
   CGPROGRAM
   #pragma surface surf Lambert alphatest:_Cutoff
   ```

3. Finally, we fill `o.Alpha` with the values we want to use on a per-pixel basis for our surface:

   ```
   void surf (Input IN, inout SurfaceOutput o)
   {
       half4 c = tex2D (_MainTex, IN.uv_MainTex);
       o.Albedo = c.rgb;
       o.Alpha = c.r;
   }
   ```

The following screenshot displays the result of our cutoff Shader with the cutoff slider at different values between 0 and 1:

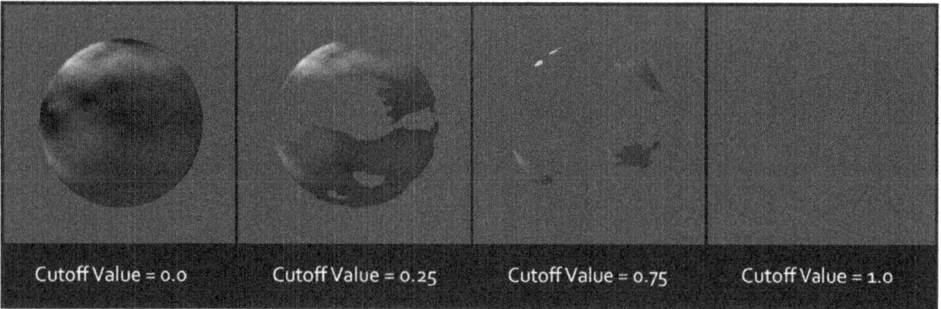

How it works...

Unity has provided us with quite a few parameters we can use with our `#pragma` directive. All of them give us the power to change and optimize our Surface Shader. It's one more reason why Surface Shaders are so powerful and efficient when it comes to writing Shaders and the iterative process.

Our cutoff shader uses a new parameter to our `#pragma` directive called `alphatest:VariableName`. This immediately sets the Shader into a simplified version of transparency. Instead of our transparency being semi-transparent, meaning each value of gray in the range of black to white affects transparency; only the value being passed by our `_CutOff` variable will determine the transparency. This means that if we put the `_CutOff` value to something like 0.4 in the **Inspector**, every value of gray below 0.4 will be considered transparent, and everything above that value will be opaque or solid.

It's advantageous to use this type of transparency when performance becomes an issue, as dealing with the blending of a semi-transparent Shader is more expensive than a cutoff transparency. On mobile devices it's the opposite, as testing the pixel values for a texture becomes quite expensive for those little GPUs. So if you are producing a mobile application with Unity3D, remember to use the semi-transparent technique and use the cutoff transparency technique sparingly.

Depth sorting with render queues

In order for us to truly understand transparency, we need to take a look at depth sorting or in simpler terms, the drawing order of objects. Unity allows us to control the order in which a particular object is drawn to the screen, so we can have a greater control of which objects render over other objects. You can think of the drawing order as being very similar to layers in Photoshop. Drawing order is especially important when dealing with transparency or elements such as user interface objects.

This recipe is going to start to reveal how you can utilize this layered approach to rendering your objects, using built-in tags provided to us by Unity. This is very important as you will gain a greater amount of control over how your objects are rendered to the game view.

Getting ready

To get started, we will need to create a few assets in order for us to learn how we can use Unity's drawing order to give us more flexibility and control in our real time renders.

1. Create a new scene and populate it with a couple of spheres, such that they are lined up in a row in whichever axis you want. Our goal is to take a look at how we can draw an object over another object regardless of its actual position in 3D space.

2. In order to see the effects of modifying an objects drawing order, we will need to have at least two Shaders. So let's create two new Shaders and name them appropriately. The demonstration Shaders are named `Depth001` and `Depth002`.

3. Your scene should look like the following screenshot. This set up will allow us to play with the order in which objects are drawn:

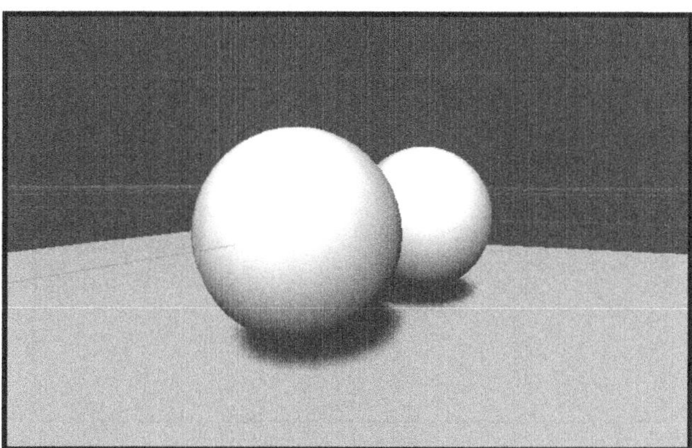

How to do it...

The actual Shader code to achieve this technique is quite simple; it just requires two new lines of code that we haven't seen before.

1. We first need to declare which render queue this object will be drawn into and to do that we need to modify our `Tags{}` block, just inside our `SubShader()`:

```
Tags { "Queue" = "Geometry-20"}
```

2. Next, we need to tell Unity that we want to control the order in which this object is drawn and that we don't want to write to the depth buffer. Add the following line of code just below the `Tags{}` line we added in the previous step:

```
ZWrite Off
```

3. With that code entered into your Shader, we can now save and return to the Unity editor to let the Shader compile. When it is finished, you will notice that one of the spheres appears behind every other object, even though its actual position in 3D space is in front of every object in the scene. The following screenshot shows the result of our depth sorting shader:

How it works...

Unity, by default, will sort your objects for you based off of the distance from the camera. So as an object gets nearer to the camera, it is going to be drawn over all objects that are further away from the camera. For most cases this works out just fine for making games, but you will find certain situations where you will want to have more control over the sorting of your objects in your scene. Using the `Tags{}` block we can control this sorting.

Unity has provided us with some default render queues, each with a unique value that directs Unity when to draw the object to the screen. These built-in render queues are called **Background**, **Geometry**, **AlphaTest**, **Transparent**, and **Overlay**. These queues weren't just created arbitrarily; they actually serve a purpose to make our lives easier when writing Shaders and interacting with the real time renderer. Refer to the following table for descriptions on the usage of each of these individual render queues:

Render queue	Render queue description	Render queue value
Background	This render queue is rendered first. It is used for skyboxes and so on.	`1000`
Geometry	This is the default render queue. This is used for most objects. Opaque geometry uses this queue.	`2000`
AlphaTest	Alpha-tested geometry uses this queue. It's different from the Geometry queue, as it's more efficient to render alpha-tested objects after all the solid objects are drawn.	`2450`

Render queue	Render queue description	Render queue value
Transparent	This render queue is rendered after Geometry and AlphaTest queues in back-to-front order. Anything alpha-blended (that is, Shaders that don't write to depth buffer) should go here, for example glass and particle effects.	`3000`
Overlay	This render queue is meant for overlay effects. Anything rendered last should go here, for example lens flares.	`4000`

So once you know which render queue your object belongs to, you can assign it's built-in render queue tag. Our Shader used the Geometry queue, so we wrote `Tags{"Queue"="Geometry"}`. But we wanted to tell our object to draw behind everything in our Geometry queue but before the background queue. So we modified the `Tags{}` block to read `Tags{"Queue"="Geometry-20"}`. Doing this tells Unity that we want to consider this object as an opaque or solid object, but render it behind every other opaque object.

Lastly, we have to declare the `Zwrite` tag to our `SubShader` block. This tells Unity that we are going to override the depth sorting of our object, and we will be assigning a new value for its render queue. So, we simply set the `Zwrite` value to `off`.

GUI and transparency

Now that we have covered the basics of creating transparent Shaders and learned how we can control the order in which objects are drawn, let's take a look at a practical production scenario in which we would need to use transparency and have control over the order in which the transparent objects are drawn.

Creating GUIs for Unity is definitely a huge task. One could use the Built-in `OnGUI()` function to create their GUI using a bunch of 2D images with alpha, and let Unity draw the images to the screen. Or, one could create an actual 3D GUI system in which you can actually see your GUI elements in the scene view, inside the Unity editor. We are going to take a look at this last approach. We need to be able to use a sheet of 2D images and place them onto 3D objects in our scene, so they can be used as GUI elements for a game.

We are also going to take a look at some issues that will pop up when using a 3D GUI approach, such as drawing order, and learn a simple way in which we can solve these issues.

Getting ready

For this recipe we will be creating a very simple GUI example, and so we are going to need to construct a sheet of GUI elements for our scene. When a GUI is created in this 3D manner, a texture sheet is created in order to save on the amount of textures we have to use. This means that all button graphics, icon graphics, and in some cases even text graphics are laid out onto a single texture with its alpha channel set to mask out where the texture sheet should be transparent and where it's opaque or semi-transparent. Refer to the following screenshot of the texture sheet we will be using for this recipe:

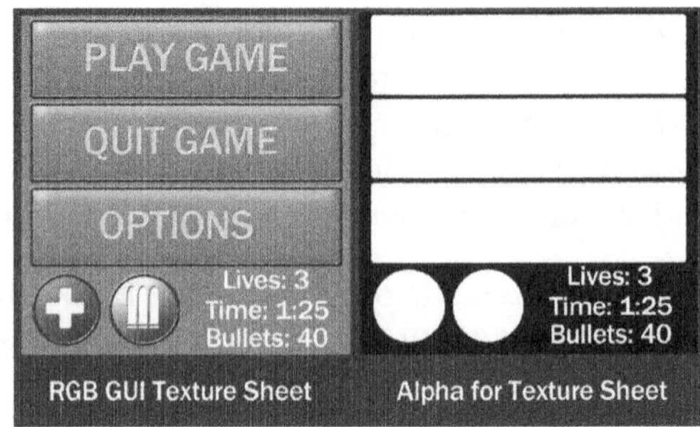

So let's start to construct our mock GUI for our Shader writing. This will allow us to simulate the kinds of things we have to think about when working on a GUI system for a production.

1. Construct a GUI texture sheet similar to the texture sheet seen in the preceding screenshot. Make sure to include the alpha texture in the alpha channel of the texture sheet.
2. We also have to create some simple geometry for our GUI. In our case, Maya was used to generate the meshes that the GUI elements sit on.
3. Create a new scene in Unity and place a plane and a directional light into the scene.
4. Then, create a new Shader and a new Material for our mock GUI and assign the Shader to the Material.
5. Now, we simply assign our Material to our GUI objects in our scene to complete the setup process.

6. When completed with the previous steps, your scene should look similar to the following screenshot. You are more than welcome to use the scene that is included with this book, but it is always a good practice to create your own:

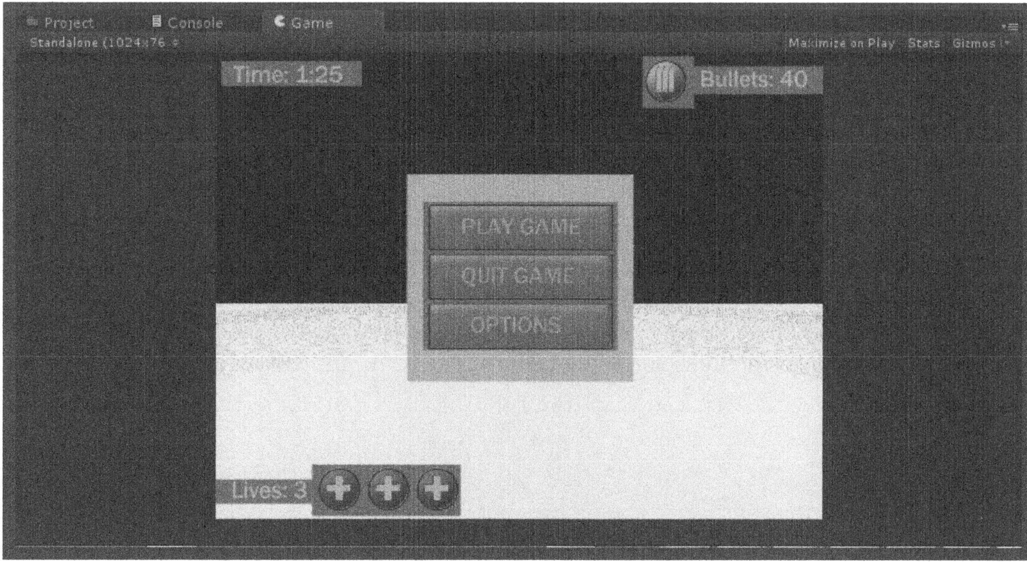

Not very interesting to look at and our alpha isn't creating the transparency effect we need in order to have a real game GUI. We need to create our GUI Shader in order for us to create a more elegant looking GUI. So let's do that now.

How to do it...

In order for our GUI to have transparency, we need to create the Shader so that we can tell Unity that these objects are transparent.

1. As usual, we need to populate our `Properties` block with the appropriate properties so that we can interact with our Shader in the Unity editor.

```
//We create our properties here so we can see them in the Unity Inspector
Properties
{
    _GUITint ("GUI Tint", Color) = (1,1,1,1)
    _GUITex ("Base (RGB) Alpha (A)", 2D) = "white" {}
    _FadeValue ("Fade Value", Range(0,1)) = 1
}
```

2. We then need to move down to our `SubShader` block and start it by setting the type of render queue we are going to be using and setting up the lighting model. You'll also notice that we have introduced some new tags to our `SubShader` block. We will cover these in the next section. For now, enter the following code at the top of your `SubShader` block:

```
//We declare our SubShader tags here so we tell Unity what type of shader
//this is going to be.
Tags { "Queue"="Transparent" "IgnoreProjector"="True" "RenderType"="Transparent"}
ZWrite Off
Cull Back
LOD 200
```

3. After our `SubShader` tags have been declared, we need to move on to our `#pragma` directives or statements, and declare our own custom lighting model and add some new arguments we haven't seen before. This will allow us to create a completely unlit surface and let the full color of the texture sheet drive the look of our GUI:

```
//Then start the CG shader and lighting model
CGPROGRAM
#pragma surface surf UnlitGUI alpha novertexlights
```

4. Our next step is to make the connection between the values in our `Properties` block to the variables in our `CGPROGRAM` block:

```
//Create a link between our properties
//and our CGPROGRAM
sampler2D _GUITex;
float4 _GUITint;
float _FadeValue;
```

5. After all of our Shader setup is completed, we have to write our **unlit lighting model**. This is fairly simple and is simply passing the color value of the texture sheet to our `SurfaceOutput` struct:

```
//Our Custom lighting model.  This is an Unlit Model
inline fixed4 LightingUnlitGUI (SurfaceOutput s, fixed3 lightDir, fixed3 viewDir, fixed atten)
{
    fixed4 c;
    c.rgb = s.Albedo;
    c.a =  s.Alpha;
    return c;
}
```

6. As always, if we are going to be using textures, we have to make sure that we get the UVs for that texture inside the `Input` struct:

```
//Process our uvs
struct Input
{
    float2 uv_GUITex;
};
```

7. Finally, we simply sample our texture and alpha values, and pass them to the `SurfaceOutput` struct inside the `surf()` function:

```
//Process the per pixel information
void surf (Input IN, inout SurfaceOutput o)
{
    half4 texColor = tex2D (_GUITex, IN.uv_GUITex);

    o.Albedo = texColor.rgb * _GUITint.rgb;
    o.Alpha = texColor.a * _FadeValue;
}
```

When finished with the Shader, you should see something very similar to the following screenshot, although if you are using your own custom geometry and texture sheet, your scene will look different. Apart from that, the Shader should be generating an effect of an unlit surface with alpha transparency:

You'll notice though that we are getting a small error in our GUI. Our background box, just behind our buttons, is actually rendering over our **Play Game** button. This is because the meshes are so close together that Unity is having a hard time discerning which object to draw first. Since the order is currently being determined by the distance from the camera, Unity is displaying the background box over the button.

8. In order for us to fix this issue, we are going to have to change the render queue on a per-material basis. We can't simply change the render queue in the Shader, as this would cause us to have to write a Shader for each queue level. We need individual control over our Materials. So, we have to write a small C# script that will allow us to achieve this effect. Let's do that now.
9. We first need to create a new C# script in order for us to achieve this fix to our GUI Shader.
10. Once you have created the script, double-click on it to open it up in MonoDevelop.
11. Our first order of business here is to tell this script to run in the editor so that we can see the effects of us changing the queue value in real time in the scene view. To achieve this, we need to declare the `[ExecuteInEditMode]` attribute before our class declaration:

```
[ExecuteInEditMode]
public class ObjectRenderQueue : MonoBehaviour
{
```

12. In order for us to change the queue level in real time, we need to create a new variable that we can change in the object's **Inspector**. So, we declare a new variable with the name `queueValue` and make it public so that it displays in the **Inspector**.

```
//Allow us to change the queue value
//in the editor
public int queueValue = 2000;
```

13. We then move on to our `Update()` function and first see if the object that this script is attached to has a Material assigned to it:

```
//First check to see if the object does in fact have
//a material
Material curMaterial = transform.renderer.sharedMaterial;
```

14. Finally, using an `if()` statement we then check to make sure our `curMaterial` variable has a Material reference in it and that it is not null. This is just to prevent any unnecessary error messages from popping up in the console window.

```
if(curMaterial)
{
    //if a material is found set the queue value
    curMaterial.renderQueue = queueValue;
}
else
{
    //if a material is not found show a debug message
    Debug.LogWarning(transform.name +
                    ": Cannot find a material to set the render queue!");
}
```

With the script completed, you can now assign it to any of our GUI elements, and adjust the queue value on the fly in the editor and see the drawing order change. Our GUI scene is now complete and all of our GUI elements are drawing in the right order. We have given ourselves a fine amount of control over the objects in our GUI, very similar to layers in Photoshop, all by creating a Shader and a small script.

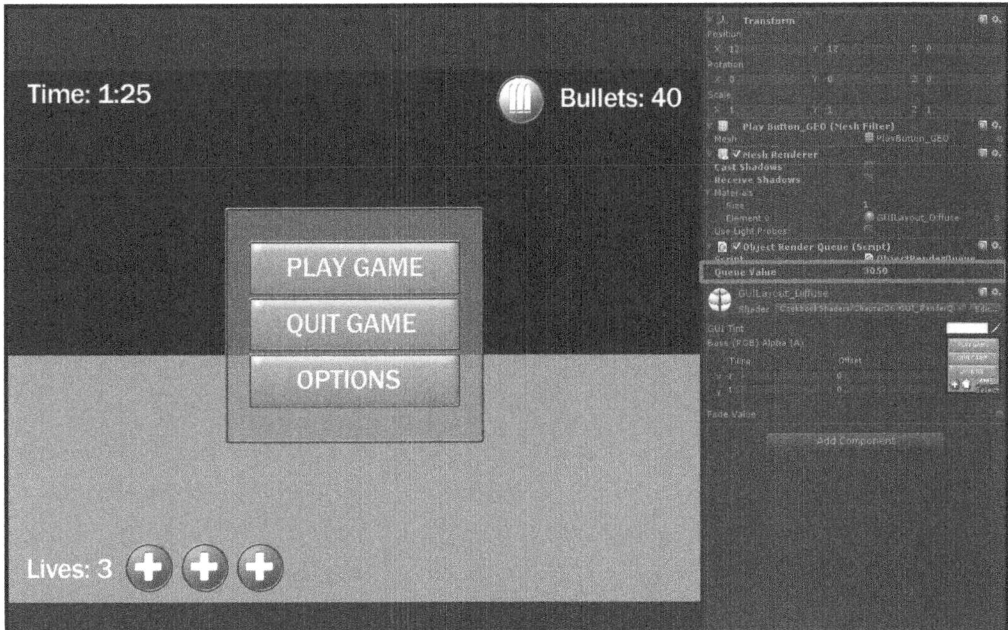

How it works...

Beginning with the GUI Shader, we have introduced a couple of new `SubShader` tags that allow us to fine tune how our Shader works with the Unity renderer. By declaring `"IgnoreProjector"="True"`, we are telling Unity that we don't want any projector type materials or textures to affect our objects or Shader. This is because we want the GUI to be separate from our scene. All the scene effects, such as projectors, should only affect objects in our game and not our GUI. The `"IgnoreProjector"` tag is one way to achieve this.

Our second new tag is the `"RenderType"="Transparent"`. Similar to the `"Queue"` tag, this tag categorizes the Shader into the transparent category for Unity's camera effects, just so Unity can give you a more organized way of sorting your objects.

The last new element to our Shader is the addition of `novertexlights` to the `#pragma` directive. This parameter tells Unity that we do not want to use any per-vertex lights or Spherical Harmonics to light our objects. In fact, we do not want to use any lights at all; so we can use this parameter to make our Shader a bit cheaper, which is exactly what we are going for when developing a 3D GUI system.

Turning our attention to the render queue script we created, the script is simply getting access to the Material attached to our object by using the `transform.renderer.sharedMaterial` code. If a Material is in fact attached to the object that the script is assigned to, that line of code will return the Material. If it cannot find a Material, it will return null.

We then check to see if the script found the Material and change the value of the render queue. If it does not find a Material, we just send a debug message to the console to make the user aware that the object needs a Material.

This is obviously a simple example of how much control you can have with transparency and the render queue, but this does gives the foundational knowledge you will need to create more robust systems of your own!

7

Vertex Magic

In this chapter you will learn about:

- Accessing a vertex color in a Surface Shader
- Animating vertices in a Surface Shader
- Using vertex color for terrains

Introduction

Shaders are absolutely necessary in order for us to render our real-time objects to the screen. It gives us the power to create very complex lighting solutions for the surfaces of those objects, but we can also use Shaders to actually modify the vertices of our objects. This becomes very advantageous as we can process these modifications to our object's vertices faster using a Shader.

The vertex function is executed once for each vertex that is sent to the **graphics processing unit** (**GPU**). Its job is to take the vertex from its 3D local space and transform it in such a way that it renders in the right location on the 2D screen. With the vertex function, we have the ability to modify elements such as the vertex position, its color, and its UV coordinate. Once the vertex function is finished modifying the vertex, it moves to the `surf()` function where per-pixel effects are applied.

Using the vertex shader, we can gain a powerful amount of control over our model to create effects such as waves on an ocean, or a waving flag, or shade our model with vertex colors. In this chapter we will be learning how to use the vertex function in a Surface Shader.

Accessing a vertex color in a Surface Shader

Let's begin this chapter by taking a look at how we can access the information of a model's vertex, using the vertex function within a Surface Shader. This will arm us with the knowledge to start utilizing the elements contained within a model's vertex, to create really useful and visually appealing effects.

A vertex in a vertex function can return information about itself that we need to be aware of. You can actually retrieve the vertices' normal directions as a `float3` value, the position of the vertex as `float3`, and you can even store color values in each vertex and return that color as `float4`. This is what we will take a look at in this recipe. We need to learn how to store color information and retrieve that stored color information, inside each vertex of a Surface Shader.

Getting ready

In order to write this Shader we are going to prepare a few assets. The following steps will set us up for creating this vertex shader:

1. In order to view the colors of a vertex, we need to have a model that has had color applied to its vertices. While you could use Unity to apply colors, you would have to write a tool to allow an individual to apply the colors or write some scripts to achieve the color application. In the case of this recipe, we simply utilized Maya to apply the colors to our model. This model is available on the book's **Support** page at `www.packtpub.com/support`.
2. Create a new scene and place the imported model into the scene.
3. Create a new Shader and Material. When completed, assign the Shader to the Material and then the Material to the imported model.

Your scene should now look similar to the following screenshot:

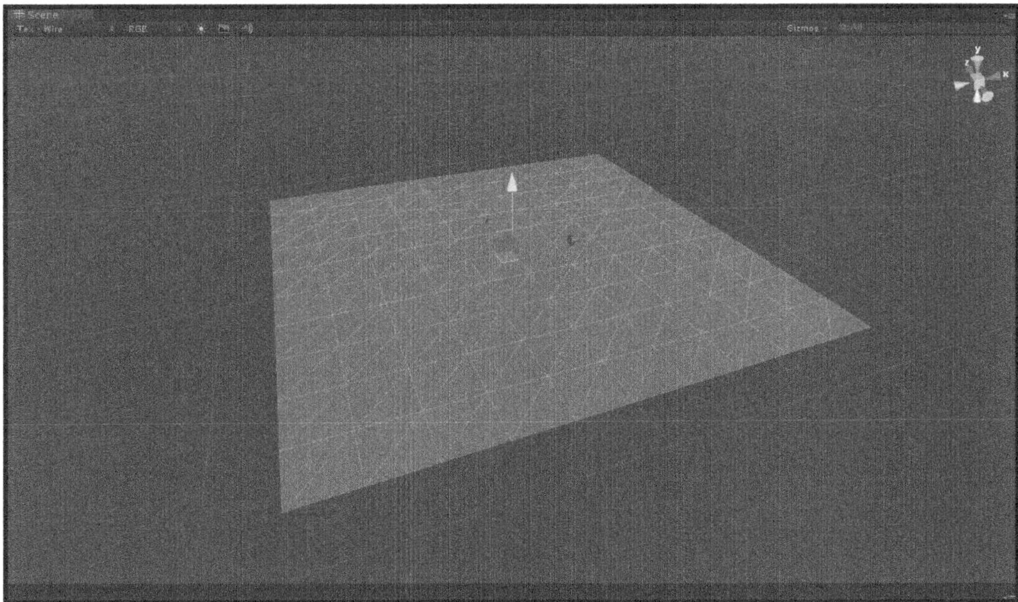

How to do it...

With our scene, the Shader, and the Material created and ready to go, we can begin to write the code for our Shader. Launch the Shader by double-clicking on it in the **Project** tab, in the Unity editor.

1. Since we are creating a very simple Shader we will not need to include *any* properties, to our `Properties` block. We will still include a global tint color, just to stay consistent with the other Shaders in this book. Enter the following code into the `Properties` block of your Shader:

```
Properties
{
    _MainTint("Global Color Tint", Color) = (1,1,1,1)
}
```

2. This next step tells Unity that we will be including a vertex function in our Shader:

```
CGPROGRAM
#pragma surface surf Lambert vertex:vert
```

3. As usual, if we have included properties in our `Properties` block, we must make sure to create a corresponding variable in our `CGPROGRAM` statement. Enter the following code just below the `#pragma` statement:

```
float4 _MainTint;
```

4. We now turn our attention to the `Input` struct. We need to add a new variable in order for our `surf()` function to access the data given to us by our `vert()` function:

```
struct Input
{
    float2 uv_MainTex;
    float4 vertColor;
};
```

5. Now we can write our simple `vert()` function to gain access to the colors stored in each vertex of our mesh:

```
void vert(inout appdata_full v, out Input o)
{
    o.vertColor = v.color;
}
```

6. Finally, we can use the vertex color data from our `Input` struct to be assigned to the `o.Albedo` parameters in the built-in `SurfaceOutput` struct:

```
void surf (Input IN, inout SurfaceOutput o)
{
    o.Albedo = IN.vertColor.rgb * _MainTint.rgb;
}
```

7. With our code completed, we can now re-enter the Unity editor and let the Shader compile. If all goes well, you should see something similar to the following screenshot:

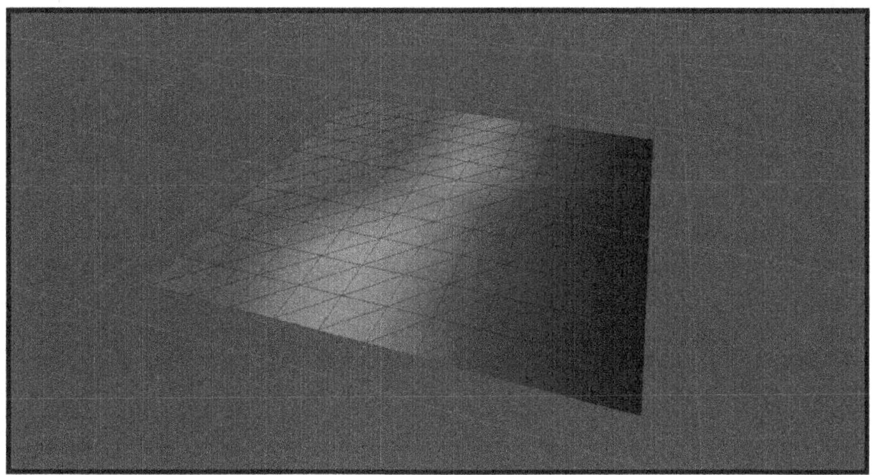

How it works...

Unity provides us with a way to access the vertex information of the model to which a Shader is attached to. This gives us the power to modify things such as the vertices' position and color. With this recipe, we have imported a mesh from Maya (though just about any 3D software application can be used), where vertex colors were added to the verts. You'll notice that by importing the model, the default material will not display the vertex colors. We actually have to write a Shader to extract the vertex color and display it on the surface of the model. Unity provides us with a lot of built-in functionality when using Surface Shaders, which make the process of extracting this vertex information quick and efficient.

Our first task is to tell Unity that we will be using a vertex function when creating our Shader. We do this by adding the `vertex:vert` parameter to the `#pragma` statement of `CGPROGRAM`. This automatically makes Unity look for a vertex function named `vert`, when it goes to compile the Shader. If it doesn't find one, Unity will throw a compiling error and ask for you to add a `vert` function to your Shader.

That brings us to our next step. We have to actually code the `vert()` function, as seen in step 5. By having this function, we can access the built-in data struct called `appdata_full`. This built-in struct is where the vertex information is stored. So, we then extract the vertex color information by passing it to our `Input` struct, by adding the code `o.vertColor = v.color`.

The `o` variable represents our `Input` struct and the `v` variable is our `appdata_full` vertex data. In this case, we are simply taking the color information from the `appdata_full` struct and putting it into our `Input` struct. Once the vertex color is in our `Input` struct, we can use it in our `surf()` function. In the case of this recipe, we simply apply the color to the `o.Albedo` parameter in the built-in `SurfaceOutput` struct.

There's more...

One can also access a fourth component from the `vert` color data. If you notice, the `vertColor` variable we declared in the `Input` struct is of type `float4`. This means we are also passing in the alpha value of the vertex colors. Knowing this, you can use it to your advantage, for the purpose of storing a fourth vertex color, to perform effects such as transparency, or to give yourself one more mask to blend in two textures. It's really up to you and your production to determine if you really need to use the fourth component, but it is worth mentioning here.

With Unity 4, we now have the ability to target Shaders to Directx 11. This is great, but it means that the compiling process for the Shaders is now a bit pickier. This means that we need to include one more line of code to our Shader, to initialize the output of the vertex information properly. The following code shows what the vertex function code looks like, if you are using Directx 11 in your Shader:

```
void vert(inout appdata_full v, out Input o)
{
    UNITY_INITIALIZE_OUTPUT(Input,o);
    o.vertColor = v.color;
}
```

By including this line of code, your vertex shader will not throw any warnings, which say that it won't compile to Directx 11 appropriately.

Animating vertices in a Surface Shader

Now that we know how to access data on a per-vertex basis, let's expand our knowledge set to include other types of data, and the position of a vertex.

Using a vertex function, we can access the position of each vertex in a mesh. This allows us to actually modify each individual vertex, while the Shader does the processing.

In this recipe we will create a Shader that will allow us to modify the positions of each vertex on a mesh with a sine wave. This technique can be used to create animations for objects such as flags or the waves on an ocean.

Getting ready

Let's gather our assets together so we can create the code for our vertex shader:

1. Create a new scene and place a plane mesh in the center of the scene.
2. Then create a new Shader and Material.
3. Finally, assign the Shader to the Material, and the Material to the plane mesh.

Your scene should look similar to the following screenshot:

How to do it...

With our scene ready to go, let's double-click on our newly created Shader to open it up in MonoDevelop:

1. Let's begin with our Shader by populating the `Properties` block:

```
Properties
{
    _MainTex ("Base (RGB)", 2D) = "white" {}
    _tintAmount ("Tint Amount", Range(0,1)) = 0.5
    _ColorA ("Color A", Color) = (1,1,1,1)
    _ColorB ("Color B", Color) = (1,1,1,1)
    _Speed ("Wave Speed", Range(0.1, 80)) = 5
    _Frequency ("Wave Frequency", Range(0, 5)) = 2
    _Amplitude ("Wave Amplitude", Range(-1, 1)) = 1
}
```

2. We now need to tell Unity that we are going to be using a vertex function by adding to the `#pragma` statement:

```
CGPROGRAM
#pragma surface surf Lambert vertex:vert
```

3. In order to access the values that have been given to us by our properties, we need to declare a corresponding variable in our `CGPROGRAM` block:

```
sampler2D _MainTex;
float4 _ColorA;
float4 _ColorB;
float _tintAmount;
float _Speed;
float _Frequency;
float _Amplitude;
float _OffsetVal;
```

4. We are going to be using the vertex position modification as a `vert` color as well. This will allow us to tint our object:

```
struct Input
{
    float2 uv_MainTex;
    float3 vertColor;
};
```

5. At this point, we can perform our vertex modification using a sine wave and the vertex function. Enter the following code after the `Input` struct:

```
void vert(inout appdata_full v, out Input o)
{
    float time = _Time * _Speed;
    float waveValueA = sin(time + v.vertex.x * _Frequency) * _Amplitude;

    v.vertex.xyz = float3(v.vertex.x, v.vertex.y + waveValueA, v.vertex.z);
    v.normal = normalize(float3(v.normal.x + waveValueA, v.normal.y, v.normal.z));
    o.vertColor = float3(waveValueA,waveValueA,waveValueA);
}
```

6. Finally, we complete our Shader by performing a `lerp` function between two colors, so we can tint the peaks and valleys of our new mesh, modified by our vertex function:

```
void surf (Input IN, inout SurfaceOutput o)
{
    half4 c = tex2D (_MainTex, IN.uv_MainTex);
    float3 tintColor = lerp(_ColorA, _ColorB, IN.vertColor).rgb;

    o.Albedo = c.rgb * (tintColor * _tintAmount);
    o.Alpha = c.a;
}
```

After completing the code for your Shader, switch back to Unity and let the Shader compile. Once compiled, you should see something similar to the following screenshot:

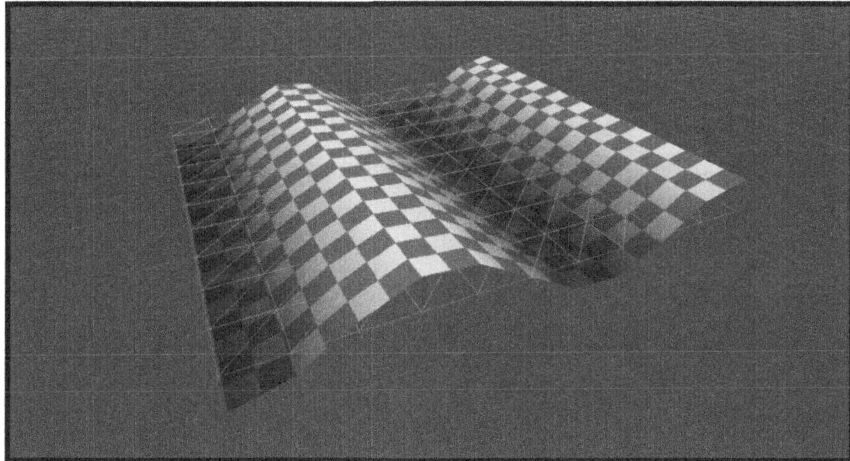

How it works...

This particular Shader uses the same concept from the last recipe except this time we are modifying the positions of the vertices in the mesh. This is really useful if you don't want to rig up simple objects, such as a flag, and then animate them using a skeleton structure or a hierarchy of transforms.

We simply create a sine wave value using the `sin()` function that is built into the Cg language. After calculating that value, we add it onto the `y` value of each vertex position, creating a wave-like effect.

We also did a little bit of modification to the normal on the mesh, just to give it more realistic shading, based on the sine wave value.

You will start to see how easy it is to perform more complex vertex effects by utilizing the built-in vertex parameters that Surface Shaders give us.

Using vertex color for terrains

One of the most common uses of vertex information is by creating more realistic-looking terrains or environments. This is done by using each channel of the RGBA vertex color to blend into different textures. This is very efficient since you don't have to import yet another texture to blend into the other textures. You'll see this technique in just about every game that deals with outdoor terrains and structures.

This particular recipe will demonstrate a more advanced way of performing this blend by using a grayscale image or heightmap to add more detail to the vertex blending.

Getting ready

Let's take a moment to get our scene together and gather a few textures we will need:

1. Create a new scene and import a mesh from a 3D application that has vertex colors applied to it. We used Maya for this example.
2. Place your imported mesh into the new scene and create a single directional light.
3. Finally, create a new Shader and Material. Then, assign the Shader to the Material and the Material to the imported mesh.

How to do it...

Once you have your new scene created, double-click on the Shader to open it up in MonoDevelop.

1. Let's create the properties we will need in order to give the users of this Shader more control over the final visual effect:

```
Properties
{
    _MainTex ("Base (RGB)", 2D) = "white" {}
    _SecondaryTex ("Secondary Texture", 2D) = "white"{}
    _HeightMap ("HeightMap", 2D) = "white" {}
    _Value ("Value", Range(1, 20)) = 3
}
```

2. We then need to tell Unity that we will be including a vertex function in our Surface Shader with the following code:

```
CGPROGRAM
#pragma surface surf Lambert vertex:vert
```

3. Let's then create variables that will connect our `CGPROGRAM` statements to our `Properties` block:

```
sampler2D _MainTex;
sampler2D _SecondaryTex;
sampler2D _HeightMap;
float _Value;
```

4. Since we are going to be using a few more textures and our vertex colors, we will need to fill out the `Input` struct with a few more parameters:

```
struct Input
{
    float2 uv_MainTex;
    float2 uv_SecondaryTex;
    float3 vertColor;
};
```

5. We then need to create our vertex function. This is simple since all we have to do in this Shader is get the vertex color and pass it to the `Input` struct:

```
void vert (inout appdata_full v, out Input o)
{
    o.vertColor = v.color.rgb;
}
```

6. Now we can turn our attention to the `surf()` function. Here, we will need to sample the texture first so that we have them ready for the blending part of this function:

```
//Sample our textures
half4 base = tex2D (_MainTex, IN.uv_MainTex);
half4 secondTex = tex2D (_SecondaryTex, IN.uv_SecondaryTex);
float4 height = tex2D(_HeightMap, IN.uv_MainTex);
```

7. We then want to process our blending value based on the red channel of our vertex colors and the heightmap:

```
//perform blending
float redChannel = 1-IN.vertColor.r;
float rHeight = height.r * redChannel;
float invertHeight = 1-height.r;
float finalHeight = (invertHeight * redChannel)*4;
float finalBlend = saturate(rHeight + finalHeight);
```

8. Our next step is to calculate a falloff value for our vertex blend, so that we can add one more level of detail to our texture blending:

```
//Let's create more detail in how the vertex colors
//blend.  Either very hard edge or very soft.
float hardness = ((1-IN.vertColor.g) * _Value)+1;
finalBlend = pow(finalBlend, hardness);
```

9. Finally, we need to lerp our two textures with our final blending value and pass the color to our `SurfaceOutput` struct:

```
//Produce the final color
float3 finalColor = lerp(base, secondTex, finalBlend);

o.Albedo = finalColor;
o.Alpha = base.a;
```

When your Shader has completed compiling, you should see a result similar to the result in the following image:

How it works...

This Shader is definitely a bit more complex, but you'll notice that we don't have to do much in the vertex function itself. We are simply passing the vertex colors off to the `surf()` function, so we can perform per-pixel operations with our vertex colors. The reason for this, as you might be able to notice, is that the vertex colors by themselves do offer us enough visual detail to create very convincing blending. By default, the vertex colors create a very blocky blending that can only be fixed by adding more vertices to the mesh and that isn't always a feasible thing.

So, we take in the vertex colors and multiply it with a grayscale image that is the height of the base texture we want to blend another texture type over. By running the vertex colors and the heightmap through the algorithm in step 7, we can add another level of visual detail to our blending that fakes the effect of one texture type blending into the base texture type. In our case, the snow texture is blending into the little crevasses in our base stone texture.

This technique has recently been made popular by games such as Uncharted and Gears of War, and is now available for you to use in your game projects!

8 Mobile Shader Adjustment

In the next two chapters we are going to take a look at making the Shaders we write performance-friendly for different platforms. We won't be talking about any one platform specifically, but we are going to begin to break down the elements of the Shaders we can adjust to make them more optimized for mobile, and make them more efficient on any platform in general. These techniques range from understanding what Unity offers you in terms of built-in variables that reduce the overhead of the Shaders' memory to learning about ways in which we can make our own Shader code more efficient. This chapter will cover the following sections:

- What is a cheap Shader?
- Profiling our Shaders
- Modifying your Shaders for mobile

Introduction

Learning the art of optimizing your Shaders will come up in just about any game project you work on. There will always come a point in any production, where a Shader needs to be optimized or it needs to use fewer textures but produce the same effect. As a technical artist, or Shader programmer, you have to understand these core fundamentals to optimize your Shaders so that you can increase the performance of your game, while still achieving the same visual fidelity. Having this knowledge can also help in setting the way in which you write your Shader from the start. For instance, by knowing that the game built using your Shader will be played on a mobile device, we can automatically set all our lighting functions to use a half vector as the view direction, or set all of our float variable types to fixed or half. These and many other techniques all contribute to your Shaders running efficiently on your target hardware. Let's begin our journey and start learning how to optimize our Shaders.

What is a cheap Shader?

When first asked what a cheap Shader is, it might be a little tough to answer, since there are many elements that go into the making of a more efficient Shader. It could be the amount of memory used up by your variables. It could be the amount of textures the Shader is using. It could also be that our Shader is working fine, but we can actually produce the same visual effect with half the amount of data, by reducing the amount of code we are using or the data we are creating. We are going to explore a few of these techniques in this recipe and show how they can be combined to make your Shader fast and efficient but still produce the high quality visuals everyone expects from games today, whether mobile or PC.

Getting ready

In order to get this recipe started, we need to gather a few resources together. So, let's perform the following tasks:

1. Create a new scene and fill it with a simple sphere object and a single directional light.
2. Create a new Shader and Material and assign the Shader to the Material.
3. We then need to assign the Material we just created to our sphere object, in our new scene.
4. Finally, modify the Shader so that it uses a diffuse texture, a normal map, and includes your own custom lighting function:

```
Shader "Cookbook/Chapter08/OptimizedShader001"
{
    Properties
    {
        _MainTex ("Base (RGB)", 2D) = "white" {}
        _NormalMap ("Normal Map", 2D) = "bump" {}
    }

    SubShader
    {
        Tags { "RenderType"="Opaque" }
        LOD 200

        CGPROGRAM
        #pragma surface surf SimpleLambert

        sampler2D _MainTex;
        sampler2D _NormalMap;

        struct Input
        {
            float2 uv_MainTex;
            float2 uv_NormalMap;
        };

        inline float4 LightingSimpleLambert (SurfaceOutput s, float3 lightDir, float atten)
        {
            float diff = max (0, dot (s.Normal, lightDir));

            float4 c;
            c.rgb = s.Albedo * _LightColor0.rgb * (diff * atten * 2);
            c.a = s.Alpha;
            return c;
        }

        void surf (Input IN, inout SurfaceOutput o)
        {
            float4 c = tex2D (_MainTex, IN.uv_MainTex);

            o.Albedo = c.rgb;
            o.Alpha = c.a;
            o.Normal = UnpackNormal(tex2D(_NormalMap, IN.uv_NormalMap));
        }
        ENDCG
    }
    FallBack "Diffuse"
}
```

This shows the result of modifying our default Shader we created in step 1.

You should now have a setup similar to the following image. This setup will allow us to take a look at some of the basic concepts that go into optimizing Shaders using Surface Shaders in Unity:

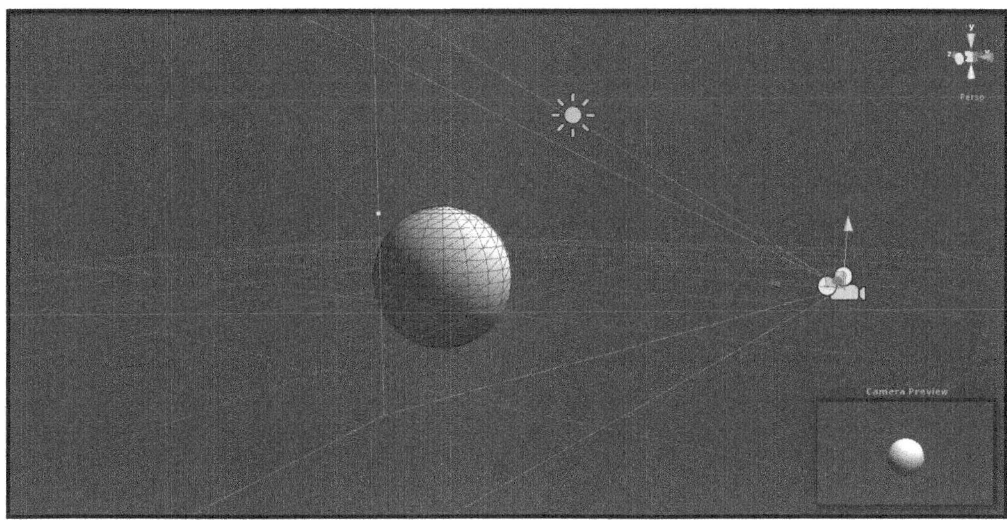

How to do it...

We are going to build a simple diffuse Shader to take a look at a few ways in which you can optimize your Shaders in general.

First we'll optimize our variable types, so that they use less memory when they are processing data:

1. Let's begin with the `Input` struct in our Shader. Currently, our UVs are being stored in a variable of type `float2`. We need to change that to use `half2` instead:

```
struct Input
{
    half2 uv_MainTex;
    half2 uv_NormalMap;
};
```

2. We can then move to our lighting function and reduce the variable's memory footprint by changing their types to the following:

```
inline fixed4 LightingSimpleLambert (SurfaceOutput s, fixed3 lightDir, fixed atten)
{
    fixed diff = max (0, dot (s.Normal, lightDir));

    fixed4 c;
    c.rgb = s.Albedo * _LightColor0.rgb * (diff * atten * 2);
    c.a = s.Alpha;
    return c;
}
```

3. Finally, we can complete this optimization pass by updating the variables in our `surf()` function:

```
void surf (Input IN, inout SurfaceOutput o)
{
    fixed4 c = tex2D (_MainTex, IN.uv_MainTex);

    o.Albedo = c.rgb;
    o.Alpha = c.a;
    o.Normal = UnpackNormal(tex2D(_NormalMap, IN.uv_NormalMap));
}
```

4. Now that we have our variables optimized, we are going to take advantage of a built-in lighting function variable, so we can control how lights are processed by this Shader. By doing this, we can greatly reduce the amount of lights the Shader processes. Modify the `#pragma` statement in your Shader with the following code:

```
CGPROGRAM
#pragma surface surf SimpleLambert noforwardadd
```

5. We can optimize this further by sharing UVs between the normal map and the diffuse texture. To do this, we simply change the UV lookup in our `UnpackNormal()` function to use the `_MainTex` UVs instead of the UVs of `_NormalMap`:

```
void surf (Input IN, inout SurfaceOutput o)
{
    fixed4 c = tex2D (_MainTex, IN.uv_MainTex);

    o.Albedo = c.rgb;
    o.Alpha = c.a;
    o.Normal = UnpackNormal(tex2D(_NormalMap, IN.uv_MainTex));
}
```

6. Since we have removed the need for the normal map UVs, we need to make sure we remove the normal map UV code from the `Input` struct:

```
struct Input
{
    half2 uv_MainTex;
};
```

7. Finally, we can further optimize this Shader by telling the Shader that it only works with certain renderers:

```
CGPROGRAM
#pragma surface surf SimpleLambert exclude_path:prepass noforwardadd
```

The result of our optimization passes show us that we really don't notice a difference in the visual quality, but we have reduced the amount of time it takes for this Shader to be drawn to the screen. We will learn about finding out how much time it takes for a Shader to render in the next section, but the idea to focus on here is that we achieve the same result with less data. So keep this in mind when creating your Shaders. The following image shows us the final result of our Shader:

How it works...

Now that we have seen the ways in which we can optimize our Shaders, let's dive in a bit deeper and really understand why all of these techniques are working, and look at a couple of other techniques you can try for yourself.

Let's first focus our attention to the size of the data that each variable is storing when we declare them. If you are familiar with programming, you will understand that you can declare values or variables with different sizes using data types. This means that a float actually has the maximum size in memory. Let's look at these variable types in more detail:

- `float`: This is a full 32-bit precision value and is the slowest of the three different types we see here. It also has its corresponding values of `float2`, `float3`, and `float4`.
- `half`: This is a reduced 16-bit floating point value and is suitable for storing UV values, color values, and is much faster than using a `float` value. It has its corresponding values like the `float` type, which are `half2`, `half3`, and `half4`.
- `fixed`: This value is the smallest in size of the three types, but can be used for lighting calculations, colors, and has the corresponding values of `fixed2`, `fixed3`, and `fixed4`.

Our second phase of optimizing our simple Shader was to declare the `noforwardadd` value to our `#pragma` statement. This is basically a switch that automatically tells Unity that any object with this particular Shader only receives per-pixel light from a single directional light. Any other lights that are calculated by this Shader will be forced to be processed as per-vertex lights using spherical harmonic values produced internally by Unity. This is especially obvious when we place another light in the scene to light our sphere object because our Shader is doing a per-pixel operation by using the normal map.

This is great, but what if you wanted to have a bunch of directional lights in the scene and want to have control over which of those lights are used for the main per-pixel light? Well, if you notice, each light has a **Render Mode** drop-down menu. If you click on this drop-down menu, you will see a couple of flags that can be set. These are **Auto**, **Important**, and **Not Important**. By selecting a light, you can tell Unity that a light should be considered more as a per-pixel light, than a per-vertex light, by setting its render mode to **Important** and vice versa. If you leave a light set to **Auto**, you will let Unity decide the best course of action.

Place another light in your scene and remove the texture that is currently in the main texture for our Shader. You will notice that the second point light does not react with the normal map, only the directional light we created first. The concept here is that you save on per-pixel operations by just calculating all extra lights as vertex lights, and save performance by just calculating the main directional light as a per-pixel light. The following image visually demonstrates this concept as the point light is not reacting with the normal map:

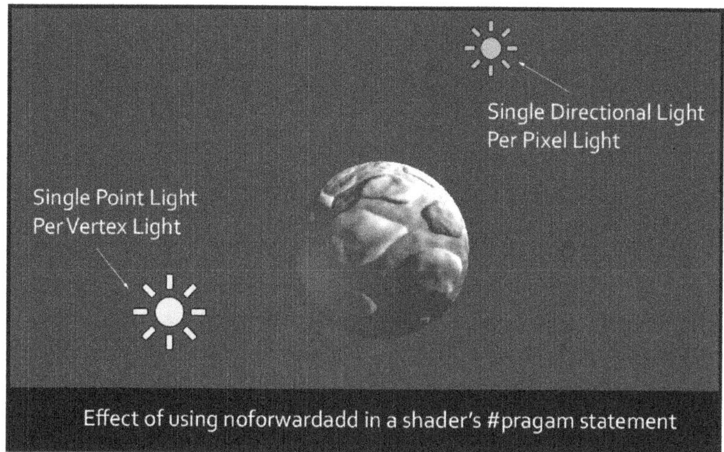

Effect of using noforwardadd in a shader's #pragam statement

Finally, we did a bit of a cleanup and simply told the normal map texture to use the main texture's UV values, and we got rid of the line of code that pulled in a separate set of UV values specifically for the normal map. This is always a good way to simplify your code and clean up any unwanted data.

We also declared `exclude_pass: prepass` in our `#pragma` statement, so that this Shader wouldn't accept any custom lighting from the deferred renderer. This means we can only really use this Shader effectively in the forward renderer, which is set in the main camera's settings.

By taking a bit of time, you will be amazed at how much a Shader can be optimized. You have seen how we can pack grayscale textures into a single RGBA texture, as well as using lookup textures to fake lighting. There are many ways in which a Shader can be optimized, which is why it is always an ambiguous question to ask in the first place; but knowing these different optimization techniques, you can cater your Shaders to your game and to your target platform, ultimately resulting in very streamlined Shaders and a nice steady frame rate.

Profiling your Shaders

Now that we know how we can reduce the overhead that our Shaders might take up, let's take a look at how to find problematic Shaders in a scene where you might have a lot of Shaders, or a lot of objects, Shaders, and scripts, all running at the same time. To find a single object or a single Shader among a whole game can be quite daunting, but Unity provides us with its built-in Profiler. This allows us to actually see on a frame-by-frame basis what is happening in the game, and lets us see each item being used by the GPU and the CPU.

Using the Profiler we can isolate only items such as Shaders, geometry, and general rendering items by using their interface to create blocks of profiling jobs. We can filter out items till we are looking at the performance of just a single object. This then lets us see the effects on the CPU and GPU that the object has while it is performing its functions at runtime.

Let's take a look at the different sections of the Profiler and learn how to debug our scenes and most importantly our Shaders.

Getting ready

Let's begin using our Profiler by getting a few assets ready and launching the **Profiler** window:

1. Let's use the scene from the last recipe and launch the Unity Profiler from **Window** | **Profiler** or by using *Ctrl* + *7*.
2. Let's also duplicate our sphere a couple more times to see how that affects our rendering.

You should see something similar to the following screenshot:

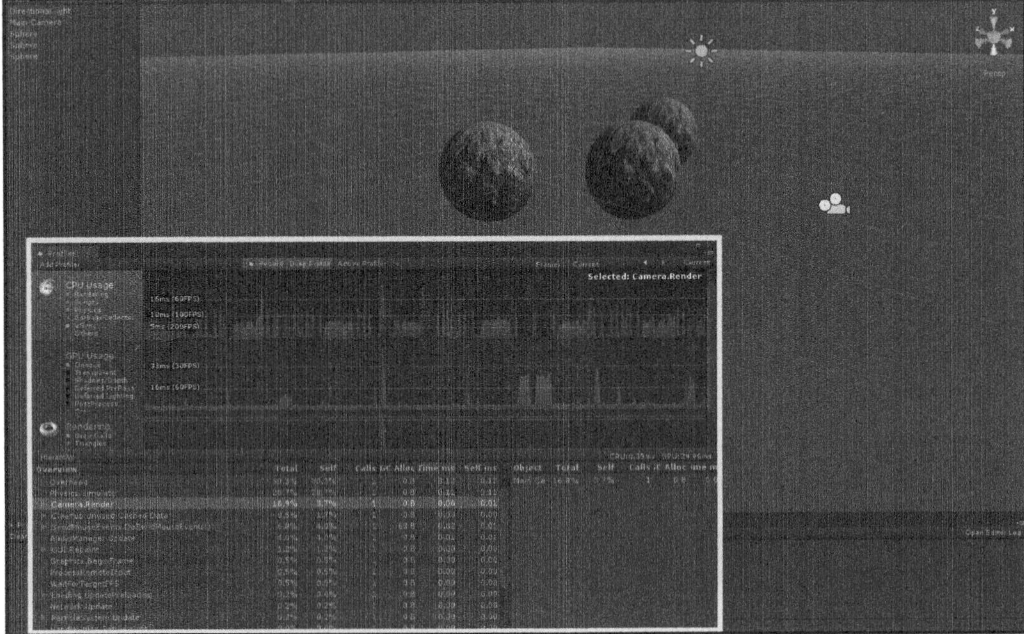

How to do it...

To begin using the Profiler, we will first take a look at some of the UI elements of this window. Before we hit play, let's take a look at how to get the information we need from the Profiler.

1. First, click on the larger blocks in the **Profiler** window called **GPU Usage**, **CPU Usage**, and **Rendering**. You will find these blocks in the left-hand side of the upper window as shown in the following screenshot:

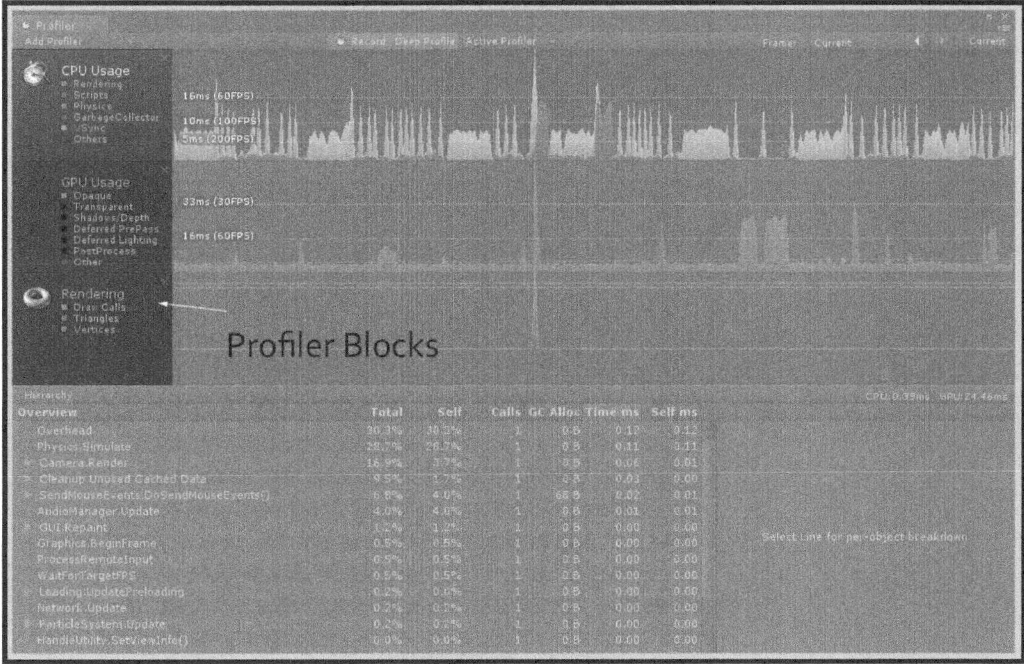

Using these blocks we can see different data specific to those major functions of our game. The **CPU Usage** block shows us what most of our scripts are doing as well as the physics, and overall rendering. The **GPU Usage** block gives us detailed information about the elements that are specific to our lighting, shadows, and render queues. Finally, the **Rendering** block gives us information about the draw calls and amount of geometry we have in our scene at any one frame.

By clicking on each of these blocks, we can isolate out the type of data we see during our profiling session.

2. Now click on the tiny colored blocks inside one of these profile blocks and hit play or *Ctrl* + *P* to run the scene.

   This lets us dive down even deeper into our profiling session, so that we can filter out what is being reported back for us. While the scene is running, uncheck all of the boxes except for **Opaque** in the **GPU Usage** block. Notice how we can now just see how much time is being used to render just the objects that are set to the render queue of **Opaque**.

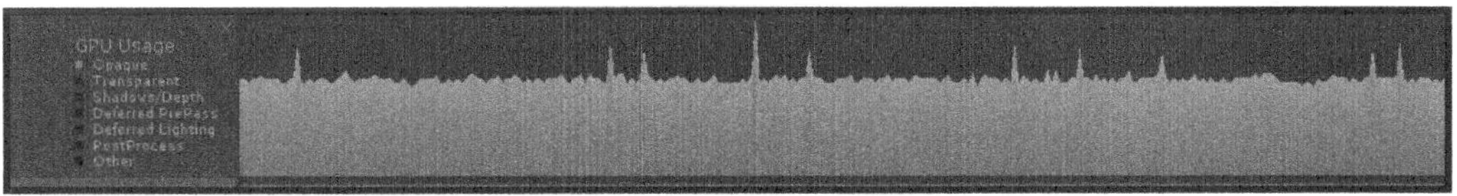

3. Another great function of the **Profiler** window is the action of clicking-and-dragging in the graph view. This will automatically pause your game so that you can further analyze a certain spike in the graph, to find out exactly which items are causing the performance problem. Click-and-drag around in the graph view to pause the game and see the effect of using this functionality:

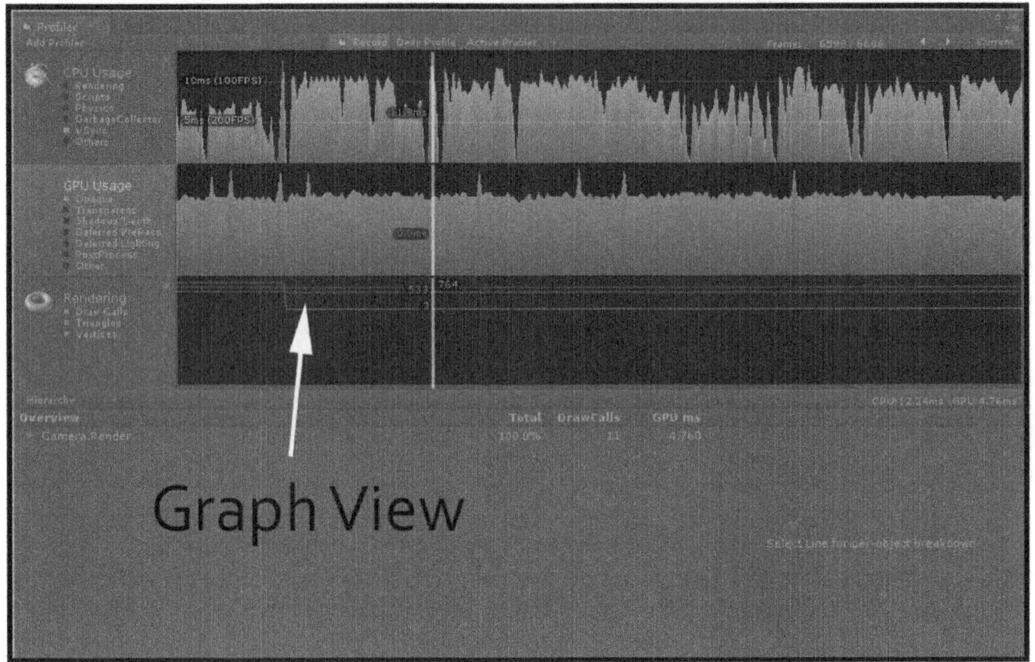

4. Turning our attention now toward the lower half of the **Profiler** window, you will notice that there is a drop-down item available, when we have the **GPU Usage** block selected. We can expand this to get even more detailed information about the current active profiling session and in this case, more information about what the camera is currently rendering and how much time it is taking up:

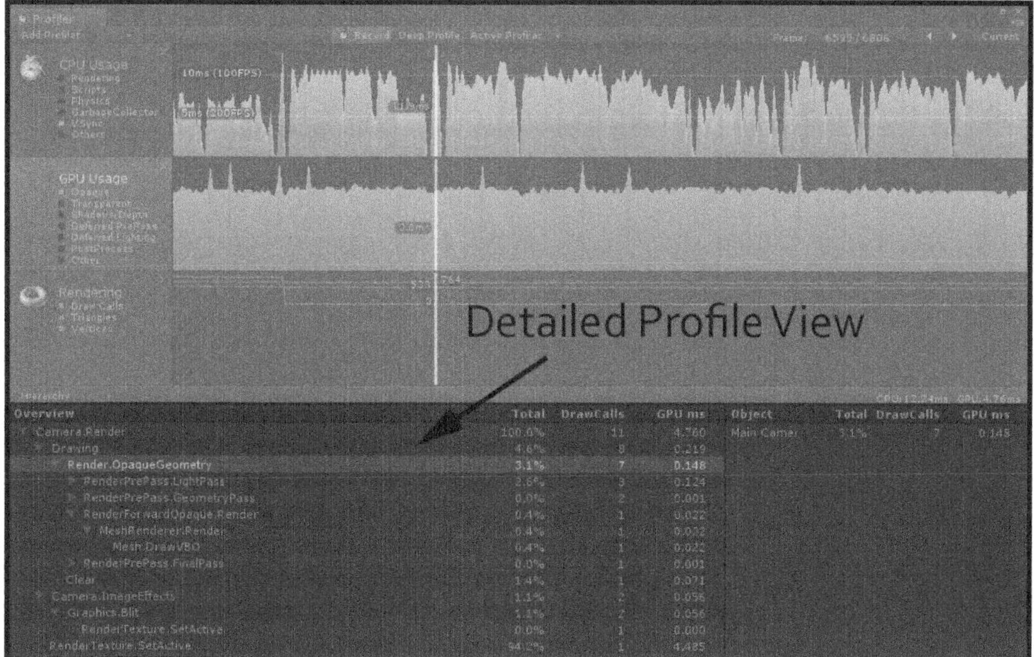

This gives us a complete look into the inner workings of what Unity is processing at this particular frame. In this case we can see that our three spheres with our optimized Shader are taking roughly 0.14 milliseconds to draw to screen, they are taking up seven draw calls, and this process is taking 3.1 percent of the GPU's time every frame. It's this type of information we can use to diagnose and solve performance issues with regard to Shaders. Let's conduct a test to see the effects of adding one more texture to our Shader and blending two diffuse textures together using a `lerp` function. You will see in the **Profiler** window the effects pretty clearly.

5. Modify the `Properties` block of your Shader with the following code to give us another texture to use:

```
Properties
{
    _MainTex ("Base (RGB)", 2D) = "white" {}
    _BlendTex ("Blend Texture", 2D) = "white" {}
    _NormalMap ("Normal Map", 2D) = "bump" {}
}
```

6. Then let's feed our texture to our `CGPROGRAM` statement:

```
sampler2D _MainTex;
sampler2D _BlendTex;
sampler2D _NormalMap;
```

7. Now it's time to update our `surf()` function accordingly so we blend our texture diffuse textures together:

```
void surf (Input IN, inout SurfaceOutput o)
{
    fixed4 c = tex2D (_MainTex, IN.uv_MainTex);
    fixed4 blendTex = tex2D (_BlendTex, IN.uv_MainTex);

    c = lerp(c, blendTex, blendTex.r);

    o.Albedo = c.rgb;
    o.Alpha = c.a;
    o.Normal = UnpackNormal(tex2D(_NormalMap, IN.uv_MainTex));
}
```

Once you save your modifications in your Shader and return to Unity's editor, we can run our game and see the increase in milliseconds of our new Shader. Press play once you have returned to Unity and let's take a look at the results in our **Profiler** window:

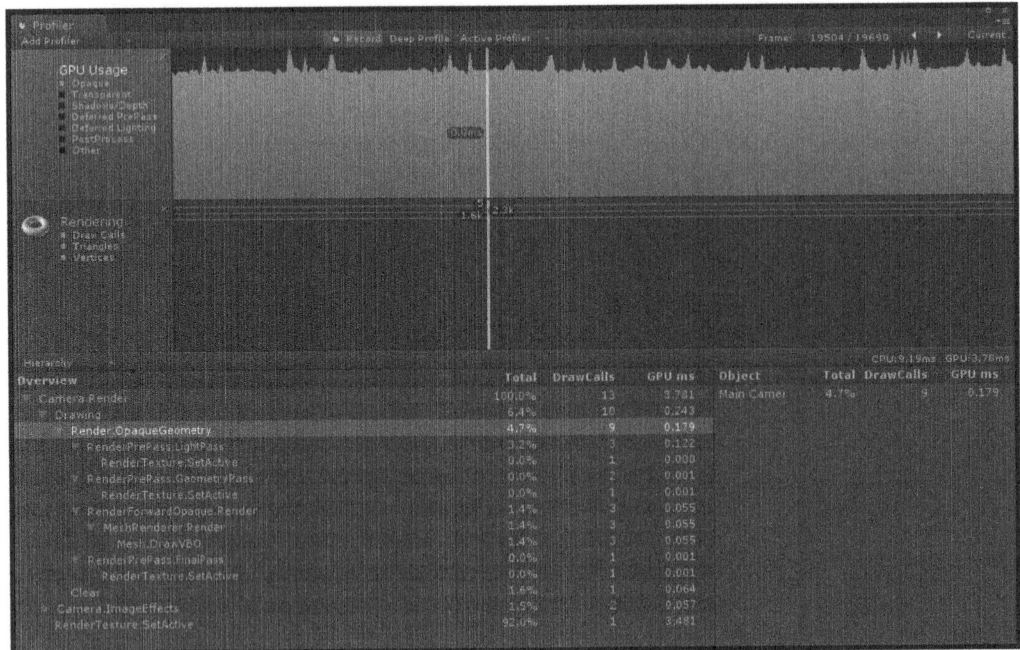

You can see now that the amount of time to render our **Opaque** Shaders in this scene is taking 0.179 milliseconds, up from 0.140 milliseconds. By adding another texture and using the `lerp()` function, we increased the render time for our spheres. While it's a small change, imagine having 20 Shaders all working in different ways on different objects.

Using the information given here you can more quickly pin point areas that are causing performance decreases, and solve those issues by using the techniques from the previous recipe.

How it works...

While it's completely out of scope of this book to describe how this tool actually works internally, we can surmise that Unity has given us a way to view the computer's performance while our game is running. Basically this window is tied very tightly to the CPU and the GPU to give us real-time feedback of how much time is being taken for each of our scripts, our objects, and our render queues. Using this information we have seen that we can track the efficiency of our Shader writing to eliminate problematic areas and code.

There's more...

It is also possible to profile specifically for mobile platforms. Unity provides us with a couple of extra features when the Android or iOS build target is set in **Build Settings**. We can actually get real-time information from our mobile devices while the game is running. This becomes very useful because you are able to profile directly on the device itself, instead of profiling directly in your editor. To find out more about this process, see Unity's documentation at the following link:

`http://docs.unity3d.com/Documentation/Manual/MobileProfiling.html`

Modifying your Shaders for mobile

Now that we have seen quite a broad set of techniques for making really optimized Shaders, let's take a look at writing a nice, high quality Shader targeted for a mobile device. It is actually quite easy to make a few adjustments to the Shaders we have written so that they run faster on a mobile device. This includes elements such as using the `approxview` or `halfasview` lighting function variables. We can also reduce the amount of textures we need and even apply better compression for the textures we are using. By the end of this section, we will have a nicely optimized, normal-mapped Specular Shader for use in our mobile games.

Getting ready

Before we begin, let's get a fresh new scene made up and fill it up with some objects to apply our mobile Shader to:

1. Create a new scene and fill it with a default sphere and a single directional light.
2. Create a new Material and a Shader, and assign the Shader to the Material.
3. Finally assign the material to our sphere object in our scene.

When completed you should have a scene similar to the one in the following image:

How to do it...

For this recipe we will write a mobile-friendly Shader from scratch and discuss the elements that make it more mobile-friendly:

1. Let's first populate our `Properties` block with the needed textures. In this case we are going to use a single diffuse texture with the gloss map in its alpha channel, plus a normal map and a slider for Specular intensity:

```
Properties
{
    _Diffuse ("Base (RGB) Specular Amount (A)", 2D) = "white" {}
    _SpecIntensity ("Specular Width", Range(0.01, 1)) = 0.5
    _NormalMap ("Normal Map", 2D) = "bump"{}
}
```

2. Our next task is to set up our `#pragma` declarations. This will simply turn certain features of the Surface Shader on and off, ultimately making the Shader cheaper or more expensive:

```
CGPROGRAM
#pragma surface surf MobileBlinnPhong exclude_path:prepass nolightmap noforwardadd halfasview
```

3. We then need to make the connection between our `Properties` block and our `CGPROGRAM` statements. Though, this time we are going to use the fixed variable type for our Specular-intensity slider to reduce its memory usage:

```
sampler2D _Diffuse;
sampler2D _NormalMap;
fixed _SpecIntensity;
```

4. In order for us to map our textures to the surface of our object, we need to get some UVs. In this case we are only going to get one set of UVs to keep the amount of data in our Shader down to a minimum:

```
struct Input
{
    half2 uv_Diffuse;
};
```

5. The next step is to fill in our lighting function using a few new input variables that are available to us by using the new `#pragma` declarations:

```
inline fixed4 LightingMobileBlinnPhong (SurfaceOutput s, fixed3 lightDir, fixed3 halfDir, fixed atten)
{
    fixed diff = max (0, dot (s.Normal, lightDir));
    fixed nh = max (0, dot (s.Normal, halfDir));
    fixed spec = pow (nh, s.Specular*128) * s.Gloss;

    fixed4 c;
    c.rgb = (s.Albedo * _LightColor0.rgb * diff + _LightColor0.rgb * spec) * (atten*2);
    c.a = 0.0;
    return c;
}
```

6. Finally, we complete the Shader by creating the `surf()` function and processing the final color of our surface:

```
void surf (Input IN, inout SurfaceOutput o)
{
    fixed4 diffuseTex = tex2D (_Diffuse, IN.uv_Diffuse);
    o.Albedo = diffuseTex.rgb;
    o.Gloss = diffuseTex.a;
    o.Alpha = 0.0;
    o.Specular = _SpecIntensity;
    o.Normal = UnpackNormal(tex2D(_NormalMap, IN.uv_Diffuse));
}
```

When completed with the code portion of this recipe, save your Shader and return to the Unity editor to let the Shader compile. If no errors occurred, you should see a result similar to the following image:

How it works...

So, let's begin the description of this Shader by explaining what it does and doesn't do. First, it excludes the deferred lighting pass. This means if you created a lighting function that was connected to the deferred renderer's prepass, it wouldn't use that particular lighting function and it would look for the default lighting function such as the ones we have been creating thus far in this book.

This particular Shader does not support light mapping by Unity's internal light mapping system. This just keeps the Shader from trying to find light maps for the object the Shader is attached to, making the Shader more performance-friendly, because it is not having to perform the light mapping check.

We included the `noforwardadd` declaration, so that we only process per-pixel textures with a single directional light. All other lights are forced to become per-vertex lights and will not be included in any per-pixel operations you might do in the `surf()` function.

Finally, we are using the `halfasview` declaration to tell Unity that we aren't going to use the main `viewDir` parameter found in a normal lighting function. We instead are going to use the half vector as the view direction and process our Specular with that. This becomes much faster for the Shader to process since it will be done on a per-vertex basis. It isn't completely accurate when it comes to simulating Specular in the real world, but visually on a mobile device it looks just fine and the Shader is more optimized.

Techniques such as these make a Shader more efficient and cleaner code-wise. Always make sure you are using only the data you need while weighing that against your target hardware and the visual quality the game requires. In the end, it becomes a cocktail of these techniques that ultimately make up your Shaders for your games.

9

Making Your Shader World Modular with CgIncludes

This chapter will reveal the following:

- CgInclude files that are built into Unity
- Creating a CgInclude file to store lighting models
- Building Shaders with #define directives

Introduction

As we have taken our journey through the process of writing Shaders, we have seen how to achieve many varieties of techniques and effects, but we still write very similar code over and over again. When in a production environment, time is precious and creating Shaders quickly and efficiently in an iterative manner is crucial to meeting the demands of a game production. This is where CgInclude files come into play. They allow us to create a framework of code that can be re-used over and over again, making our Shader writing environment modular.

Actually, we have already been using a couple of built-in CgInclude files to write our Surface Shaders. Anytime we use the built-in Lambert or BlinnPhong lighting models, we are using code snippets and functions from CgInclude files that Unity has already created for us. This reduces the amount of coding we have to do at our end and keeps a nice level of consistency in your lighting and effects over all your Shaders.

By understanding and writing your own CgInclude files for your Shader development environment, the process of creating Shaders will become fast and easy to modify whenever needed. So let's continue our Shader writing journey by taking a look at what Unity has already provided us in terms of lighting models, functions, and built-in state variables.

CgInclude files that are built into Unity

Our first step into writing our own CgInclude files is to understand what Unity is already providing us for Shaders. By writing Surface Shaders there is a lot happening underneath the hood, which makes the process of writing Surface Shaders so efficient. We can see this code in the included CgInclude files found in your Unity install folder at `Editor | Data | CGIncludes`. All the files contained within that folder do their part to render our objects with our Shaders on to the screen. Some of these files take care of shadows and lighting, some take care of helper functions, and some manage platform dependencies. Without them, our Shader writing experience would be much more laborious.

You can find a list of information Unity has provided to us at the following link:

`http://docs.unity3d.com/Documentation/Components/SL-BuiltinIncludes.html`

Let's begin the process of understanding these built-in CgInclude files, using some of the built-in helper functions from the `UnityCG.cginc` file.

Getting ready

Before we start diving into the meat of writing the Shader, we need to get a few items set up in our scene. Let's create the following and then open the Shader in MonoDevelop:

1. Create a new scene and fill it with a simple sphere model.
2. Create a new Shader and Material.
3. Attach the new Shader to the new Material and assign the Material to the sphere.
4. Then, let's create a directional light and position it above our sphere.
5. Finally, we are going to want to open the `UnityCG.cginc` file from Unity's `CgInclude` folder located in Unity's install directory. This will let us analyze some of the helper function's code so we can better understand what is happening when we use them.

6. You should have a simple scene set up for working on the Shader. Refer to the following screenshot as an example:

How to do it...

With the scene prepared, we can now begin the process of experimenting with some of the built-in helper functions included with the `UnityCG.cginc` file. Double-click on the Shader that was created for this scene to open it in MonoDevelop and insert the code given in the following steps:

1. Add the following code to the `Properties` block of the new Shader file. We will need a single texture and a single slide for our example Shader:

```
Properties
{
    _MainTex ("Base (RGB)", 2D) = "white" {}
    _DesatValue ("Desaturate", Range(0,1)) = 0.5
}
```

2. We then need to make sure we create the data connection between our `Properties` block and our `CGPROGRAM` block, with the following code placed after the `CGPROGRAM` declaration and `#pragma` directives:

```
sampler2D _MainTex;
fixed _DesatValue;
```

3. Finally, we just have to update our `surf()` function to include the following code. We introduce a new function that we haven't seen yet, which is built into Unity's `UnityCG.cginc` file:

```
void surf (Input IN, inout SurfaceOutput o)
{
    half4 c = tex2D (_MainTex, IN.uv_MainTex);

    c.rgb = lerp(c.rgb,Luminance(c.rgb), _DesatValue);

    o.Albedo = c.rgb;
    o.Alpha = c.a;
}
```

With the Shader code modified you should see something similar to the following screenshot. We have simply used a helper function, built into Unity's CgInclude file, to give us an effect of desaturating the main texture of our Shader:

How it works...

Using the built-in helper function named `Luminance()`, we are able to quickly get a desaturation or gray scale effect on our Shaders. This is all possible because the `UnityCG.cginc` file is automatically brought into our Shader since we are using a Surface Shader.

If you search through the `UnityCG.cginc` file, opened in MonoDevelop, you will find the implementation of this function at line 276. The following screenshot shows the code from the file:

```
274
275 // Converts color to luminance (grayscale)
276 inline fixed Luminance( fixed3 c )
277 {
278     return dot( c, fixed3(0.22, 0.707, 0.071) );
279 }
280
```

Since this function is included in this file and Unity automatically compiles with this file, we can use the function in our code as well, thereby reducing the amount of code we have to write over and over again.

If you notice there is also a `Lighting.cginc` file that Unity comes with. This file houses all the lighting models that we use when we declare something like `#pragma Surface surf Lambert`. Sifting through this file reveals that all the built-in lighting models are defined here for re-use and modularity.

Creating a CgInclude file to store lighting models

Knowing about the built-in CgInclude files is great, but what if we wanted to build our own CgInclude files to store our own lighting models and helper functions? We can in fact create our own CgInclude files, but we need to learn a little more code syntax before we can start to use them efficiently in our Shader writing pipelines. Let's take a look at the process of creating a new CgInclude file from scratch.

Getting ready

Using the same scene, Shader, and Material, let's walk through the process of generating a new item for this recipe.

1. Begin by creating a new text file and call it something like `MyCgInclude.txt`.
2. Then change its file extension to `.cginc`. Windows will give you a warning message saying that the file may become unusable, but it will still work.
3. Import that new `.cginc` file into your Unity project and let it compile. If all goes well, you will see that Unity knew to compile it to a CgInclude file.

We are now ready to begin creating our own custom CgInclude code. Simply double-click on the CgInclude file you created to open in MonoDevelop.

How to do it...

With our CgInclude file open, we can begin to enter the code that will get it working with our Surface Shaders. The following code will get our CgInclude file ready for use within our Surface Shaders and allow us to continually add more code to it as we develop more Shaders:

1. We begin our CgInclude file with what is called a preprocessor directive. These are statements like `#pragma` and `#include`. In this case, we want to define a new set of code that will be executed if our Shader includes this file in its compiler directives. Enter the following code at the top of your CgInclude file:

```
#ifndef MY_CG_INCLUDE
#define MY_CG_INCLUDE
```

2. We then always need to make sure we close our `#ifndef` or `#ifdef` with an `#endif` to close the definition check, just like an `if` statement needs to be closed with two brackets in C#. Enter the following code just after the `#define` directive:

```
#endif
```

3. At this point we just need to fill in the guts of the CgInclude file. So we finish off our CgInclude file by entering in the following code:

```
//Custom Built-in Variables
fixed4 _MyColor;

//lighting models
inline fixed4 LightingHalfLambert (SurfaceOutput s, fixed3 lightDir, fixed atten)
{
    fixed diff = max (0, dot (s.Normal, lightDir));

    diff = (diff + 0.5)*0.5;

    fixed4 c;
    c.rgb = s.Albedo * _LightColor0.rgb * ((diff * _MyColor.rgb) * atten * 2);
    c.a = s.Alpha;
    return c;
}
```

4. With that completed, you now have your very first CgInclude file. With just this little bit of code we can greatly reduce the amount of code we have to re-write, and we can begin to store lighting models we use all the time here so that we never lose them. Your CgInclude file should look similar to the following screenshot:

```
#ifndef MY_CG_INCLUDE
#define MY_CG_INCLUDE

//Custom Built-in Variables
fixed4 _MyColor;

//lighting models
inline fixed4 LightingHalfLambert (SurfaceOutput s, fixed3 lightDir, fixed atten)
{
    fixed diff = max (0, dot (s.Normal, lightDir));

    diff = (diff + 0.5)*0.5;

    fixed4 c;
    c.rgb = s.Albedo * _LightColor0.rgb * ((diff * _MyColor.rgb) * atten * 2);
    c.a = s.Alpha;
    return c;
}

#endif
```

There are a couple more steps we need to complete before we can fully utilize this CgInclude file. We simply need to tell the current Shader we are working with to use this file and its code. To complete the process of creating and using CgInclude files, let's complete the next set of steps.

5. If we turn our attention to our Shader we need to tell our `CGPROGRAM` block to include our new CgInclude file, so we can access the code it contains. Modify the directives of our `CGPROGRAM` block to include the following code:

```
CGPROGRAM
#include "MyCGInclude.cginc"
#pragma surface surf Lambert
```

6. Our current Shader is currently using the built-in Lambert lighting model, but we want to use the Half Lambert lighting model we created in our CgInclude. Since we include the code from our CgInclude file, we can use the Half Lambert lighting model with the following code:

```
CGPROGRAM
#include "MyCGInclude.cginc"
#pragma surface surf HalfLambert
```

7. Finally, we have also declared a custom variable in our CgInclude file to show that we can set up default variables for our Shaders to use. To see this in action, enter the following code into the `Properties` block of your Shader:

```
Properties
{
    _MainTex ("Base (RGB)", 2D) = "white" {}
    _DesatValue ("Desaturate", Range(0,1)) = 0.5
    _MyColor ("My Color", Color) = (1,1,1,1)
}
```

When we return to Unity, the Shader and CgInclude file will compile, and if you do not see any errors, you will notice that in fact we are using our new Half Lambert lighting model and a new color swatch appeared in our Materials **Inspector**. The following screenshot shows the result of using our CgInclude file:

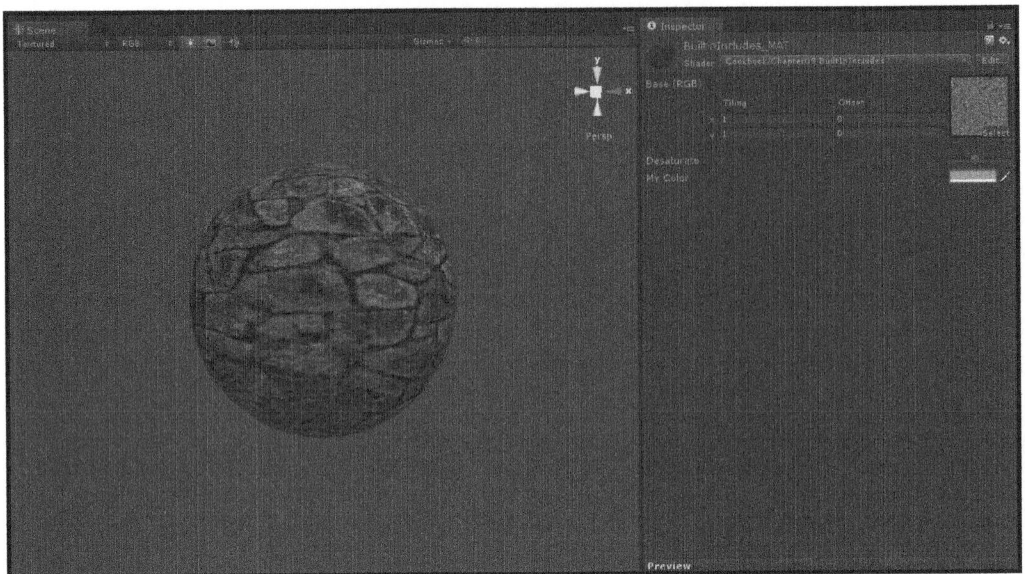

How it works...

When using Shaders, we can include other sets of code by using the `#include` preprocessor directive. This tells Unity that we want to let the current Shader use the code from within the included file in the Shader, that's the reason why these files are called CgInclude files. We are including snippets of Cg code using the `#include` directive.

Once we declare the `#include` directive and Unity is able to find the file in the project, Unity will then look for code snippets that have been defined. This is where we start to use the `#ifndef` directive and `#endif` directive. When we declare the `#ifndef` directive we are simply saying, *if not defined, define something with a name*. In this recipe's case, we said we wanted to `#define MY_CG_INCLUDE`. So if Unity doesn't find a definition called `MY_CG_INCLUDE`, it goes and creates it when the CgInclude file is compiled, thereby giving us access to the code that follows. The `#endif` simply says that this is the end of this definition, so stop looking for more code.

You can now see how powerful this becomes, since we can now store all of our lighting models and custom variables in one file, and greatly reduce the amount of code we have to write. The real power is when you can begin to give your Shaders the flexibility by defining multiple states of functions within the CgInclude files.

Building Shaders with #define directives

We have seen how we can use Unity's built-in CgInclude files, and we have seen how to construct our very own simple CgInclude file to house all of our lighting models, variables, and helper functions. Now, let's turn our focus to a more dynamic and efficient way to use CgIncludes to make our Shader more modular and to have states we can switch on and off as needed.

To demonstrate this we will change our Half Lambert lighting model we created in the last recipe, to include a definition for Half Lambert. So if we do decide to define a Shader with Half Lambert, our lighting model will update to a Half Lambert diffuse and not a standard **NdotL lighting model**.

Let's see how this works in the following sections, using the assets we have already created. We will just modify their contents with just a little bit of code.

How to do it...

We begin this section by turning our focus over to our CgInclude file. We want to somehow tell the lighting model to have two states.

1. Our first state will be a normal NdotL diffuse lighting model and our second state will be a Half Lambert lighting model. Modify your CgInclude file to include the following code:

```
#ifndef MY_CG_INCLUDE
#define MY_CG_INCLUDE

//Custom Built-in Variables
fixed4 _MyColor;


//lighting models
inline fixed4 LightingCustomLambert (SurfaceOutput s, fixed3 lightDir, fixed atten)
{
    fixed diff = max (0, dot (s.Normal, lightDir));

    #ifdef HalfLambert
    diff = (diff + 0.5)*0.5;
    #endif

    fixed4 c;
    c.rgb = s.Albedo * _LightColor0.rgb * ((diff * _MyColor.rgb) * atten * 2);
    c.a = s.Alpha;
    return c;
}

#endif
```

2. Then in our Shader, we need to update the directives in our CGPROGRAM block:

```
CGPROGRAM
#define HalfLambert

#include "MyCGInclude.cginc"
#pragma surface surf CustomLambert
```

3. Save your CgInclude file and your Shader and return to Unity to let them compile. If all went well, you shouldn't see a difference. This is because we are telling Unity to define a directive called `HalfLambert`, and if it finds one in any of the included files it will use that snippet of code.
4. Return to your Shader and just comment out the new definition we made. Then save and return to Unity to let it compile.

```
CGPROGRAM
//#define HalfLambert

#include "MyCGInclude.cginc"
#pragma surface surf CustomLambert
```

If all went well, you should see that our Shader is now using a standard NdotL lighting model. This is because we aren't defining the `HalfLambert` directive anymore, so Unity will skip that snippet of code when compiled. This makes our Shader writing more flexible and more efficient, since we don't have to constantly re-write or delete out large sections of code. The following screenshot shows the results of this new modularity in our Shader writing:

How it works...

As you can see, the amount of code needed at this point is really minimal. We can create many variations of our lighting models using these simple techniques. By using the `#ifdef` directive, we are telling Unity to look for the name of the definition following the `#ifdef` statement; in this case we used `HalfLambert`.

When we declare the `#define` directive in our Shader, it tells Unity that it needs to look for this definition in any of the included files. If it finds this particular definition then it will include that snippet of code until it finds a `#endif` directive. You can imagine how important the naming of these definitions becomes as you need to make sure you aren't using a definition already included.

The power of using CgInclude files makes it more efficient to write Shaders, not only because we save on the amount of code we have to write in our actual Surface Shaders, but it becomes a way to store the vast amounts of lighting models. This makes it easier to recall a lighting model or to modify it further with multiple states. Imagine trying to remember all of the lighting models from this book, or documenting them in a notepad for use later on. Using CgInclude files will make you a more productive Shader writer as well as more organized.

10

Screen Effects with Unity Render Textures

In this chapter, we will learn the following:

- Setting up the screen effects script system
- Brightness, saturation, and contrast with screen effects
- Basic Photoshop-like blend modes with screen effects
- Overlay blend mode with screen effects

Introduction

One of the most impressive aspects of learning to write Shaders is the process of creating your own screen effects, also known as **post effects**. With these screen effects, we can create stunning looking real-time images with Bloom, Motion Blur, HDR effects, and so on. Most modern games out on the market today make heavy use of these screen effects, for their **depth of field** (**DOF**) effects, their bloom effects, and even their color correction effects.

Throughout this chapter we will learn how to build up the script system that gives us the control to create these screen effects. We will learn about render textures, what the depth buffer is, and how to create effects that give you Photoshop-like control over the final rendered image of your game. By utilizing screen effects for your games, you not only round out your Shader-writing knowledge, but you will gain the power to create your own incredible real-time renders with Unity.

Setting up the screen effects script system

The process of creating screen effects is one in which we grab a full screen image (or texture) use a Shader to process its pixels on the GPU, then send it back to Unity's renderer to apply it to the whole rendered image of the game. This allows us to perform per-pixel operations to the rendered image of the game in real time, giving us a more global artistic control.

Imagine if you had to go through and adjust each material on each object in your game to just adjust the contrast of the final look of your game. While not impossible, this would take a bit of labor to perform. By utilizing a screen effect, we can adjust the screen's final look as a whole, thereby giving us a more Photoshop-like control over our game's final appearance.

In order to get a screen effect system up and running we have to set up a single script to act as the courier of the game's current rendered image or what Unity calls the **render texture**. By utilizing this script to pass the render texture to a Shader, we can create a flexible system to create screen effects. For our first screen effect, we are going to create a very simple grayscale effect, where we can make our game look black and white. Let's take a look at how this is done.

Getting ready

In order to get our screen effects system up and running, we need to begin by creating a few assets for our current Unity project. By doing this we will set ourselves up for the steps in the following sections:

1. In the current project, we need to create a new C# script and call it `TestRenderImage.cs`.
2. Create a new Shader and call it `ImageEffect.shader`.
3. Create a simple sphere in the scene and assign it a new Material. This new Material can be anything, but for our example we decided to make a simple red, Specular Material.
4. Finally, create a new directional light and save the scene.

With all of our assets ready, you should have a simple scene setup, which looks similar to the following image:

How to do it...

In order to make our grayscale screen effect to work we need a script and a Shader. So, we will complete these two new items here and fill them with the appropriate code to produce our first screen effect. Our first task is to complete the C# script. This will get the whole system running. After that we will complete the Shader and see the results of our screen effect. Let's complete our script and Shader using the following steps:

1. Open the `TestRenderImage.cs` C# script and let's begin by entering in a few variables that we will need to store important objects and data. Enter the following code into the very top of the `TestRenderImage` class:

```
public class TestRenderImage : MonoBehaviour
{
    #region Variables
    public Shader curShader;
    public float grayScaleAmount = 1.0f;
    private Material curMaterial;
    #endregion
```

2. In order for us to edit the screen effect in real time, when the Unity editor isn't playing, we need to enter the following line of code just above the declaration of the `TestRenderImage` class:

```
[ExecuteInEditMode]
public class TestRenderImage : MonoBehaviour
{
```

3. Since our screen effect is using a Shader to perform the pixel operations on our screen image, we have to create a material to run the Shader. Without it, we can't access the properties of the Shader. For this we will create a C# property to check for a material, then create one if it doesn't find one. Enter the following code just after the declaration of the variables from step 1:

```
#region Properties
Material material
{
    get
    {
        if(curMaterial == null)
        {
            curMaterial = new Material(curShader);
            curMaterial.hideFlags = HideFlags.HideAndDontSave;
        }
        return curMaterial;
    }
}
#endregion
```

4. We now want to set up some checks in our script, to see if the current target platform that we are building the Unity game to actually supports image effects. If it doesn't find anything at the start of this script, the script will disable itself:

```
void Start()
{
    if(!SystemInfo.supportsImageEffects)
    {
        enabled = false;
        return;
    }

    if(!curShader && !curShader.isSupported)
    {
        enabled = false;
    }
}
```

5. To actually grab the rendered image from the Unity renderer, we need to make use of the following built-in function that Unity provides us, called `OnRenderImage()`. Enter the following code so we can have access to the current render texture:

```
void OnRenderImage(RenderTexture sourceTexture, RenderTexture destTexture)
{
    if(curShader != null)
    {
        material.SetFloat("_LuminosityAmount", grayScaleAmount);
        Graphics.Blit(sourceTexture, destTexture, material);
    }
    else
    {
        Graphics.Blit(sourceTexture, destTexture);
    }
}
```

6. Our screen effect has a variable called `grayScaleAmount`, which we can use to control how much grayscale we want for our final screen effect. So, in this case, we need to make the value go from 0 - 1, where 0 is no grayscale effect and 1 is full grayscale effect. We will perform this operation in the `Update()` function, so that it sets every frame this script is running on:

```
void Update()
{
    grayScaleAmount = Mathf.Clamp(grayScaleAmount, 0.0f, 1.0f);
}
```

7. Finally, we complete our script by doing a little bit of cleanup on objects we created when the script started:

```
void OnDisable()
{
    if(curMaterial)
    {
        DestroyImmediate(curMaterial);
    }
}
```

At this point we can now apply this script to the camera if it compiled without errors in Unity. So, let's apply the `TestRenderImage.cs` script to our main camera in our scene. You should see the `grayScaleAmount` value and a field for a Shader, but the script throws an error to the console window. It says that it is missing an instance to an object and so won't process appropriately. If you remember from step 4, we are doing some checks to see if we have a Shader and if the current platform supports the Shader. Since we haven't given the screen effect script a Shader to work with, then the `curShader` variable is just null, which throws the error.

Let's continue our screen effects system by completing the Shader:

1. To begin our Shader, we will populate our properties with some variables, so we can send data to this Shader:

```
Properties
{
    _MainTex ("Base (RGB)", 2D) = "white" {}
    _LuminosityAmount ("GrayScale Amount", Range(0.0, 1)) = 1.0
}
```

2. Our Shader is now going to utilize pure Cg Shader code, instead of utilizing Unity's built-in Surface Shader code. This will make our screen effect more optimized as we only need to work with the pixels of the render texture. So, we will create a new pass block in our Shader and fill it with some new `#pragma` statements that we haven't seen before:

```
SubShader
{
    Pass
    {
        CGPROGRAM
        #pragma vertex vert_img
        #pragma fragment frag
        #pragma fragmentoption ARB_precision_hint_fastest
        #include "UnityCG.cginc"
```

3. In order to access the data being sent to the Shader from the Unity editor, we need to create the corresponding variables in our `CGPROGRAM` statement:

```
        uniform sampler2D _MainTex;
        fixed _LuminosityAmount;
```

4. Finally, all we need to do is set up our pixel function, in this case called `frag()`. This is where the meat of the screen effect is. This function will process each pixel of the render texture, and return a new image back to our `TestRenderImage.cs` script:

```
fixed4 frag(v2f_img i) : COLOR
{
    //Get the colors from the RenderTexture and the uv's
    //from the v2f_img struct
    fixed4 renderTex = tex2D(_MainTex, i.uv);

    //Apply the Luminosity values to our render texture
    float luminosity = 0.299 * renderTex.r + 0.587 * renderTex.g + 0.114 * renderTex.b;
    fixed4 finalColor = lerp(renderTex, luminosity, _LuminosityAmount);


    return finalColor;
}
```

Once the Shader is complete, return to Unity and let it compile to see if any errors occurred. If not, assign the new Shader to the `TestRenderImage.cs` script, and change the value of the grayscale amount variable. You should see the game view go from a colored version of the game to a grayscale version of the game. The following image demonstrates this screen effect:

With that complete, we now have an easy way to test out new screen effect shaders, without having to write our whole screen effect system over and over again. Let's dive a little deeper and learn about what's going on with the render texture and how it is processed throughout its existence.

How it works...

To get a screen effect up and running inside of Unity, we need to create a script and a Shader. The script drives the real-time update in the editor, but is also responsible for capturing the render texture from the main camera, and passing it to the Shader. Once the render texture gets to the Shader, we can use the Shader to perform per-pixel operations.

At the start of the script we perform a few checks to make sure the current selected build platform actually supports screen effects and the Shader itself. There are instances where a current platform will not support screen effects or the Shader that we are using. So the checks we do in the `Start()` function make sure we don't get any errors, if the platform doesn't support the screen system.

Once the script passes those checks, we initiate the screen effects system by calling the built-in function `OnRenderImage()`. This function is responsible for grabbing the render texture, giving it to the Shader using the `Graphics.Blit()` function, and returning the processed image back to the Unity renderer. You can find out more information on these two functions at the following URLs:

- **OnRenderImage** (`http://docs.unity3d.com/Documentation/ScriptReference/MonoBehaviour.OnRenderImage.html`)
- **Graphics.Blit** (`http://docs.unity3d.com/Documentation/ScriptReference/Graphics.Blit.html`)

Once the current render texture reaches the Shader, the Shader takes it, processes it through the `frag()` function, and returns the final color for each pixel.

You can see how powerful this becomes as it gives us Photoshop-like control over the final rendered image of our game. These screen effects work sequentially, like Photoshop layers in the camera. When you place these screen effects one after the other, they will be processed in that order. These are just the bare bones steps to get a screen effect working, but it is the core of how the screen effects system works.

There's more...

Now that we have our simple screen effect system up and running, let's take a look at some of the other useful information we can obtain from Unity's renderer:

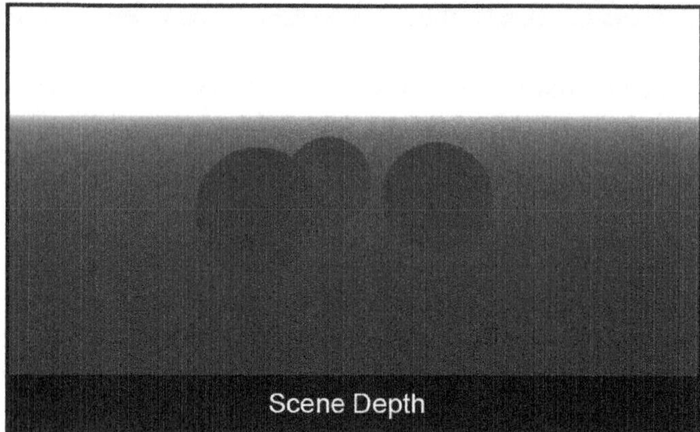

We can actually get the depth of everything in our current game by turning on Unity's built-in depth mode. Once this is turned on, we can use the depth information for a lot of different effects. Let's take a look at how this is done:

1. Create a new Shader and call it `SceneDepth_Effect`. Then double-click on this Shader to open it up in the MonoDevelop editor.
2. We will create the main texture property and a property to control the power of the scene depth effect. Enter the following code into your Shader:

```
Properties
{
    _MainTex ("Base (RGB)", 2D) = "white" {}
    _DepthPower ("Depth Power", Range(1, 5)) = 1
}
```

3. Now we need to create the corresponding variables in our `CGPROGRAM` statement. We are going to add one more variable called `_CameraDepthTexture`. This is a built-in variable that Unity has provided us through the use of the `UnityCG` CgInclude file. It gives us the depth information from the camera:

```
Pass
{
    CGPROGRAM
    #pragma vertex vert_img
    #pragma fragment frag
    #pragma fragmentoption ARB_precision_hint_fastest
    #include "UnityCG.cginc"

    uniform sampler2D _MainTex;
    fixed _DepthPower;
    sampler2D _CameraDepthTexture;
```

4. We complete our depth shader by utilizing a couple more built-in functions that Unity provides us, the `UNITY_SAMPLE_DEPTH()` function and the `linear01Depth()` function. The first function actually gets the depth information from our `_CameraDepthTexture` and produces a single `float` value for each pixel. The `Linear01Depth()` function then makes sure that the values are within the 0 to 1 range. By taking this final depth value to a power, we can control where the mid-value on the 0 to 1 range sits in the scene based on the camera position:

```
fixed4 frag(v2f_img i) : COLOR
{
    //Get the colors from the RenderTexture and the uv's
    //from the v2f_img struct
    float d = UNITY_SAMPLE_DEPTH( tex2D(_CameraDepthTexture, i.uv.xy) );
    d = pow(Linear01Depth(d), _DepthPower);

    return d;
}
```

5. With our Shader complete, let's turn our attention over to our screen effects script. We need to add the `depthPower` variable to the script so we can let users change the value in the editor:

```
#region Variables
public Shader curShader;
private Material curMaterial;

public float depthPower = 1.0f;
#endregion
```

6. Our `OnRenderImage()` function then needs to be updated so that it passes the right value to our Shader:

```
void OnRenderImage(RenderTexture sourceTexture, RenderTexture destTexture)
{
    if(curShader != null)
    {
        material.SetFloat("_DepthPower", depthPower);
        Graphics.Blit(sourceTexture, destTexture, material);
    }
    else
    {
        Graphics.Blit(sourceTexture, destTexture);
    }
}
```

7. To complete our depth screen effect, we need to tell Unity to turn on the depth rendering inside the current camera. This is simply done by setting the main camera's `depthTextureMode` variable:

```
void Update()
{
    Camera.main.depthTextureMode = DepthTextureMode.Depth;
    depthPower = Mathf.Clamp(depthPower, 0, 5);
}
```

With all the code set up, save your script and Shader and return to Unity to let them both compile. If no errors were encountered, you should see a similar result to the following image:

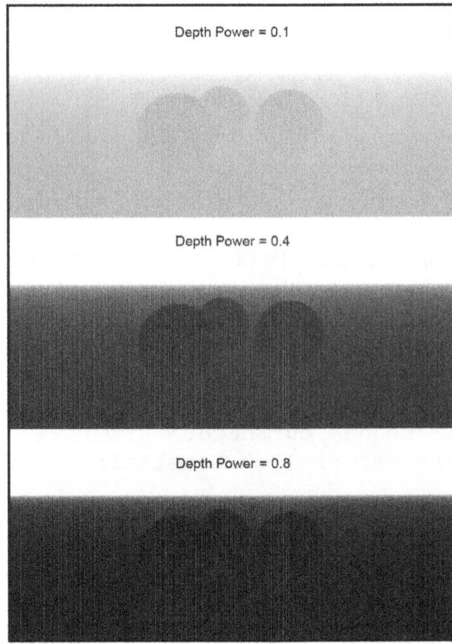

Brightness, saturation, and contrast with screen effects

Now that we have our screen effects system up and running, we can begin to learn how to create more involved pixel operations to perform some of the more common screen effects found in games today.

Using a screen effect to adjust the overall final colors of your game is crucial in giving artists a final global control over the final look of the game. Techniques such as color adjustment sliders to adjust the intensity for the reds, blues, and greens of the final rendered game, or techniques such as putting a certain tone of color over the whole screen as seen in something like a sepia film effect.

For this particular recipe we are going to cover some of the more core color adjustment operations we can perform on an image. These are brightness, saturation, and contrast. Learning how to code these color adjustments gives us a good base for learning the art of screen effects.

Getting ready

To begin we are going to need to create a couple of new assets. We can utilize the same scene as our test scene, but we will need a new script and a new Shader:

1. Create a new script and call it `BSC_ImageEffect`.
2. Create a new Shader called `BSC_Effect`.
3. Now we simply need to copy the code we had from the C# script, in the previous recipe, into our new C# script. This will allow us to just focus on the math for the brightness, saturation, and contrast effects.
4. Copy the code from the Shader in the previous recipe into our new Shader.
5. Create a couple of new objects in the scene and set up some different colored diffuse materials and randomly assign them to the new objects in the scene. This will give us a good range of colors to test our new screen effect.

When completed, you should have a scene similar to the following screenshot:

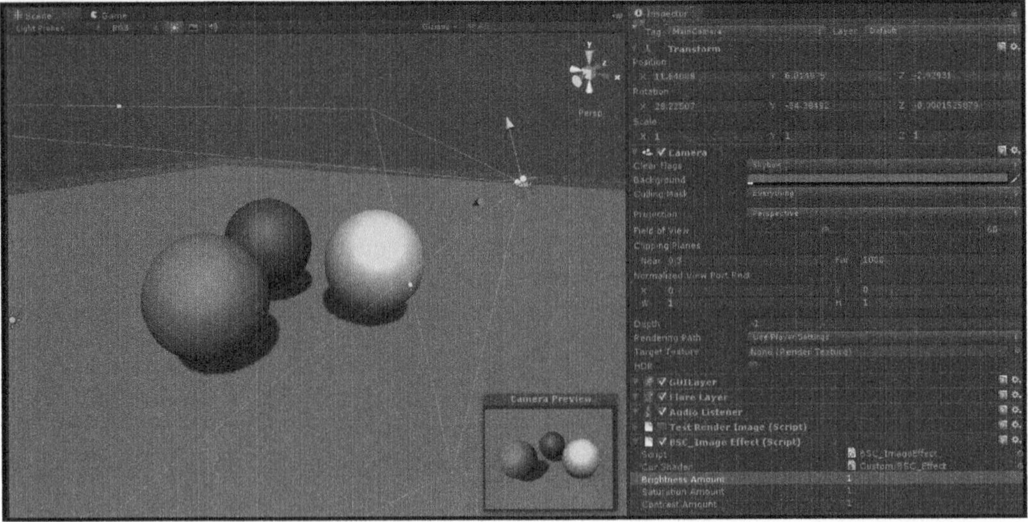

How to do it...

Now that we have completed our scene setup and have created our new script and Shader. We can begin to fill in the code necessary to achieve brightness, saturation, and a contrast screen effect. We will be focusing on just the pixel operation and variable setup for our script and Shader, as getting a screen effect system up and running is described in the previous recipe:

1. Let's begin by launching our new Shader and new script into MonoDevelop. Simply double-click on the two files in the project view to perform this action.
2. Editing the Shader first makes more sense so that we know what kinds of variables we will need for our C# script. Let's begin this by entering in the appropriate properties for our brightness, saturation, and contrast effect. Remember, we need to keep the `_MainTex` property in our Shader as that is the property the render texture targets when creating screen effects.

```
Properties
{
    _MainTex ("Base (RGB)", 2D) = "white" {}
    _BrightnessAmount ("Brightness Amount", Range(0.0, 1)) = 1.0
    _satAmount ("Saturation Amount", Range(0.0, 1)) = 1.0
    _conAmount ("Contrast Amount", Range(0.0, 1)) = 1.0
}
```

3. As usual, in order for us to access the data coming in from our properties into our CGPROGRAM statement, we need to create the corresponding variables in the CGPROGRAM statement:

```
Pass
{
    CGPROGRAM
    #pragma vertex vert_img
    #pragma fragment frag
    #pragma fragmentoption ARB_precision_hint_fastest
    #include "UnityCG.cginc"

    uniform sampler2D _MainTex;
    fixed _BrightnessAmount;
    fixed _satAmount;
    fixed _conAmount;
```

4. Now we need to create the operations that will perform the brightness, saturation, and contrast effects. Enter the following new function into our Shader just above the frag() function. Don't worry if it doesn't make sense just yet; all the code will be explained in the next section:

```
float3 ContrastSaturationBrightness(float3 color, float brt, float sat, float con)
{
    // Increase or decrease these values to
    //adjust r, g and b color channels separately
    float AvgLumR = 0.5;
    float AvgLumG = 0.5;
    float AvgLumB = 0.5;

    //Luminance coefficients for getting luminance from the image
    float3 LuminanceCoeff = float3(0.2125, 0.7154, 0.0721);

    //Operation for brightness
    float3 AvgLumin = float3(AvgLumR, AvgLumG, AvgLumB);
    float3 brtColor = color * brt;
    float intensityf = dot(brtColor, LuminanceCoeff);
    float3 intensity = float3(intensityf, intensityf, intensityf);

    //Operation for saturation
    float3 satColor = lerp(intensity, brtColor, sat);

    //Operation for contrast
    float3 conColor = lerp(AvgLumin, satColor, con);
    return conColor;
}
```

5. Finally, we just need to update our `frag()` function to actually use the `ContrastSaturationBrightness()` function. This will process all the pixels of our render texture and pass it back to our script:

```
fixed4 frag(v2f_img i) : COLOR
{
    //Get the colors from the RenderTexture and the uvs
    //from the v2f_img struct
    fixed4 renderTex = tex2D(_MainTex, i.uv);

    //Apply the Brightness, saturation, contrast operations
    renderTex.rgb = ContrastSaturationBrightness(renderTex.rgb,
                                                  _BrightnessAmount,
                                                  _satAmount,
                                                  _conAmount);

    return renderTex;
}
```

With the code entered into the Shader, return to the Unity editor to let the new Shader compile. If there are no errors, we can return to MonoDevelop to work on our script. Let's begin this by creating a couple new lines of code that will send the proper data to our Shader:

1. Our first step in modifying our script is to add the proper variables that will drive the values of our screen effect. In this case we will need a slider for brightness, a slider for saturation, and a slider for contrast:

```
#region Variables
public Shader curShader;
public float brightnessAmount = 1.0f;
public float saturationAmount = 1.0f;
public float contrastAmount = 1.0f;
private Material curMaterial;
#endregion
```

2. With our variables set up, we now need to tell the script to pass their data to the Shader. We do this in the `OnRenderImage()` function:

```
void OnRenderImage(RenderTexture sourceTexture, RenderTexture destTexture)
{
    if(curShader != null)
    {
        material.SetFloat("_BrightnessAmount", brightnessAmount);
        material.SetFloat("_satAmount", saturationAmount);
        material.SetFloat("_conAmount", contrastAmount);

        Graphics.Blit(sourceTexture, destTexture, material);
    }
    else
    {
        Graphics.Blit(sourceTexture, destTexture);
    }
}
```

3. Finally, all we need to do is clamp the values of the variables within a range that is reasonable. These clamp values are entirely by preference, so you can use whichever values you see fit:

```
void Update()
{
    brightnessAmount = Mathf.Clamp(brightnessAmount, 0.0f, 2.0f);
    saturationAmount = Mathf.Clamp(saturationAmount, 0.0f, 2.0f);
    contrastAmount = Mathf.Clamp(contrastAmount, 0.0f, 3.0f);
}
```

With the script completed and the Shader finished up, we simply assign our script to our main camera and our Shader to the script, and you should see the effects of brightness, saturation, and contrast by manipulating the slider values. The following image shows a result you can achieve with this screen effect:

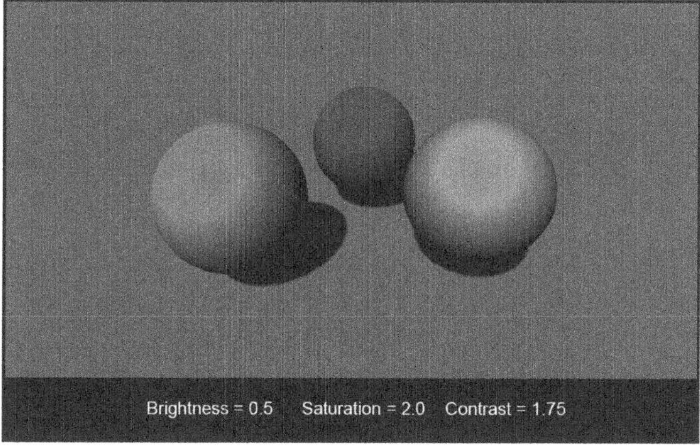

The following image shows another example of what can be done by adjusting the colors of the render image:

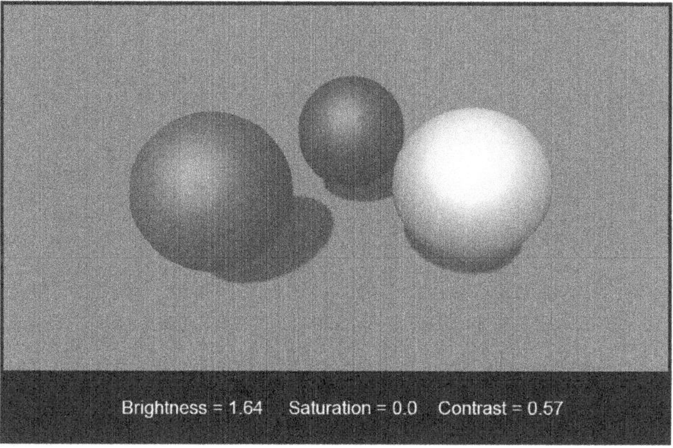

How it works...

Since we now know how the basic screen effects system works, let's just cover the per-pixel operations we created in the `ContrastSaturationBrightness()` function.

The function starts by taking in a few arguments. The first and most important is the current render texture. The other arguments simply adjust the overall effect of the screen effect, and are represented by sliders in the screen effects section in the **Inspector** tab. Once the function receives the render texture and the adjustments values, it declares a few constant values that we use to modify and compare against the original render texture.

The `luminanceCoeff` variable is storing the values that will give us the overall brightness of the current image. These coefficients are based on the CIE color matching functions and are pretty standard throughout the industry. We can find the overall brightness of the image by getting the dot product of the current image dotted with these luminance coefficients. Once we have the brightness, we simply use a couple of `lerp` functions to blend from the grayscale version of the brightness operation, and have the original image multiplied by the brightness value being passed into the function.

Screen effects like this one are crucial to achieving high quality graphics for your games, as they let lets you tweak the final look of your game without having to edit each Material in your current game scene.

Basic Photoshop-like blend modes with screen effects

Screen effects aren't just limited to adjusting the colors of a rendered image from our game. We can also use them to combine other images with our render texture. This technique is no different than creating a new layer in Photoshop and choosing a blend mode to blend two images together, or in our case, a render texture. This becomes a very powerful technique, since it gives the artists in a production environment, a way to simulate their blending modes in game, rather than just in Photoshop.

For this particular recipe, we are going to take a look at some of the more common blend modes, such as **Multiply**, **Add**, and **Overlay**. You will see how simple it is to have the power of Photoshop blend modes inside your game.

Getting ready

To begin we have to get our assets ready again. So let's follow the next few steps to get our screen effects system up and running for our new blend mode screen effect:

1. Create a new script and call it `BlendMode_ImageEffect`.
2. Create a new Shader and call it `BlendMode_Effect`.

3. Now we simply need to copy the code we had from the C# script in the *Setting up the screen effects script system* recipe of this chapter, into our new C# script. This will allow us to just focus on the math for the brightness, saturation, and contrast effect.
4. Copy the code from the Shader in the same recipe of this chapter, into our new Shader.
5. Finally, we will need another texture with which we will perform our blend mode effect. In this recipe we are going to use a grunge type texture. This will make the effect very obvious when we are testing it out.

The following image is the grunge map used in the making of this effect. We'll need to find a texture with enough detail and a nice range of grayscale values to test our new effect.

How to do it...

The first blend mode we will implement is the Multiply blend mode as seen in Photoshop. Let's begin by modifying the code in our Shader first. So, launch the Shader into MonoDevelop by double-clicking on it in Unity's project view.

1. We need to add in some new properties so that we have a texture to blend with and a slider for an opacity value. Enter the code from the following image into your new Shader:

```
Properties
{
    _MainTex ("Base (RGB)", 2D) = "white" {}
    _BlendTex ("Blend Texture", 2D) = "white"{}
    _Opacity ("Blend Opacity", Range(0,1)) = 1
}
```

2. Enter the corresponding variables into our `CGPROGRAM` statement, so that we can access the data from our `Properties` block:

```
Pass
{
    CGPROGRAM
    #pragma vertex vert_img
    #pragma fragment frag
    #pragma fragmentoption ARB_precision_hint_fastest
    #include "UnityCG.cginc"

    uniform sampler2D _MainTex;
    uniform sampler2D _BlendTex;
    fixed _Opacity;
```

3. Finally, we modify our `frag()` function so that it performs the multiply operation on our two textures:

```
fixed4 frag(v2f_img i) : COLOR
{
    //Get the colors from the RenderTexture and the uv's
    //from the v2f_img struct
    fixed4 renderTex = tex2D(_MainTex, i.uv);
    fixed4 blendTex = tex2D(_BlendTex, i.uv);

    //Perform a multiply Blend mode
    fixed4 blendedMultiply = renderTex * blendTex;

    //Adjust amount of Blend Mode with a lerp
    renderTex = lerp(renderTex, blendedMultiply, _Opacity);

    return renderTex;
}
```

4. Save the Shader and return to the Unity editor to let the new Shader code compile and check for errors. If no errors occurred, double-click on the C# script file to launch it into the MonoDevelop editor.

5. In our script file we need to create the corresponding variables as well. So we will need a texture, so we can assign one to the Shader, and a slider to adjust the final amount of the blend mode we want to use:

```
#region Variables
public Shader curShader;
public Texture2D blendTexture;
public float blendOpacity = 1.0f;
private Material curMaterial;
#endregion
```

6. We then need to send our variable data to the Shader through the `OnRenderImage()` function:

```
void OnRenderImage(RenderTexture sourceTexture, RenderTexture destTexture)
{
    if(curShader != null)
    {
        material.SetTexture("_BlendTex", blendTexture);
        material.SetFloat("_Opacity", blendOpacity);

        Graphics.Blit(sourceTexture, destTexture, material);
    }
    else
    {
        Graphics.Blit(sourceTexture, destTexture);
    }
}
```

7. To complete the script, we simply fill in our `Update()` function so that we can clamp the value of the `blendOpacity` variable between a value of 0.0 and 1.0:

```
void Update()
{
    blendOpacity = Mathf.Clamp(blendOpacity, 0.0f, 1.0f);
}
```

With that completed, we assign the screen effect script to our main camera and our screen effect shader to our script so that it has a Shader to use for the per-pixel operations. Finally, in order for the effect to be fully functional, the script and Shader starts looking for a texture. You can assign any texture to the texture field in the **Inspector** tab for the screen effect script. Once that texture is in place, you will see the effect of multiplying this texture over the games rendered image. The following image demonstrates the screen effect:

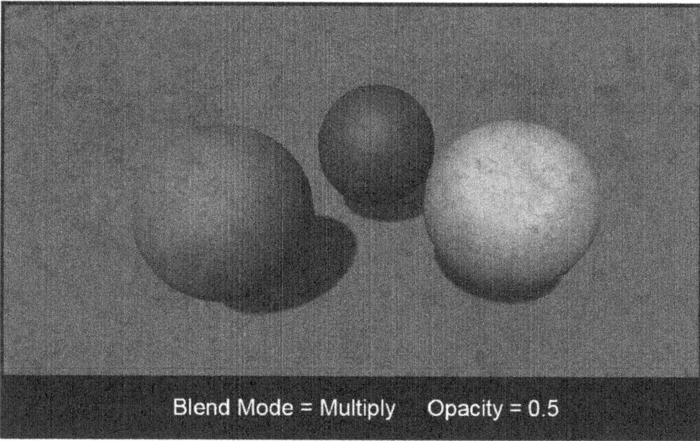

The following image demonstrates a higher intensity of Opacity, making the multiplied image much more apparent over our render image:

With our first blend mode set up we can begin to add a couple of simpler blend modes to get a better understanding of how easy it is to add more effects and really fine-tune the final result in your game. But first let's break down what is happening here.

How it works...

Now we are starting to gain a lot of power and flexibility in our screen effects programming. I am sure you can start to understand how much one can do with this simple system in Unity. We can literally replicate the effects of Photoshop layer blending modes in our game to give artists the flexibility they need to achieve high quality graphics in a short amount of time.

With this particular recipe we looked at how to multiply two images together, add two images together, and perform a screen-blending mode, using just a little bit of math. When working with blend modes, one has to think on a per-pixel level. For instance, when we are using a Multiply blend mode, we literally take each pixel from the original render texture and multiply them with each pixel of the blend texture. The same goes for the Add blend mode. It is just a simple math operation of adding each pixel from the source texture, or render texture, to the blend texture.

The screen blend mode is definitely a bit more involved, but it is doing the same thing. It takes each image, the render texture and the blend texture, inverts them both, then multiplies them together, and then inverts them again to achieve the final look. Just like Photoshop blends its textures together, using blend modes, we can do the same with screen effects.

There's more...

Let's continue this recipe by adding a couple more blend modes to our screen effect:

1. In the screen effect shader, let's add the following code to our `frag()` function and change the value we are returning to our script. We will also need to comment out the Multiply blend so that we don't return that as well:

```
fixed4 frag(v2f_img i) : COLOR
{
    //Get the colors from the RenderTexture and the uvs
    //from the v2f_img struct
    fixed4 renderTex = tex2D(_MainTex, i.uv);
    fixed4 blendTex = tex2D(_BlendTex, i.uv);

    //Perform a multiply Blend mode
    //fixed4 blendedMultiply = renderTex * blendTex;
    fixed4 blendedMultiply = renderTex + blendTex;

    //Adjust amount of Blend mode with a lerp
    renderTex = lerp(renderTex, blendedMultiply, _Opacity);

    return renderTex;
}
```

2. Save the Shader file in MonoDevelop and return to the Unity editor to let the Shader compile. If no errors occurred, you should see a result similar to the following image. This is a simple Add blending mode:

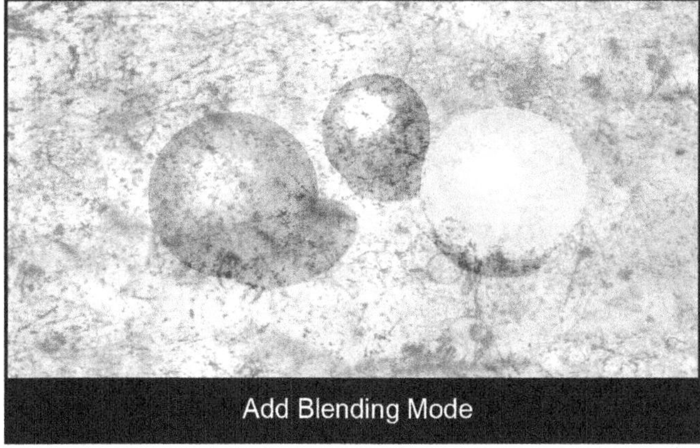

As you can see, this has the opposite effect of the Multiply because we are adding the two images together.

3. Finally, let's add one more blend mode, called a `Screen Blend`. This one is a little bit more involved from a math standpoint, but still simple to implement. Enter the following code into the `frag()` function of our Shader:

```
fixed4 frag(v2f_img i) : COLOR
{
    //Get the colors from the RenderTexture and the uv's
    //from the v2f_img struct
    fixed4 renderTex = tex2D(_MainTex, i.uv);
    fixed4 blendTex = tex2D(_BlendTex, i.uv);

    //Perform a multiply Blend mode
    //fixed4 blendedMultiply = renderTex * blendTex;
    //fixed4 blendedAdd = renderTex + blendTex;
    fixed4 blendedScreen = (1.0 - ((1.0 - renderTex) * (1.0 - blendTex)));

    //Adjust amount of Blend Mode with a lerp
    renderTex = lerp(renderTex, blendedScreen, _Opacity);

    return renderTex;
}
```

The following image demonstrates the results of using a Screen type blend mode to blend two images together in a screen effect:

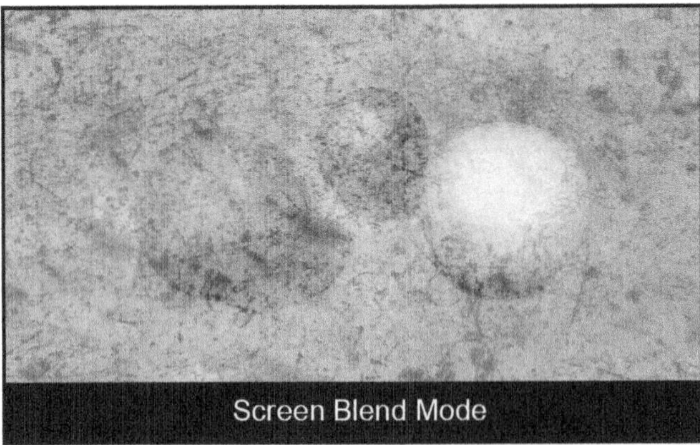

The Overlay blend mode with screen effects

For our final recipe we are going to take a look at another type of blend mode, the Overlay blend mode. This blending actually makes use of some conditional statements that determine the final color of each pixel in each channel. So, the process of using this type of blend mode needs a bit more coding to get working. Let's take a look at how this is done in the following few sections.

Getting ready

For this last screen effect we will need to set up our two scripts like the ones we have in the previous recipes in this chapter. For this recipe we will just be using the same scene we have been using, so that we don't have to create a new one.

1. Create a new script file called `Overlay_ImageEffect`, and a Shader file called `Overlay_Effect`.
2. Copy the code from the previous C# script file into our new script file.
3. Copy the code from the previous Shader file into our new Shader file.
4. Assign the `Overlay_ImageEffect` script to the main camera and `Overlay_Effect` to the script component in the **Inspector** tab.
5. Finally, double-click on the script and the Shader files to open them up in the MonoDevelop editor.

How to do it...

We begin our Overlay screen effect just as we have done for most of the recipes in this chapter; we get the code of our Shader up and running without errors. We can then modify our script file to feed the correct data into the Shader.

1. We first need to set up our properties in our `Properties` block. We will use the same properties from the last few recipes in this chapter:

```
Properties
{
    _MainTex ("Base (RGB)", 2D) = "white" {}
    _BlendTex ("Blend Texture", 2D) = "white"{}
    _Opacity ("Blend Opacity", Range(0,1)) = 1
}
```

2. We then need to create the corresponding variables inside our `CGPROGRAM` statement:

```
Pass
{
    CGPROGRAM
    #pragma vertex vert_img
    #pragma fragment frag
    #pragma fragmentoption ARB_precision_hint_fastest
    #include "UnityCG.cginc"

    uniform sampler2D _MainTex;
    uniform sampler2D _BlendTex;
    fixed _Opacity;
```

3. In order for the Overlay blend effect to work, we are going to have to process each pixel from each channel individually. To do that, in a Shader we have to write a custom function that will take in a single channel, such as the red channel for instance, and perform the Overlay operation. Enter the following code into the Shader just below the variable declarations:

```
fixed OverlayBlendMode(fixed basePixel, fixed blendPixel)
{
    if(basePixel < 0.5)
    {
        return (2.0 * basePixel * blendPixel);
    }
    else
    {
        return (1.0 - 2.0 * (1.0 - basePixel) * (1.0 - blendPixel));
    }
}
```

4. Finally, we need to update our `frag()` function to process each channel of our textures, to perform the blending:

```
fixed4 frag(v2f_img i) : COLOR
{
    //Get the colors from the RenderTexture and the uv's
    //from the v2f_img struct
    fixed4 renderTex = tex2D(_MainTex, i.uv);
    fixed4 blendTex = tex2D(_BlendTex, i.uv);

    fixed4 blendedImage = renderTex;

    blendedImage.r = OverlayBlendMode(renderTex.r, blendTex.r);
    blendedImage.g = OverlayBlendMode(renderTex.g, blendTex.g);
    blendedImage.b = OverlayBlendMode(renderTex.b, blendTex.b);

    //Adjust amount of Blend Mode with a lerp
    renderTex = lerp(renderTex, blendedImage, _Opacity);

    return renderTex;
}
```

5. With the code completed in the Shader, our effect should be working. Save the Shader and return to the Unity editor to let the Shader compile. Our script is already set up, so we don't have to modify it any further. Once the Shader compiles, you should see a result similar to the following image:

Overlay Blend Mode

How it works...

Our Overlay blend mode is definitely a lot more involved, but if you break down the function, you will notice that it is simply a Multiply blend mode and a Screen blend mode. It's just that in this case we are doing a conditional check to apply one or the other blend mode to a pixel.

With this particular screen effect, when the Overlay function receives a pixel, it looks to see if it is less than 0.5. If it is, we apply a modified Multiply blend mode to that pixel; if it's not, we apply a modified screen blend mode to the pixel. We do this for each pixel for each channel, giving us the final RGB pixel values for our screen effect.

As you can see, there are many things that can be done with screen effects. It really just depends on the platform and the amount of memory you have allocated for screen effects. Usually this is determined throughout the course of a game project, so have fun and get creative with your screen effects.

11
Gameplay and Screen Effects

In this chapter, we will cover the following:

- Creating an old movie screen effect
- Creating a night vision screen effect

Introduction

If you are reading this book, you are most likely a person that has played a game or two in your time. One of the aspects to real-time games is the effect of immersing a player into a world to make it feel as if they were actually playing in the real world. The more modern games make heavy use of screen effects to achieve this immersion.

With screen effects, we can turn the mood of a certain environment from calm to scary, just by changing the look of the screen. Imagine walking into a room, which is contained within a level, then the game takes over and goes into a cinematic moment. Many modern games will turn on different screen effects to change the mood of the current moment. Understanding how to create effects triggered by gameplay is next in our journey of Shader writing.

In this chapter, we are going to take a look at some of the more common gameplay screen effects. We are going to learn how to change the look of the game from normal to an old movie effect, and we are going to take a look at how many first-person shooter games apply their night vision effects to the screen. With each of these recipes, we are going to look at how to hook these up to game events, so that they are turned on and off as the game's current presentation needs it.

Creating an old movie screen effect

Many games are set in different times. Some take place in fantasy worlds, or future sci-fi worlds, and some even take place in the old west, where film cameras were just being developed and the movies that people watched were black and white or sometimes tinted with what is called a sepia effect. The look is very distinct, and we are going to replicate that look using a screen effect in Unity.

There are a few steps to achieving this look and as just making the whole screen black and white or gray scale, we need to break down this effect into its component parts. If we analyze some reference footage of an old movie, we can begin to do this. Let's take a look at the following image and break down the elements that make up the old movie look:

We constructed this image using a few reference images found online. It is always a good idea to try and utilize Photoshop to construct images like this, to aid you in creating a plan for your new screen effect. Performing this process not only tells us the elements we will have to code in, but it also gives us a quick way to see which blending modes work and how we will construct the layers of our screen effect. The Photoshop file we created for this recipe is included in this book's support page at `www.packtpub.com/support` and is called `OldFilmEffect_Research_Layout.psd`.

Getting ready

Now that we know what we have to make, let's take a look at how each of the layers is combined to create the final effect and gather some resources for our Shader and screen effect script.

- **Sepia Tone**: This is a relatively simple effect to achieve, as we just need to bring all the pixel colors of the original render texture to a single color range. This is easily achieved by using the luminance of the original image and adding a constant color. Our first layer will look like the following image:

- **Vignette effect**: We can always see some sort of soft border around old films, when they are being projected with an old movie projector. This is caused because the bulb being used for the movie projector has more brightness in the middle than it does at the edges of the film. This effect is generally called a Vignette effect and is our second layer in our screen effect. We can achieve this with an overlaid texture over the whole screen. The following image demonstrates what this layer looks like isolated out as a texture:

- **Dust and scratches**: The third and final layer in our old movie screen effect is the dust and scratches. This layer will utilize two different tiled textures, one for scratches and one for dust. The reason is that we will want to animate these two textures over time at different tiling rates. This will give the effect that the film is moving along and there are small scratches and dust on each frame of the old film. The following image demonstrates this effect isolated out to its own texture:

Let us get our screen effect system ready with the preceding textures. Perform the following steps:

1. Gather up a Vignette texture and some dust and scratches textures, like the ones we just saw.
2. Create a new script called `OldFilmEffect.cs` and a new Shader called `OldFilmEffectShader.shader`.
3. With our new files created, fill in the code necessary to get the screen effect system up and running. For reference on how to do that see *Chapter 10, Screen Effects with Unity Render Textures*.

Finally, with our screen effect system up and running and our textures gathered, we can begin the process of recreating this old film effect.

How to do it...

Our individual layers for our old film screen effect are quite simple, but when combined we get some very visually stunning effects. Let's run through how to construct the code for our script and our Shader, then we can step through each line of code and learn why things are working the way they are. At this point you should have the screen effects system up and running, as we will not be covering how to set that up in this recipe.

1. We will begin by entering the code to our script. Our first block of code we will enter will define our variable we want to expose to the **Inspector**, to let the user of this effect adjust it as they see fit. We can also use our mocked-up Photoshop file as reference when deciding what we will need to expose to the **Inspector** of this effect. Enter the following code into your effect script:

```
#region Variables
public Shader oldFilmShader;

public float OldFilmEffectAmount = 1.0f;

public Color sepiaColor = Color.white;
public Texture2D vignetteTexture;
public float vignetteAmount = 1.0f;

public Texture2D scratchesTexture;
public float scratchesYSpeed = 10.0f;
public float scratchesXSpeed = 10.0f;

public  Texture2D dustTexture;
public float dustYSpeed = 10.0f;
public float dustXSpeed = 10.0f;

private Material curMaterial;
private float randomValue;
#endregion
```

2. Next, we need to fill in the contents of our `OnRenderImage()` function. Here, we will be passing the data from our variables to our Shader, so that the Shader can then use that data in the processing of the render texture:

```
void OnRenderImage(RenderTexture sourceTexture, RenderTexture destTexture)
{
    if(oldFilmShader != null)
    {
        material.SetColor("_SepiaColor", sepiaColor);
        material.SetFloat("_VignetteAmount", vignetteAmount);
        material.SetFloat("_EffectAmount", OldFilmEffectAmount);

        if(vignetteTexture)
        {
            material.SetTexture("_VignetteTex", vignetteTexture);
        }

        if(scratchesTexture)
        {
            material.SetTexture("_ScratchesTex", scratchesTexture);
            material.SetFloat("_ScratchesYSpeed", scratchesYSpeed);
            material.SetFloat("_ScratchesXSpeed", scratchesXSpeed);
        }

        if(dustTexture)
        {
            material.SetTexture("_DustTex", dustTexture);
            material.SetFloat("_dustYSpeed", dustYSpeed);
            material.SetFloat("_dustXSpeed", dustXSpeed);
            material.SetFloat("_RandomValue", randomValue);
        }

        Graphics.Blit(sourceTexture, destTexture, material);
    }
    else
    {
        Graphics.Blit(sourceTexture, destTexture);
    }
}
```

3. To complete the script portion of this effect, we simply need to make sure we clamp the values of the variables that need to have a clamped range, instead of being any value.

```
void Update()
{
    vignetteAmount = Mathf.Clamp01(vignetteAmount);
    OldFilmEffectAmount = Mathf.Clamp(OldFilmEffectAmount, 0f, 1.5f);
    randomValue = Random.Range(-1f,1f);
}
```

4. With our script complete, let's turn our attention to our Shader file. We need to create the corresponding variables, which we created in our script, in our Shader. This will allow the script and the Shader to communicate with one another. Enter the following code into the `Properties` block of the Shader:

```
Properties
{
    _MainTex ("Base (RGB)", 2D) = "white" {}
    _VignetteTex ("Vignette Texture", 2D) = "white"{}
    _ScratchesTex ("Scartches Texture", 2D) = "white"{}
    _DustTex ("Dust Texture", 2D) = "white"{}
    _SepiaColor ("Sepia Color", Color) = (1,1,1,1)
    _EffectAmount ("Old Film Effect Amount", Range(0,1)) = 1.0
    _VignetteAmount ("Vignette Opacity", Range(0,1)) = 1.0
    _ScratchesYSpeed ("Scratches Y Speed", Float) = 10.0
    _ScratchesXSpeed ("Scratches X Speed", Float) = 10.0
    _dustXSpeed ("Dust X Speed", Float) = 10.0
    _dustYSpeed ("Dust Y Speed", Float) = 10.0
    _RandomValue ("Random Value", Float) = 1.0
}
```

5. Then as usual, we need to add those same variable names to our `CGPROGRAM` block, so that the `Properties` block can communicate with the `CGPROGRAM` block:

```
SubShader
{
    Pass
    {
        CGPROGRAM
        #pragma vertex vert_img
        #pragma fragment frag
        #pragma fragmentoption ARB_precision_hint_fastest
        #include "UnityCG.cginc"

        uniform sampler2D _MainTex;
        uniform sampler2D _VignetteTex;
        uniform sampler2D _ScratchesTex;
        uniform sampler2D _DustTex;
        fixed4 _SepiaColor;
        fixed _VignetteAmount;
        fixed _ScratchesYSpeed;
        fixed _ScratchesXSpeed;
        fixed _dustXSpeed;
        fixed _dustYSpeed;
        fixed _EffectAmount;
        fixed _RandomValue;
```

6. Now, we simply fill in the guts of our `frag()` function so that we process the pixels for our screen effect. To start with, let's get the Render Texture and the Vignette texture passed to us by the script:

```
fixed4 frag(v2f_img i) : COLOR
{
    //Get the colors from the RenderTexture and the uvs
    //from the v2f_img struct
    half2 renderTexUV = half2(i.uv.x, i.uv.y + (_RandomValue * _SinTime.z * 0.005));
    fixed4 renderTex = tex2D(_MainTex, renderTexUV);

    //Get the pixels from the Vignette Texture
    fixed4 vignetteTex = tex2D(_VignetteTex, i.uv);
```

7. We then need to add the process for the dust and scratches by entering the following code:

```
//Process the Scratches UV and pixels
half2 scratchesUV = half2(i.uv.x + (_RandomValue * _SinTime.z * _ScratchesXSpeed),
                          i.uv.y + (_Time.x * _ScratchesYSpeed));
fixed4 scratchesTex = tex2D(_ScratchesTex, scratchesUV);

//Process the Dust UV and pixels
half2 dustUV = half2(i.uv.x + (_RandomValue * (_SinTime.z * _dustXSpeed)),
                     i.uv.y + (_RandomValue * (_SinTime.z * _dustYSpeed)));
fixed4 dustTex = tex2D(_DustTex, dustUV);
```

8. The Sepia Tone process is next on our list:

```
// get the luminosity values from the render texture using the YIQ values.
fixed lum = dot (fixed3(0.299, 0.587, 0.114), renderTex.rgb);

//Add the constant color to the lum values
fixed4 finalColor = lum + lerp(_SepiaColor, _SepiaColor +
                               fixed4(0.1f,0.1f,0.1f,1.0f), _RandomValue);
```

9. Finally, we combine all of our layers and colors, to return the final screen effect texture:

```
    //Create a constant white color we can use to adjust opacity of effects
    fixed3 constantWhite = fixed3(1,1,1);

    //Composite together the different layers to create final Screen Effect
    finalColor = lerp(finalColor, finalColor * vignetteTex, _VignetteAmount);
    finalColor.rgb *= lerp(scratchesTex, constantWhite, (_RandomValue));
    finalColor.rgb *= lerp(dustTex.rgb, constantWhite, (_RandomValue * _SinTime.z));
    finalColor = lerp(renderTex, finalColor, _EffectAmount);

    return finalColor;
}

ENDCG
```

10. With all of our code entered and no errors, you should have a result very similar to the following image. Hit **Play** in the Unity editor to see the effects of the dust and scratches and the slight image shift we give the Screen Effect.

How it works...

Now, let's walk through each of the layers in this Screen Effect and break down why each of the lines of code is working the way it is, and get more insight as to how we can add more to this Screen Effect.

Now that our old film screen effect is working, let's step through the lines of code in our `frag()` function as all the other code should be pretty self-explanatory at this point in the book.

Just like our Photoshop layers, our Shader is processing each layer and then compositing them together, so while we go through each layer, try to imagine how the layers in Photoshop work. Keeping this concept in mind always helps when developing new screen effects.

Here, we have the first set of lines of code in our `frag()` function:

```
fixed4 frag(v2f_img i) : COLOR
{
    //Get the colors from the RenderTexture and the uvs
    //from the v2f_img struct
    half2 distortedUV = barrelDistortion(i.uv);
    fixed4 renderTex = tex2D(_MainTex, distortedUV);
    fixed4 vignetteTex = tex2D(_VignetteTex, i.uv);
```

The first line of code, just after the `frag()` function declaration, is the definition of how the UVs should work for our main render texture, or the actual rendered frame of our game. As we are looking to fake the effect of an old film style, we want to adjust the UVs of our render texture, every frame, such that they flicker. This flickering simulates how the winding of the film's projector is a just a bit off. This tells us that we need to animate the UVs and that is what this first line of code is doing.

We use the built-in `_SinTime` variable, which Unity provides us, to get a value between -1 and 1. We then multiply this by a very small number, in this case `0.005`, to reduce the intensity of the effect. The final value is then multiplied again by the `_RandomValue` variable, which we generate in the Effect script. This value bounces back and forth between -1 and 1, as well to basically flip the direction of the motion back and forth.

Once our UVs are built and stored in the `renderTexUV` variable, we can sample the render texture using a `tex2D()` function. This operation then gives us our final render texture, which we can use to process further in the rest of the Shader.

Moving on to the last line in the previous image, we simply do a straight sample of the vignette texture using the `tex2D()` function. We don't need to use the animated UVs we already created, as the vignette texture will be tied to the motion of the camera itself and not to the flickering of the camera film.

The following code snippet illustrates the second set of lines of code in our `frag()` function:

```
//Process the Scratches UV and pixels
half2 scratchesUV = half2(i.uv.x + (_RandomValue * _SinTime.z * _ScratchesXSpeed),
                          i.uv.y + (_Time.x * _ScratchesYSpeed));
fixed4 scratchesTex = tex2D(_ScratchesTex, scratchesUV);

//Process the Dust UV and pixels
half2 dustUV = half2(i.uv.x + (_RandomValue * (_SinTime.z * _dustXSpeed)),
                     i.uv.y + (_RandomValue * (_SinTime.z * _dustYSpeed)));
fixed4 dustTex = tex2D(_DustTex, dustUV);
```

These lines of code are almost exactly like the previous lines of code, in which we need to generate unique animated UV values to modify the position of our screen effect layers. We simply use the built-in `_SinTime` value to get a value between -1 and 1, multiply it by our random value, and then by another multiplier to adjust the overall speed of the animation. Once those UV values are generated, we can then sample our dust and scratches texture using these new animated values.

Our next set of code handles the creation of the colorizing effect for our old film screen effect. The following code snippet demonstrates these lines:

```
// get the luminosity values from the render texture using the YIQ values.
fixed lum = dot (fixed3(0.299, 0.587, 0.114), renderTex.rgb);

//Add the constant color to the lum values
fixed4 finalColor = lum + lerp(_SepiaColor, _SepiaColor +
                              fixed4(0.1f,0.1f,0.1f,1.0f), _RandomValue);
```

With this set of code, we are creating the actual color tinting of the entire render texture. To accomplish this, we first need to turn the render texture in the gray scale version of itself. To do that, we can use the luminosity values given to us by the YIQ values. YIQ values are the color space used by the NTSC color TV system. Each letter in YIQ actually stores color constants that are used by TVs to adjust the color for readability. For more information on the YIQ values refer to the following links:

- http://en.wikipedia.org/wiki/YIQ
- http://www.blackice.com/colorspaceYIQ.htm
- http://dcssrv1.oit.uci.edu/~wiedeman/cspace/me/infoyiq.html

While it is not necessary to actually know the reasons for this color scale, it should be known that the Y value in the YIQ is the constant luminance values for any image. So, we can generate a gray-scale image of our render texture by taking each pixel of the render texture and dotting it with our luminance values. That is what the first line in this set is doing.

Once we have the luminance values, we can simply add on the color we want to tint the image with. This color is passed from our script, into our Shader, then into our CGPROGRAM block, where we can add it on to our gray scale render texture. Once completed, we will have a perfectly tinted image.

Finally, we create the blending between each of our layers in our screen effect. The following code snippet shows the set of code we are looking at:

```
    //Create a constant white color we can use to adjust opacity of effects
    fixed3 constantWhite = fixed3(1,1,1);

    //Composite together the different layers to create finsl Screen Effect
    finalColor = lerp(finalColor, finalColor * vignetteTex, _VignetteAmount);
    finalColor.rgb *= lerp(scratchesTex, constantWhite, (_RandomValue));
    finalColor.rgb *= lerp(dustTex.rgb, constantWhite, (_RandomValue * _SinTime.z));
    finalColor = lerp(renderTex, finalColor, _EffectAmount);

    return finalColor;
}

ENDCG
```

Our last set of code is relatively simple and doesn't really need a ton of explanation. In short, it is simply multiplying all the layers together to reach our final result. Just like we multiplied our layers together in Photoshop, we multiply them together in our Shader. Each layer is processed through a `lerp()` function so that we can adjust the opacity of each layer, which gives more artistic control over the final effect. The more tweaks one can offer, the better when it comes to screen effects.

Creating a night vision screen effect

Our next screen effect is definitely a more popular one. The night vision screen effect is seen in Call of Duty Modern Warfare, Halo, and just about any first-person shooter out in the market today. It is the effect of brightening the whole image using that very distinct lime green color.

In order to achieve our night vision effect, we need to break our effect down using Photoshop. It is a simple process of finding some reference images online and composing a layered image to see what kinds of Blending modes you will need, or in which order we will need to combine our layers. The following image shows the result of performing just this process in Photoshop:

Let's begin to break down our rough Photoshop-composite image into its component parts so that we can better understand the assets we will have to gather. In the next section, we will cover the process of doing just that.

Getting ready

Let's begin this screen effect by again breaking down our effect into its component layers. Using Photoshop, we can construct a layered image to better illustrate how we can go about capturing the effect of night vision.

- **Tinted green**: Our first layer in our screen effect is the iconic green color, found in just about every night vision image. This will give our effect that signature night vision look.

- **Scan lines**: To increase the effect of this being a new type of display for the player, we include scan lines over the top of our tinted layer. For this, we will use a texture created in Photoshop and let the user tile it so that the scan lines can be bigger or smaller.

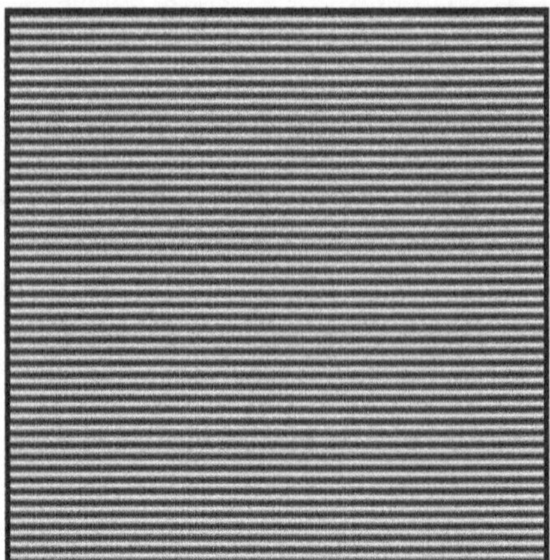

- **Noise**: Our next layer is a simple noise texture that we tile over the tinted image and the scan lines, to break up the image and to add even more detail to our effect. This layer simply emphasizes that digital read out look.

- **Vignette**: The last layer in our night vision effect is the vignette. If you look at the night vision effect in Call of Duty Modern Warfare, you will notice that it uses a vignette that fakes the effect of looking down a scope. We will do that for this screen effect.

Let's create a screen effect system by gathering our textures. Perform the following steps:

1. Gather up a vignette texture, a noise texture, and a scan line texture, like the ones we just saw.
2. Create a new script called `NightVisionEffect.cs` and a new Shader called `NightVisionEffectShader.shader`.
3. With our new files created, fill in the code necessary to get the screen effect system up and running. For instructions on how to do that, refer to *Chapter 10, Screen Effects with Unity Render Textures*.

Finally, with our Screen Effect system up and running and our textures gathered, we can begin the process of recreating this old film effect.

How to do it...

With all of our assets gathered and our screen effect system running smoothly, let's begin to add the code necessary to both the script and the Shader. We will begin our coding with the `NightVisionEffect.cs` script; so double-click on that file now to open it up in MonoDevelop.

1. We need to create a few variables that will allow the user of this effect to adjust it in the script's **Inspector**. Enter the following code into the `NightVisionEffect.cs` script:

```
#region Variables
public Shader nightVisionShader;

public float contrast = 2.0f;
public float brightness = 1.0f;
public Color nightVisionColor = Color.white;

public Texture2D vignetteTexture;

public Texture2D scanLineTexture;
public float scanLineTileAmount = 4.0f;

public Texture2D nightVisionNoise;
public float noiseXSpeed = 100.0f;
public float noiseYSpeed = 100.0f;

public float distortion = 0.2f;
public float scale = 0.8f;

private float randomValue = 0.0f;
private Material curMaterial;
#endregion
```

2. Next, we need to complete our `OnRenderImage()` function so that we are passing the right data to the Shader, in order for the Shader to process the screen effect properly. Complete the `OnRenderImage()` function with the following code:

```
void OnRenderImage(RenderTexture sourceTexture, RenderTexture destTexture)
{
    if(nightVisionShader != null)
    {
        material.SetFloat("_Contrast", contrast);
        material.SetFloat("_Brightness", brightness);
        material.SetColor("_NightVisionColor", nightVisionColor);
        material.SetFloat("_RandomValue", randomValue);
        material.SetFloat("_distortion", distortion);
        material.SetFloat("_scale",scale);

        if(vignetteTexture)
        {
            material.SetTexture("_VignetteTex", vignetteTexture);
        }

        if(scanLineTexture)
        {
            material.SetTexture("_ScanLineTex", scanLineTexture);
            material.SetFloat("_ScanLineTileAmount", scanLineTileAmount);
        }

        if(nightVisionNoise)
        {
            material.SetTexture("_NoiseTex", nightVisionNoise);
            material.SetFloat("_NoiseXSpeed", noiseXSpeed);
            material.SetFloat("_NoiseYSpeed", noiseYSpeed);
        }

        Graphics.Blit(sourceTexture, destTexture, material);
    }
    else
    {
        Graphics.Blit(sourceTexture, destTexture);
    }
}
```

3. To complete the `NightVisionEffect.cs` script, we simply need to make sure that we clamp certain variables so that they stay within a range. These ranges are arbitrary and can be changed at a later time. These are just values that worked well.

```
void Update()
{
    contrast = Mathf.Clamp(contrast, 0f,4f);
    brightness = Mathf.Clamp(brightness, 0f, 2f);
    randomValue = Random.Range(-1f,1f);
    distortion = Mathf.Clamp(distortion, -1f,1f);
    scale = Mathf.Clamp(scale, 0f, 3f);
}
```

4. We can now turn our attention over to the Shader portion of this screen effect. Open the Shader, if you haven't already, and begin by entering the following properties in the `Properties` block:

```
Properties
{
    _MainTex ("Base (RGB)", 2D) = "white" {}
    _VignetteTex ("Vignette Texture", 2D) = "white"{}
    _ScanLineTex ("Scan Line Texture", 2D) = "white"{}
    _NoiseTex ("Noise Texture", 2D) = "white"{}
    _NoiseXSpeed ("Noise X Speed", Float) = 100.0
    _NoiseYSpeed ("Noise Y Speed", Float) = 100.0
    _ScanLineTileAmount ("Scan Line Tile Amount", Float) = 4.0
    _NightVisionColor ("Night Vision Color", Color) = (1,1,1,1)
    _Contrast ("Contrast", Range(0,4)) = 2
    _Brightness ("Brightness", Range(0,2)) = 1
    _RandomValue ("Random Value", Float) = 0
    _distortion ("Distortion", Float) = 0.2
    _scale ("Scale (Zoom)", Float) = 0.8
}
```

5. To make sure that we are passing the data from our `Properties` block into our `CGPROGRAM` block, we need to make sure to declare them with the same name inside the `CGPROGRAM` block.

```
SubShader
{
    Pass
    {
        CGPROGRAM
        #pragma vertex vert_img
        #pragma fragment frag
        #pragma fragmentoption ARB_precision_hint_fastest
        #include "UnityCG.cginc"

        uniform sampler2D _MainTex;
        uniform sampler2D _VignetteTex;
        uniform sampler2D _ScanLineTex;
        uniform sampler2D _NoiseTex;
        fixed4 _NightVisionColor;
        fixed _Contrast;
        fixed _ScanLineTileAmount;
        fixed _Brightness;
        fixed _RandomValue;
        fixed _NoiseXSpeed;
        fixed _NoiseYSpeed;
        fixed _distortion;
        fixed _scale;
```

6. Our effect is also going to include a lens distortion to further convey the effect that we are looking through a lens and the edges of the image are being distorted by the angle of the lens. Enter the following function just after the variable decelerations in the `CGPROGRAM` block:

```
float2 barrelDistortion(float2 coord)
{
    // lens distortion algorithm
    // See http://www.ssontech.com/content/lensalg.htm

    float2 h = coord.xy - float2(0.5, 0.5);
    float r2 = h.x * h.x + h.y * h.y;
    float f = 1.0 + r2 * (_distortion * sqrt(r2));

    return f * _scale * h + 0.5;
}
```

7. We can now concentrate on the meat of our `NightVisionEffect` shader. Let's start this by entering the code that is necessary to get the render texture and the vignette texture. Enter the following code into the `frag()` function of our Shader:

```
fixed4 frag(v2f_img i) : COLOR
{
    //Get the colors from the RenderTexture and the uv's
    //from the v2f_img struct
    half2 distortedUV = barrelDistortion(i.uv);
    fixed4 renderTex = tex2D(_MainTex, distortedUV);
    fixed4 vignetteTex = tex2D(_VignetteTex, i.uv);
```

8. The next step in our `frag()` function is to process the scan lines and noise textures and apply the proper animated UVs to them:

```
//Process scan lines and noise
half2 scanLinesUV = half2(i.uv.x * _ScanLineTileAmount, i.uv.y * _ScanLineTileAmount);
fixed4 scanLineTex = tex2D(_ScanLineTex, scanLinesUV);

half2 noiseUV = half2(i.uv.x + (_RandomValue * _SinTime.z * _NoiseXSpeed),
                      i.uv.y + (_Time.x * _NoiseYSpeed));
fixed4 noiseTex = tex2D(_NoiseTex, noiseUV);
```

9. To complete all of our layers in the screen effect, we simply need to process the luminance value of our render texture, and then apply the night vision color to it to achieve that iconic night vision look:

```
// get the luminosity values from the render texture using the YIQ values.
fixed lum = dot (fixed3(0.299, 0.587, 0.114), renderTex.rgb);
lum += _Brightness;
fixed4 finalColor = (lum *2) + _NightVisionColor;
```

10. Lastly, we will combine all the layers together and return the final color of our night vision effect:

```
        //Final output
        finalColor = pow(finalColor, _Contrast);
        finalColor *= vignetteTex;
        finalColor *= scanLineTex * noiseTex;

        return finalColor;
    }

    ENDCG
```

When you have finished entering the code, return to the Unity editor to let the script and the Shader to compile. If there are no errors, hit **Play** in the editor to see the results. You should see something similar to the following image:

How it works...

The night vision effect is actually very similar to the old film screen effect, which shows us just how modular we can make these components. Just by simply swapping out the textures we are using for overlays and changing the speed at which our tiling rates are being calculated, we can achieve very different results using the same code.

The only difference with this effect is the fact that we are including a lens distortion to our screen effect. So let's break this down, so that we can get a better understanding of how it works.

The following code snippet illustrates the code used in processing our lens distortion. It is a snippet of code provided to us by the makers of SynthEyes, and the code is freely available to use in your own effects:

```
float2 barrelDistortion(float2 coord)
{
    // lens distortion algorithm
    // See http://www.ssontech.com/content/lensalg.htm

    float2 h = coord.xy - float2(0.5, 0.5);
    float r2 = h.x * h.x + h.y * h.y;
    float f = 1.0 + r2 * (_distortion * sqrt(r2));

    return f * _scale * h + 0.5;
}
```

When breaking down the `barrelDistortion()` function, the first line of code finds the center of the render texture image. Once we have the center of the image, we can then apply a stretching to the pixels as they get further away from the center of the image. So, we fake the effect of the main render texture being distorted by the angle of a lens. Quite a nice effect when applied to screen effects like the night vision effect.

Once the UVs have been processed to compute the fake stretching, we can continue with the Shader just like we have before, applying UV animation and pixel operations to achieve our final night vision effect.

See also

- The following link takes you to the page which describes the lens distortion effect:

  Lens Distortion: `http://www.ssontech.com/content/lensalg.htm`

Index

Symbols

A

B

C

M

N

O

P

R

S

T

U

V

W

Z

About Packt Publishing

Packt, pronounced 'packed', published its first book "*Mastering phpMyAdmin for Effective MySQL Management*" in April 2004 and subsequently continued to specialize in publishing highly focused books on specific technologies and solutions.

Our books and publications share the experiences of your fellow IT professionals in adapting and customizing today's systems, applications, and frameworks. Our solution based books give you the knowledge and power to customize the software and technologies you're using to get the job done. Packt books are more specific and less general than the IT books you have seen in the past. Our unique business model allows us to bring you more focused information, giving you more of what you need to know, and less of what you don't.

Packt is a modern, yet unique publishing company, which focuses on producing quality, cutting-edge books for communities of developers, administrators, and newbies alike. For more information, please visit our website: `www.packtpub.com`.

Writing for Packt

We welcome all inquiries from people who are interested in authoring. Book proposals should be sent to `author@packtpub.com`. If your book idea is still at an early stage and you would like to discuss it first before writing a formal book proposal, contact us; one of our commissioning editors will get in touch with you.

We're not just looking for published authors; if you have strong technical skills but no writing experience, our experienced editors can help you develop a writing career, or simply get some additional reward for your expertise.

HTML5 Game Development with GameMaker

ISBN: 978-1-84969-410-0 Paperback: 364 pages

Experience a captivating journey that will take you from creating a full-on shoot 'em up to your first social web browser game

1. Build browser-based games and share them with the world
2. Master the GameMaker Language with easy to follow examples
3. Every game comes with original art and audio, including additional assets to build upon each lesson.

Unity 3.x Scripting

ISBN: 978-1-84969-230-4 Paperback: 292 pages

Write efficient, reusable scripts to build custom characters, game environments, and control enemy AI in your Unity game

1. Make your characters interact with buttons and program triggered action sequences
2. Create custom characters and code dynamic objects and players' interaction with them
3. Synchronize movement of character and environmental objects
4. Add and control animations to new and existing characters

Torque 3D Game Development Cookbook

ISBN: 978-1-84969-354-7 Paperback: 380 pages

Over 80 practical recipes and hidden gems for getting the most out of the Torque 3D game engine

1. Clear step-by-step instruction and practical examples to advance your understanding of Torque 3D and all of its sub-systems
2. Explore essential topics such as graphics, sound, networking and user input
3. Helpful tips and techniques to increase the potential of your Torque 3D games

---

Mastering UDK Game Development

ISBN: 978-1-84969-560-2 Paperback: 290 pages

Eight projects specifically designed to help you exploit the Unreal Development Kit to its full potential

1. Guides you through advanced projects that help augment your skills with UDK by practical example
2. Comes complete with all the art assets and additional resources that you need to create stunning content
3. Perfect for level designers who want to take their skills to the next level

Please check **www.PacktPub.com** for information on our titles

Lightning Source UK Ltd.
Milton Keynes UK
UKOW06f0353260713

214369UK00004B/148/P